KW-719-484

SCIENTIFIC EVIDENCE AND EXPERT TESTIMONY HANDBOOK

A Guide for Lawyers, Criminal Investigators and Forensic Specialists

By

RONALD F. BECKER, J.D.

Department of Criminal Justice
Southwest Texas State University
San Marcos, Texas

CHARLES C THOMAS • PUBLISHER, LTD.
Springfield • Illinois • U.S.A.

WEYMOUTH COLLEGE
LIBRARY

ACC 0 8 SEP 2006
No.

CLASS 345 .06
No. B

Published and Distributed Throughout the World by

CHARLES C THOMAS • PUBLISHER, LTD.
2600 South First Street
Springfield, Illinois 62794-9265

This book is protected by copyright. No part of
it may be reproduced in any manner without
written permission from the publisher.

© *1997 by* CHARLES C THOMAS • PUBLISHER, LTD.
ISBN 0-398-06761-9   (cloth)
ISBN 0-398-06762-7   (paper)

Library of Congress Catalog Card Number: 96-53287

With THOMAS BOOKS *careful attention is given to all details of manufacturing
and design. It is the Publisher's desire to present books that are satisfactory as to their
physical qualities and artistic possibilities and appropriate for their particular use.*
THOMAS BOOKS *will be true to those laws of quality that assure a good name
and good will.*

Printed in the United States of America
SC-R-3

Library of Congress Cataloging-in-Publication Data

Becker, Ronald F.
    Scientific evidence and expert testimony handbook : a guide for
lawyers, criminal investigators and forensic specialists / by Ronald
F. Becker.
        p.   cm.
    Includes bibliographical references and index.
    ISBN 0-398-06761-9 (cloth). — ISBN 0-398-06762-7 (pbk.)
    1. Evidence, Expert—United States.   2. Evidence, Criminal—
United States.   3. Forensic sciences—United States.   I. Title.
KF9674.B43   1997
345.73'067—dc21
                                                                    96-53287
                                                                          CIP

FOREWORD

Whether you have practiced criminal law for years or are stepping into a courtroom for the first time, the need for scientific evidence and expert witnesses is ever increasing. In the technological future we can only expect that need to increase. Most lawyers are not scientists, nor do they have a scientific background. When confronted with that quandary, many lawyers seek reference materials that will assist in preparation of scientific testimony. Often those materials are written by scientists for scientists, easy for scientists to understand but perhaps elusive for the layman. Ronald Becker's book, *Scientific Evidence and Expert Testimony Handbook*, has something of interest for every trial lawyer, laboratory technician, investigating police officer, and testifying expert. From fingerprint analysis, identification, lifting and comparison to blood spatter patterns and accident reconstruction, the book sets out the significant developments in the field in a way that stands out for its readability, practicality, and applicability. The section on firearms identification is as comprehensive as any but written in a conversational style that lends to understanding and reduces ambiguity and unnecessary jargon. It will not make you a firearms expert, but it should make you comfortable in questioning a firearms expert.

A need for a book like this is obvious: Countless crimes would go undetected, unsolved, or unproven without the benefit of forensic science. But lawyers need more than the evidence itself. They need to understand what story the evidence tells about the crime, the criminal, the crime scene, the investigators and the technicians who handled the evidence. Once the story is told, lawyers need to know how to use the evidence to its best advantage. That advantage can only be had by presenting evidence through the expert witness. Many a case that should have been illustrative was somehow made incomprehensible in translation from legalize to language of the expert. This book demonstrates the use of language to communicate rather than to inadvertently build obstacles to communication and understanding. When the lawyer examining an expert witness is sure of the technical ground upon which he/she stands, that lawyer, through the expert, will paint a picture that the jury can understand and believe. This book provides the tools to paint a picture in bold, even, and forcible strokes that a jury not only will understand but more importantly will find interesting and to which they will attend. You would be hard pressed to find another volume that more thoroughly explores forensic science in a way that criminal lawyers, prosecutors, police, and experts can digest and use.

THOMAS L. KRAMPITZ
Executive Director
Texas District and County Attorneys Association

PREFACE

Many readers may ask how this book could be written without significant reference to the homicide of Nicole Brown Simpson and Ronald Goldman, the forensic trial of the century. That absence was not accidental. Nothing that contributed to the advancement of forensic science resulted from the trial other than making the public aware of what a forensic scientist is and does. Unfortunately, the battle between defense and prosecution experts convinced the public that forensic science is illusory and that forensic scientists are confused and perhaps dishonest. Little was learned of the day-to-day work of forensic scientists that has advanced the field of criminal investigation and perpetrator identification. Nothing was learned of the vast number of crimes that are cleared because of forensic science and forensic scientists. For a short time in the sun, forensic science received national attention. Hopefully that attention can be refocused on the contribution of forensic science and scientists instead of the media feeding frenzy attempting to "sound bite" their way into living rooms.

The portions of this book dealing with science are largely dependent upon the work of a variety of forensic scientists and the work of Dr. Richard Safferstein specifically. My expertise is that of a trial lawyer and criminal investigator. I am not a scientist and am mathematically challenged. My interest in science and forensic science particularly grew while working as a police investigator. My appreciation for science and scientific expert witnesses grew from the need to retain, examine, and cross-examine expert witnesses in a personal injury trial practice. Cases involving biomechanical engineers, medical examiners, pathologists, petroleum engineers, and various medical specialists taught me that with assistance and study a lawyer could conduct intelligent direct and cross-examinations of highly technical professionals. Applying work and trial experience, I have attempted to understand what forensic scientists do, how they do it, and then explain it in a language that lawyers, jurors, and police investigators can understand.

During my private practice, I discovered that there were few library resources available to assist in a nontechnical understanding of specific areas of forensic science. Those resources that were available were generally written for forensic scientists or forensic science students by forensic scientists. Few available resources provided the knowledge needed to prepare a forensic scientist to testify or for a lawyer to prepare himself for direct and cross-examination of a forensic scientist. The legal materials that were available to assist a lawyer in fashioning questions necessary to convince the court that a forensic expert was qualified and his testimony necessary had little reference to the scientific aspects of the prospective testimony.

This book will hopefully provide lawyers, criminal investigators, and forensic specialists with a reference book that will advise them of their respective roles and responsibilities when advancing forensic testimony in the context of a criminal trial.

R.F.B.

ACKNOWLEDGMENTS

Lawyers often are criticized for demonstrating the same traits society has deemed acceptable in itself. Greed, aggression, and intolerance were not invented by lawyers and have become "legal tender" because society finds them useful. In the minds of most, they stand above lawyers and their pursuit of the dollar. People derive tremendous satisfaction degrading a once honorable profession by telling jokes or recounting the most recent sensationalized media report of lawyer misconduct.

This book was motivated by the men and women who have taken on the burden of "court champion." Who for reasons known only to themselves have forsaken pursuit of significant financial gain and assumed the mantle of representative of the people. Without their inspiration this book could not have been written.

More specifically, the Kendall County, Texas, County Attorney, Pamela McKay, has provided me with insight into the thought processes of a criminal prosecutor. Watching her take a personal interest in the victims of domestic violence and drunk driving gave me some insight into what maintains these dedicated professionals. Pam, as my wife, has provided an up-close and personal portrait of the evolution of a prosecutor. I have had the opportunity to watch her grow from a "baby prosecutor" into a professional who takes pride in her work and the people for whom that work is done. Without her dedication, I would never have recognized that there is a group of unsung heroes out there, and they are called prosecutors.

Writing a book is a time-consuming process. My primary responsibilities as an associate professor are to the Criminal Justice Department at Southwest Texas State University. Our teaching schedule can be adjusted to allow for scholarship activities. To Joy Pollock, our Department Chair, and to Gene Martin, our School Dean, I owe a debt of gratitude for adjusting my schedule to allow me to write this book. Joy Pollock also provided support and direction. Her expertise as author and editor has been invaluable in my evolution as an author.

A hearty thanks to my editor, William Bried, who brought order out of chaos. His patience with someone grammatically challenged was appreciated. I would like to assure him that his job in the future will be easier as a result of his subtle instruction, but I would probably be lying. Once grammatically challenged, always grammatically challenged.

CONTENTS

SCIENTIFIC EVIDENCE AND EXPERT TESTIMONY HANDBOOK

Chapter 1

INTRODUCTION

The Age of Technology

Science and technology have made life easier and simultaneously more complex. Computers lightened the burden of many in the workplace but concomitantly extracted excruciating pain for many in becoming computer literate. Computers opened technical realms that previously were available only to those seeking specialized knowledge in specialized places. The Internet gives anyone who is computer literate access to technical forums of the most obscure nature through a world-wide repository. Science and technology have expanded at an exponential rate and the computer is the only tool that allows us to keep up.

Police use computers to enhance video images; to establish serial killer data bases; to catalog, compare, and store fingerprints, blood, and DNA samples. Forensic specialists testify about "blood spatter" and "trace evidence." Criminal justice curriculums are evolving to include courses in forensic anthropology, criminalistics, statistics, research methods, computer science, and forensics.

The criminal trial courtroom has not been immune to the impact of science and technology. Court administrators juggle dockets with computers. Court statistics are often a product of computer networks established for enhanced communication and coordination. Judges are attending continuing judicial education seminars dealing with computers, scientific evidence, and expert testimony. Judges are admitting a greater and more diverse array of experts into their courtrooms than ever before.

Scientific evidence can come before the jury only from the mouth of an expert witness. Occasionally, controversy surrounds a particular scientific or pseudoscientific practice bringing into question whether such a practice or procedure is in fact scientific. The United States Court of Appeals set forth a rule that has been followed for years, known as the Frye test. The Frye test simply postulated that scientific evidence could not be admitted until it had gained general acceptance in the particular field to which it belonged (*Frye v. United States,* 293 F. 1013, 1923). It is this test that has been used in determining the scientific validity of hypnosis, polygraphs, battered women's syndrome, DNA printing, and others. Many courts have paid little attention to the Frye standard and employed individual judicial discretion in the determination of what is scientific and what is not. The United States Supreme Court has decided that Federal Rule of Evidence 702 supersedes the Frye test (*Daubert v. Merrell-Dow Pharmaceuticals, Inc.,* 113 S. Ct. 2793, 1993). Rule 702 deals with the admissibility of expert testimony and provides that:

> if scientific, technical, or other specialized knowledge will assist the trier of fact to understand the evidence or to determine a fact in issue, a witness qualified as an expert by knowledge, skill, experience, training or education may testify thereto in the form of an opinion or otherwise.

If Frye is no longer the standard, then what standard is to apply? That Frye was replaced by the Federal Rules of Evidence does not imply that there are no restrictions on scientific testimony. Under the rules, the trial judge must ensure that any and all scientific testimony or evidence admitted is not only relevant, but reliable (*Daubert v. Merrell-Dow Pharmaceuticals, Inc.,* 113 S.Ct. 2795, 1993). The trial judge must consider whether (1) the technique employed is replicable, (2) has been subjected to peer review and publication, and (3) to what extent the technique has been accepted by the scientific community.

The standards set forth by McCormick in his article entitled "Scientific Evidence: Defining a New Approach to Admissibility" would provide greater guidance in determining the probative value of proffered scientific evidence. McCormick offers eleven factors to be applied in a probative analysis of the admissibility of scientific evidence:

1. The potential error rate in using the technique;
2. The existence and maintenance of standards governing its use;
3. Presence of safeguards in the characteristics of the technique;
4. Analogy to other scientific techniques whose results are admissible;
5. The extent to which the technique has been accepted by scientists in the field involved;
6. The nature and breadth of the inference adduced;
7. The clarity and simplicity with which the technique can be described and its results explained;
8. The extent to which the basic data are verifiable by the court and jury;

9. The availability of other experts to test and evaluate the technique;
10. The probative significance of the evidence in the circumstances of the case;
11. The care with which the technique was employed in the case (McCormack, 1982).

The simplest test to apply to any suggested scientific procedure is the replicability of the procedure and the opportunity to test the validity of test results. Applying such standards will reduce the arbitrary discretion of trial courts in admitting astrological and junk food influences on defendants.

The United States Supreme Court has opened the floodgates of scientific experts as the result of a recent decision. The rigid standard that has been applied historically to the admissibility of "scientific evidence" has been abandoned. The new standard has been incorporated into the Federal Rules of Evidence embracing virtually any area of expertise that the presiding judge believes may assist in understanding the issues in dispute, from the violence inducing properties of Twinkies and astrological influences. As a result "expert testimony" has become a "growth industry."

Courts are becoming more reliant on scientific evidence. This reliance appears to be the product of three correlative factors:

1. The ever-increasing dependence of society on technology to provide answers;
2. The original infusion of funds by the federal government into the Law Enforcement Assistance Administration (LEAA) for the upgrade of law enforcement and the development of forensic applications; and
3. The United States Supreme Court, under Chief Justice Earl Warren, restricted the admissibility of evidence under the Fourth, Fifth and Sixth Amendments that had been secured under traditional police methods and admonished that new investigative skills need be developed and applied to criminal investigations (Farley, 1993).

The number of criminal trials relying in whole or part on scientific evidence and expert testimony has increased dramatically. In a 1980 survey of judges and attorneys by the National Center for State Courts, 44 percent of those responding stated that at least 30 percent of the cases in which they were involved required the introduction of scientific evidence or expert testimony (National Center for State Courts Report, Study to Investigate Use of Scientific Evidence, 1980). The police conduct that the Supreme Court was concerned about in the above mentioned cases has to a large extent been replaced by forensic investigation and evidence.

More professionals are using more of their time to testify in criminal and civil cases. Hourly expert witness fees may exceed $600.00 per hour. Professional bar journals abound with advertisements for expert trial assistance from medical malpractice cases to criminal drug cases. The classified section of many bar journals, heretofore the purview of those seeking to fill legal positions, is rapidly giving way to "experts" hawking their wares.

In the midsts of a technical revolution in the courtroom, police, investigators, prosecutors, defense lawyers, jurors and judges prepare to do battle by focusing on scientific circumstantial evidence admitted or refuted by "expert witnesses." For every prosecution or plaintiff's expert, there will be an equally credentialed opposing expert ready and willing to take exception to the work of prosecution and plaintiff experts. Many advertisements should read "fast gun for hire." If an expert cannot be found to refute a prosecutor's scientific evidence, then one will be found who can assist in confabulation, obfuscation, confusion, and delay (justice delayed is sanction delayed, not necessarily justice denied). It is axiomatic in criminal defense trial practice to argue the facts if the case law is against you, argue the law if the facts are against you, and delay and confuse when both the case law and the facts are against you. One of the best sources of confusion in a criminal trial is an expert witness for the defense who can make the easily understood absolutely indecipherable. It is discouraging to discover that other professions and professionals can be held in the same disdain as are many lawyers (money can have that effect).

Too often the name of the expert witness game is "the price is right"; if you have the right price, there is an expert somewhere, someplace willing to provide testimony regardless of how tenuous the defense. Although a "growth industry," it would be erroneous to presume that any "expert" is capable of giving credible expert testimony. If it was easy anyone could and would do it.

The balance in the system to thwart unqualified, unnecessary, and incompetent experts is cross examination. Although the quality of advocacy varies, there is a maxim that generally holds true: as the stakes increase, so does the quality of advocacy, especially in those cases where counsel is privately retained. It is a matter of time before a marginal expert witness who continues to professionally testify is pummelled at the hands of a competent cross-examiner. Once humiliated during a vigorous cross examination the "expert" will find an easier way to make a living.

Unfortunately, the language of science and technology can be lost on judges, juries, and lawyers. This book will attempt to simplify the concepts and the methods used to present these concepts.

Many expert witnesses testify as a direct result of working for a state agency. Forensic scientists working in crime laboratories, medical examiners, police evidence technicians, police investigators, and laboratory specialists must testify as an integral part of the services they provide. No additional compensation is provided. Often these men and women will have to do battle with well-paid, hired specialists for the defense. Although sale of this book is unrestricted, it is to these professionals and to prosecutors nationwide that this book is addressed.

REFERENCES

Farley, M. Legal standards for the admissibility of novel scientific evidence. Saferstein, R. ed. *Forensic Science Handbook*, Vol III. 1993. Englewood Cliffs, New Jersey: Regents/Prentice Hall.

McCormick, C. Scientific evidence: Defining a new approach to admissibility, 67 *Iowa L. Rev.* 879:911–912, 1982.

National Center for State Courts Report, *Study to Investigate Use of Scientific Evidence*, vol. 7, No. 8, Aug. 1980.

Table of Cases

Daubert v Merrell-Dow Pharmaceuticals, Inc., 113 S Ct. 2786, 1993.

Frye v United States, 293 F. 1013 (D.C. Cir. 1923).

Chapter 2

GETTING EXPERT TESTIMONY
BEFORE THE COURT

In most courts, in most states, and in most jurisdictions, lay witnesses and expert witnesses are allowed to testify. Under the Federal Rules of Evidence which most states have adopted, lay testimony generally is restricted to what the witness has seen or may reflect an opinion as to the character for truthfulness and/or violence of the defendant, the victim, or another witness. Most courts will allow lay witnesses to testify as to the nonviolent nature of the victim. It is not to these witnesses that the responsibility of expressing opinions on causation, intent, motive, or other ultimate issues involved in criminal or civil trials falls. Expert witnesses are allowed a latitude unique in the examination of witnesses. However, that latitude must first be shown to be warranted.

The Rules

Federal Rules 702 through 705 provide the framework within which an expert witness will be allowed to testify. That framework provides that:

1. That the witness has knowledge, skill, or training to form an expert opinion that will assist the trier of fact (judge or jury) to understand evidence or to establish a fact in issue, i.e., was the latent fingerprint lifted at the scene left there by the defendant (Rule 702).
2. An expert's opinion(s) may be based on facts or data compiled or provided by the expert himself (Rule 703).
3. An expert's opinion(s) may be based on information (fact or data) provided to the expert prior to or at the time of the expert's testimony (Rule 703).
4. An expert's opinion must be based on the type of facts or data that expert's ordinarily rely upon (Rule 703).

5. An expert's opinion may address an ultimate fact issue (Rule 704).
6. An expert's opinion as to that ultimate issue is not required to be accepted by the jury (Rule 704).
7. An expert need not state upon what facts her opinion is based (Rule 705).
8. An expert must disclose the facts upon which her opinion is based when required by the court or when asked on cross-examination (Rule 705).

Qualification

Before a witness is allowed to express her opinions pursuant to Federal Rules 702 through 705, she must first be qualified as an expert. With the assistance of the attorney offering the witness as an expert, an examination of the witness' credentials will be conducted. The nature of the qualifying questions will vary from specialty to specialty, generally the questions will focus on the following areas:

a. training
b. education
c. seminars and workshops
d. licensure
e. certification
f. board membership
g. diplomate status
h. professional experience
i. professional organization affiliations
j. teaching experience
k. publication record
l. expert witness experience

Although this is a list of broad areas of inquiry, as we address areas of specialty in subsequent chapters the qualification questions will be specific to the area of expertise. In most instances, a current resume will be helpful to the parties and to refresh recollection. When supplying a resume it is imperative that the resume be accurate, complete, and truthful. Exaggeration is unacceptable. Cross-examination may be based on a thorough investigation of the resume or a prior resume used in another case or context. There are only two ways to disqualify a potential expert:

1. demonstrating to the satisfaction of the court that the expert is not professionally qualified to render opinions in the pending case or that expert testimony is unnecessary, and
2. impeaching the credibility of the prospective witness.

Trial lawyers will often avoid the time-consuming necessity of qualifying an expert witness by agreeing to stipulate to the court that the witness is acceptable as an expert in the specific area for which he is qualified. Why would a lawyer pass up the opportunity to parade an expert's credentials before the jury? If both parties are calling experts and one is substantially better qualified than the other, the attorney with the least qualified expert may suggest that "in the sake of saving court time," a stipulation should be entered agreeing the witness is an expert. However, the lawyer with the better qualified expert would be foolish to miss the opportunity to describe her experts' qualifications. Although it may be easier and save time, an experts' credentials may impress a jury or judge when compared to one not as well qualified. If both experts are comparatively qualified, it may be advantageous to stipulate qualifications of the respective witnesses. Many lawyers will seek stipulation as to expertise because they are not confident in establishing the appropriate predicate or lack enthusiasm for conducting the voir dire or cross-examination of an opposing expert.

Foundation

Once the witness has been qualified as an expert, before her opinion can be solicited, it must first be shown that her opinion was based on data:

    a. perceived prior to the hearing,
    b. perceived during the hearing,
    c. made known to the witness prior to the hearing, or
    d. made known to the witness at the time of the hearing.

Firsthand Knowledge

The standard sequence of questions posed by the attorney offering the expert follows a general pattern. That pattern is designed to establish a "foundation" (predicate — used interchangeably) for the opinion that will be submitted by the expert. That foundation may differ in specifics, but the general purpose and content is the same regardless of specialty.

Knowledge acquired by the expert as a result of her own efforts or perceptions is considered to be "firsthand knowledge" and is solicited by asking:

a. if there is a fact or event that the witness observed that is relevant to the opinion she is to render;

b. when that fact or event was first observed;

c. where and under what conditions the fact or event was first observed;

d. who other than the expert was present at the time of the observation;

e. were there any special techniques or services required to observe the fact or event (how was the event observed);

f. what was the fact or the event that was observed; and finally

g. has the witness formed an opinion based on the observable fact or event?

Hearsay

Prior to 1985, experts were restricted to testifying to what they themselves experienced or observed and the deductions arrived at from those observations. If the fact or event was not observed by the expert, then the prospective testimony would be hearsay and she, as any other witness, could not testify based on hearsay. Recent changes in the rules of evidence on the state and federal levels allow experts to base an opinion on hearsay if that information is the type of information upon which an expert would reasonably rely. Hearsay may be viewed as an out-of-court statement made by someone other than the person testifying. Hearsay is inadmissible, subject to twenty-four exceptions, one of those being that the information is being used by an expert to assist in forming an opinion and the hearsay is information of the type that experts reasonably rely upon. That hearsay evidence may have been obtained prior to trial or during trial; the only proviso to its use is that experts in the field of the testifying expert reasonably rely on such information in forming their opinions.

The questions posed as part of the introductory foundation (or predicate) for hearsay facts or events upon which an expert has based her opinion follow a standard course:

a. certain information was provided to the expert prior to the hearing; or

b. certain information was provided to the expert during the hearing; or

c. certain information was obtained by the expert as she listened to the testimony of others at the hearing; and

d. the expert relied upon that information in part or whole in forming her opinion; and

e. the information upon which the expert has relied is the type reasonably relied upon by experts in the same field in forming such opinions.

Hypothetical Question

Historically, the expert witness could not testify as to ultimate issues; these were left for the judge or jury to decide and witnesses were not allowed to infringe upon hallowed ground. Lawyers with inventive imaginations discovered that the same factual issues involved in a case could be posed to an expert in the form of a "hypothetical" question. In theory, these were not the issues forbidden by the Rules of Evidence but pertained to a hypothetical matter that was unrelated to the case at hand. Everyone knew that the issues in the "hypothetical" question were the same issues in the case in dispute and the facts in the hypothetical question designed to provide information upon which the expert could base his answer were the same facts as those in the case at issue. Everyone associated with this ruse recognized the need for changing the Rules of Evidence to allow experts to address ultimate issues and hearsay information. When the Rules finally were changed allowing experts to testify to ultimate issues and to base their opinion on hearsay, the need for the "hypothetical" question ceased. However, many had become so enamored with the subterfuge and deceit inherent in the hypothetical question that it still abounds in courtrooms across the country. From a practical perspective, the hypothetical question can be useful if an expert is to be called as a witness before other fact witnesses testify. It is the job of fact witnesses to prove up the facts that an expert may use in her testimony. Because of schedule conflicts, a prosecutor may need to call his expert before his investigators. Not an advisable strategy, but "stuff happens." By asking the expert a hypothetical question that includes information not yet testified to, the prosecutor may later bring the fact witnesses to the stand and testify to the facts contained in the "hypothetical" question. Prepared lawyers who know how to establish evidentiary and testimonial foundations (predicates) need not resort to hypothetical questions.

Because hypothetical questions are still widely used, it is necessary to include here the foundation for a hypothetical question:

1. a hypothetical question—the facts to be assumed must be in the form of a question; and
2. based on expert knowledge, education, or training the expert is asked to draw an inference or conclusion from the information provided.

Expert Opinion

Nowhere in the above foundation has the expert been asked to express her expert opinion. All of the foregoing questions are necessary to allow the expert to assert what conclusions he or she has drawn from the facts and events upon which he or she has relied. Once those questions have been satisfactorily answered, the expert is in a legal posture to be asked her opinion. It is at this juncture that the opposing attorney may interject herself and request that the witness be examined as to credentials, facts, and events comprising the foundation, and veracity. This procedure is referred to as voir dire of an expert witness and is not to be confused with the voir dire of a jury panel. Literally voir dire means to speak the truth and applies in both situations. During this voir dire the expert can expect to have any exaggerations, bias, prejudice, or untruths delved into. The only way to prevent embarrassment of the attorney and the expert is for the attorney offering the witness to be as thorough as the opposing attorney in investigating the expert witness and her credentials.

In order for an expert to state an opinion she must first weather the voir dire. Once that has been accomplished, the witness will be returned to the offering attorney who as a matter of course should offer the witness to the court as a qualified witness in the specific area of expertise. The expert will then declare in response to the proper query that:

a. she has an opinion and
b. her opinion is based on a reasonable probability within her area of specialization.

Medical practitioners and scientists will testify to a reasonable medical probability and reasonable scientific probability respectively.

Without further explanation the witness now will be asked what her opinion or opinions are. This is obviously a rather roundabout way to get to where you are going, but the above procedure provides for information and examination of a prospective expert that over time has proven a workable method. Perhaps a bit convoluted, but once the foundation questions and response liturgy have been mastered, it is relatively painless. The expert witness not only must know what her responses to foundation questions are, but there must also be an appreciation for what the questions are attempting to accomplish so that an experienced expert can assist the unartful or inexperienced prosecutor. Absent satisfactory foundation testimony, the opposing attorney will object to the Court's acceptance of the witness and the prospective testimony. Judges have a number of ways to deal with the improper predicate:

1. disallow the testimony,
2. require counsel to continue establishing the foundation,
3. inquire of the objecting counsel what portion of the predicate is missing.

This last technique is used by judges who tend to be prosecutorial in their sympathies: the first option is employed by those judges who tend to sympathize with the defendant. The appropriate approach should be to require the prosecution to continue to attempt to establish the appropriate predicate and when it becomes apparent that the foundation is not going to be provided excuse the witness subject to being recalled at a later time. Hopefully the prosecutor will then take the time to prepare the necessary questions. It is in the interests of justice to allow all relevant testimony before the court.

Although trial techniques vary, once the expert has testified that she has an opinion, the basis for that opinion is the focus of the continuing direct examination. Documents, evidence, witness statements, defendant statements, medical examinations, forensic tests, comparisons, and psychological examinations are generally the stuff upon which experts base their opinions. Each piece of information including textbooks and reference materials, other scientists, technicians, police officers, or investigators who have assisted in arriving at the experts opinion must be addressed and its contribution to the opinion explained. The questions pertaining to the basis of the opinion may not be mined on direct examination; in some instances the prosecution may wish to leave the consideration of the basis of the opinion to the defense attorney. Although not the usual tactic, it may surprise the opposition who will have to develop the bases for opinions expressed while simultaneously trying to challenge them. This technique allows the prosecutor to redirect questions and seemingly bring order to the intentionally-created chaos. Whoever inquires into the bases of the expressed opinions will need to develop the following information:

a. Each bit of information that assisted the expert in formulating her opinion must be described and shown to have been instrumental in arriving at that formulated opinion.
b. Bit by bit, piece by piece, the puzzle should be made whole.
c. The witness should build her opinion from the bottom up, from the smallest bit of information to the next.
d. Once the whole puzzle has been constructed, it should be apparent to all present from where her opinion came.

Learned Treatises

Another latitude granted expert witnesses that is not extended to any other is the ability to refer to authoritative texts germane to the experts area of speciality and prospective opinions. Once the expert has authenticated a text as authoritative, she may then quote from those sources in support of opinions arrived at or procedures employed.

Cross-Examination

Cross examination of an expert is usually conducted to:

a. impeach the credibility of the witness;
b. impeach the qualifications of the witness;
c. impeach the testimony of the witness;
d. demonstrate to the court that the experts testimony is not relevant;
e. demonstrate to the court that the experts testimony is not necessary; or
f. question the chain of evidence.

Cross-examination can occur after the witness has been passed to the defendant or as a voir dire after basic qualifications have been established. The voir dire procedure is usually done outside the presence of the jury and confined to credentials and relevance. The defense may choose to wait until the witness is passed and conduct a cross-examination of credentials, relevance, and credibility in the presence of the jury. The later tactic is dangerous unless the defense has uncovered information that is unflattering to the expert and wants the jury to hear about it. This technique is used to avoid bringing out uncomplimentary information about the witness to the judge absent the jury, and have the judge allow the witness to testify nonetheless. The goal of the defense attorney is to prevent the expert from testifying if possible or to discredit and restrict the testimony. In an effort to accomplish these goals the defense may:

    a. File a pretrial motion in limine — a motion to be heard before trial requesting the court restrict an attorney from inquiring into a particular area in front of the jury until the judge has had an opportunity to rule on the admissibility of the evidence or line of questioning.

Often it is possible to anticipate prospective witness testimony. The limine motion is one way to assure that the questions eliciting certain testimony are not asked until it has been established that the answer is admissible thereby avoiding conjecture on the part of the jury as to what the answer to these inadmissible questions might be. The motion does not prohibit an attorney from asking certain questions. It simply requires that she advise the court that the material in the limine order is about to be pursued and that its relevance should now have been made apparent so there can be no further objection to the prospective questions.

    b. Request that an expert's testimony be restricted to the area of specialization and qualification established in the foundation and none other.

    c. Request that the expert not be allowed to testify to any hearsay upon which she may have based her opinion. The hearsay may be used in basing an opinion, but the expert cannot be used as a conduit through which hearsay evidence is brought before the jury.

    d. Request a continuance to review all the data upon which the expert has relied in forming her opinions.

    e. Challenge the data upon which the expert has relied as not the type reasonably relied upon by experts in that field.

Chapter 3

A BRIEF HISTORY OF EXPERT WITNESSES

In tracing the roots of the use of expert witnesses to resolve disputes, it is necessary to begin in the feudal era. Medieval history reveals that the way for feudalism was paved between the third and sixth centuries and established between the sixth and ninth centuries. Merovingian and Carolingian kings paid their generals and administrators with grants of land; in the ninth century these fiefs became hereditary and semi-independent (Durant, 1950). In those times, Western European society consisted of freemen, serfs, and slaves. Freemen included nobles, clerics, professional soldiers, practitioners of the professions, most merchants and artisans, and peasants who owned their land or leased it from a feudal lord. The feudal law of property was complex and unique. It recognized three forms of land possession:

1. the allod, unconditional ownership;
2. the fief—land whose use but not ownership was granted to a vassal on condition of service; and
3. tenure—where use was granted on condition of payment.

Typically, the serf tilled a plot of land owned by a lord or baron who gave him a life tenure and military protection as long as he paid an annual rent in products, labor, or money. In feudal theory only the king had absolute ownership of the land, the loftiest of nobles was only a tenant (Durant, 1950).

Feudal Experts

As disputes involving land use and succession arose, manorial courts were established to settle disputes between tenant and tenant, or between tenant and lord; disputes between lord and vassal, or lord and lord were submitted to juries of men of equal standing and of the same fief. Procedure in feudal law attempted to extend efforts to substitute public penalties for private revenge. In this regime where judges and executors

17

of law were usually illiterate, custom and law were largely one. When question arose as to law or penalty, the oldest members of the community were asked what had been the custom thereon in their youth. Age and recall being the required qualifying characteristics for admitting their learned opinion. The community itself was the chief source of law and the elders of the community were called as experts by the court to assist in a consistent application of an unwritten law and its penalties.

Truth by ordeal has a history that extends beyond the Old Testament and has been applied by aborigines of the Australian Outback, Africans, and Scandinavians (Holland, 1995). The Old Testament speaks of poison as a truth determiner and it was used in that vein in Africa and India (Holland, 1995). The ordeal was superstition applied to resolve legal disputes, the belief that a supreme being would not let an innocent suffer provided for the foundation. God or the gods were called upon to serve as an expert in assisting the trier of fact in determining guilt or innocence. The ordeal took many forms, from walking on red hot plowshares to being bound and thrown in a pond. The conventional wisdom (science?) supported the belief that witches would not allow themselves to drown and the innocent would sink. Dead but guiltless was the desired outcome. Obviously, an "expert" postulated the "fact" that bound witches float and innocent people walking across red hot plowshares will not be burned.

Trial by ordeal continued until banned by Pope Innocent III at the Fourth Lateran Council in 1216. English King Henry III adopted this prohibition into English law in 1219. In Germany the old tests persisted into the fourteenth century; it was revived again in the trials of witches in the sixteenth century.

Feudalism encouraged a revival of a ritual of Germanic history, trial by combat. England retained trial by combat in its statutes until the late nineteenth century. As early as the tenth century, paid champions were allowed to substitute for the aggrieved parties. God would decide the issue according to the justice of the accusation not the respective strength or prowess of the "experts." The use of champions cast discredit upon trial by combat and Pope Innocent III prohibited trial by combat in 1215.

The Early Inquisition

Any nation preparing for war is well advised and often does seek out minor skirmishes to prepare troops and equipment for major engagements. The Church of Rome was no exception. The continuing war on hearsay that culminated in "The Papal Inquisition" began with a series of inquisitional skirmishes that had their justification steeped in the Old Testament.

The Old Testament laid down a simple code for dealing with heretics: they were to be carefully examined; and if three reputable witnesses testified to their having "gone and served other gods," the heretics were to be led out from the city and "stoned with stones till they die" (Deut. xvii, 25).

In classical Rome, where the gods were allied with the state in close harmony, heresy and blasphemy were classed with treason, and were punishable with death. Where no accuser could be found to denounce and offender, the Roman judge summoned the suspect and made an *inquisitio*, or inquiry, into the case; from this procedure the medieval Inquisition took its form and name.

It was the general assumption of Christians that the Church had been established by the Son of God. On this assumption, any attack upon the Catholic faith was an offense against God Himself; the contumacious heretic could only be viewed as an agent of Satan, sent to undo the work of Christ; and any man or government that tolerated heresy was serving the devil. The Church looked upon heresy precisely as the state looked upon treason: it was an attack upon the very foundation of social order. "The civil law," said Pope Innocent III, "punishes traitors with confiscation of their property, and death ... All the more, then, should we excommunicate, and confiscate the property of, those who are traitors to the faith of Jesus Christ; for it is an infinitely greater sin to offend the divine majesty than to attack the majesty of the sovereign" (Durant, 1950 p. 777).

Normally, before the thirteenth century, inquisition into heresy was left to local bishops who waged local wars against a rising heresy. Berthold of Regensburg estimated there were 150 heretical sects in the thirteenth century. Most of these were harmless groups who gathered to study the Bible without the assistance of a priest and to interpret various passages as they saw fit. Many felt that priests should live in poverty as did Christ. The Franciscan movement arose as such a sect, and narrowly escaped being treated as heretical. A few heretical movements, however, did pose a direct threat to the Catholic Church and its hierarchy. The *Cathari* in France denounced the Church for its materialism and other spectral appetites. An ever growing body of disenchanted Catholics began denouncing the practices of the priests and gravitated to the *Cathari* movement. In 1167, various branches of the *Cathari* held a council of their clergy, attended by representatives from several countries. The disenfranchised nobility supported the *Cathari* in an effort to weaken the Church because of the imposing land ownership resulting from property confiscations. The people of Europe decried the leniency of the bishops in addressing heresy and demanded swift, more severe treatment of the heretic. The state, with some reluctance, joined in persecuting heretics because it feared that government would be impossible without the aid of a unified religious belief. Materialism may have played a part in the religious war on heresy. The church and state with abandon required confiscation of the property of heretics. King Robert of France had thirteen heretics burned at Orleans in 1022, the first case of capital punishment for heresy since 385. Other monarchs followed suit; Henry III of Germany hanged several *Cathari* at Goslar over the protests of the presiding bishop. In 1183, Count Philip of Flanders, in collaboration with the archbishop of Reims, sent many nobles, clerics, and knights to the stake; confiscated their property; and shared it between them.

In 1185, Pope Lucius III, dissatisfied with the negligence of the bishops in pursuing heresy, ordered them to visit their parishes at least once a year, to arrest all suspects, to reckon as guilty any who would not swear full loyalty to the Church (the *Cathari* refused to take any oaths), and to hand over such recalcitrants to the government. Papal legates were empowered to depose bishops negligent in stamping out heresy. Innocent III, in 1215, required all civil authorities, on pain of death, to swear publicly to exterminate, from the lands subject to their obedience, all heretics.

When Gregory IX mounted the papal throne (1227), he found that despite prosecutions, heresy was growing in most of Italy and France. Pope Gregory appointed a board of inquisitors, headed by a Dominican monk, to sit in Florence and bring the heretics to judgment (1227). This in effect was the beginning of the papal inquisition. The Inquisition was now officially established under the control of the popes.

After 1227, Gregory and his successors sent out an increasing number of special inquisitors to pursue heresy. Inquisitorial procedure might begin with the summary arrest of all heretics, sometimes also of all suspects; the visiting inquisitors might summon the entire adult population of a locality for a preliminary examination. Heretics who did not confess were cited before the inquisitorial court. Accused persons could be tried in their absence and condemned to death. Two condemnatory witnesses were required. After 1254, the inquisitors were required to submit all evidence to a group of men of high repute from the community. Often a board of experts (*periti*) was called upon to pass on the evidence.

In condemning the inquisition and the methods employed in extracting confessions, it should be noted that three legal precedents were established that have innured to our benefit as a result of the inquisition:

1. confessions must be voluntary;
2. a suspect cannot be convicted on the uncorroborated testimony of an accomplice; and
3. the concept of burden of proof rests upon the accusing party.

Interestingly, the rationale for using torture to solicit incriminating statements was based on a benevolent motive. The Church believed that it was necessary to prove guilt beyond not just a reasonable doubt but beyond all doubt. The only way that all doubt could be removed was through self-incrimination. The end sought was admirable; it was the means to that end that we now question.

The Common Law

In early English Common Law history, there seem to have been two modes of using expert knowledge:

1. to select as jurymen such persons as were by experience especially fitted to know the class of facts which were before them, and
2. to call to the aid of the court skilled persons whose opinion it might adopt or not as it pleased.

The first has been lost, but the second is alive and well along with a third more contemporary application of having the parties in dispute bring forth skilled persons to testify.

The first method mentioned above was to impanel a "special jury," which in this connection means a jury of persons especially fitted to judge the peculiar facts of the case in issue. The first recorded incidence of such a "special jury" took place in 1838 (*Rey v. Wyoherly*, 8 C&P. p. 262, 1838). A jury of persons especially skilled in landlord tenant relations was impanelled and their opinions were followed by the court in disposing of the matter (id.). This specially impanelled jury was no anomaly and its use in resolving trade disputes was common in the city of London throughout the fourteenth century (Riley, 1868).

The special jury continued as an institution of England. We find in 1645 that the court summoned a jury of merchants to try merchants' affairs because it was conceived they might have a better understanding of the issues in dispute than others who were not of the profession (Hand, 1901).

The second method mentioned above was to summon to the advice of the court certain skilled persons to help it out of its difficulties. In 1345, in an appeal of mayhem, the court summoned surgeons from London to aid them in learning whether or not a wound was fresh (Riley, 1868). In 1409 and 1555, documents submitted to the court, partly in Latin, prompted the justices to seek grammatical masters to assist in the interpretation and construction of the documents (*Buckley v. Thomas*, 1 Plow. 118, 1555). Lord Holt of the Kings Bench, in deciding the celebrated case of *Buller v. Crips*, asked the opinion of London merchants as to the effect of refusing negotiability of promissory notes (*Buller v. Crips*, 6 Mod. 29, 1703).

Originally, and for many years under common law trial practice, the jury had no witnesses present before them at all. They were advised of the issues in dispute and were allowed to cast about at their own discretion in gathering what facts might be available. Those facts were brought with them to the court and considered amongst the jurors during their deliberations. It was not until the middle of the fifteenth century that the courts developed the practice of summoning witnesses for the purpose of providing testimony, and it was still later that compulsory process became available (Hand, 1901).

The rules of evidence in England evolved slowly and were focused upon the regulation of what evidence the jury could see and hear. Through successive court decisions, judges gradually restricted the material witnesses might present to the jury. The rule that a witness may not testify to mere opinion was promulgate. A rule was designed to relegate the irrelevant and redundant inadmissible. The rule prohibiting witness opinions seems to have been applied as early as 1671 wherein the court said that a witness swears but to what he hath heard or seen, generally or more largely, to what hath fallen under his senses. But a Juryman swears to what he can infer and conclude from the Testimony of such Witnesses by the act and force of the Understanding, to be the Fact inquired after, which differs nothing in the Reason, though in the punishment, from what a Judge, out of various Cases consider'd by him, infers to be the Law in the Question before him. (Bushell's Case 22, Car. p. 2, 1671)

It was to this rule, prohibiting opinion evidence, that the courts excepted experts. Obviously, an anomaly in the procedural law that was the resort of the court when an issue was reached that was beyond their ken. This anomaly that inured to the benefit of the court was extended to trial adversaries in 1678 in the Case of Rex v Pembroke. (*Rex v. Pembroke*, 7 Howell, State Trials, p. 185–86, 1678. See also: *Rex v. Green*, 6 Howell, State Trials, p. 1337, 1678. Spencer Cowper's Case, State Trials, 13 Howell 1126–35, 1699). This was a trial for murder and the question was raised as to the cause and mechanism of death. Out of an abundance of caution, the court allowed both sides to present physicians, thereby balancing the latitude extended the parties. The court delegated the exception that it had reserved unto itself, to trial adversaries, in the hopes that expert opinion to assist the court could be anticipated and provided for by the litigants.

Finally, Lord Ellenborough ruled definitively upon the general question of expert opinion testimony in 1807. That ruling distinctly recognized the significance of expert testimony and placed it in its contemporary context. The case was a cause of action on a marine insurance policy. The insurer alleged fraud in the inducement of the policy in that the insurer contended that the vessel was unseaworthy at the time the policy was underwritten. The defendant offered to call several eminent surveyors, who had not seen the ship but intended to testify as to their opinions based on the facts in evidence. The plaintiff objected that this was a fact issue for the jury to decide to which witnesses might not allude. Lord Ellenborough overruled the objection and said:

> As the truth of the facts stated to them was not certainly known, their opinion might not go for much; but still it was admissible evidence. The prejudice alluded to might be removed by asking them, in cross-examination, what they should think upon the statement of facts contended for on the other side (*Beckwith v. Sydebotham*, 1 Camp, p. 116, 1807).

Lord Ellenborough thus gave birth to the fledgling industry of expert witnesses as well as the ubiquitous hypothetical question.

Contemporary Experts

Experts have been the source of insight as well as chicanery. In 1781, Sir William Herschel, the British astronomer who discovered the planet Uranus, was convinced and publicly pronounced that the "the sun was richly stored with inhabitants" (Gardner, 296:1957). Physicians of the nineteenth century were encouraged by Dr. Linard Williams, who was the medical officer to the Insurance Institute of London, to treat those with wide set eyes as horses or cows because the set of their eyes suggested they were not evolved from meat eating predators but rather from vegetarian bovine and equine (id at 301). Even the noted physicist Lord Kelvin believed that x-rays were a hoax (id at 296). Had these scientists been called as expert witnesses in their questionable areas of expertise, what havoc would have been wrecked upon an unsuspecting jury and court? What irreparable damage might have been done to the litigants? Although Sir William Herschel was an eminent astronomer, could he and should he have been allowed to testify as to the inhabitants of the sun? The credentials an expert may have should be strictly and narrowly construed in qualifying that witness to testify. Just as no responsible attorney should question an expert without some perfunctory understanding of the scientific knowledge that is central to the expected testimony, so no lawyer should accept an adversary's expert's credentials sight unseen. There is little argument that forewarned is forearmed; the presumption in dealing with expert witnesses is that credentials must be verified, not only those of the expert testifying for the opposition, but those of friendly experts as well. Precious time spent on credential verification will be well borne when puffery, exaggeration, and lies are discovered in the credentials of your adversary's hired champion. A complete verification of an expert's credentials will include a thorough perusal of all available articles, journals, texts, and depositions available authored by the expert. When state scientists and technicians are to be called, each such expert should have on file a line-by-line verification of his or her educational and occupational achievements. Puffery in a resume when seeking employment may be unethical; puffery in trial evidence is illegal and anathemical to a successful outcome.

REFERENCES

Deuteronomy Chapter 17 verse 25, *King James Edition.*

Durant, W. 1995. *The Age of Faith.* New York: Simon and Schuster.

Hand, L. Considerations regarding expert testimony. *Harvard Law Review* 1:40–58, 1901.

Gardner, M. 1957. *Fads and Fallacies in the Name of Science.* New York: Ballantine.

Holland, B. Do you swear that you will well and truly try . . . ? *Smithsonian* pp. 108–117, March, 1995.

Riley, H.T. 1868. *Memorials of London and London Life in the 13th, 14th, and 15th Centuries.* London: Longmans, Green & Co.

Table of Cases

Beckwith v. Sydebotham, 1 Camp. p. 116, 1807.

Buckley v. Thomas, 1 Plow. p. 118, 1555.

Buller v. Crips, 6 Mod. p. 29, 1703.

Bushell's Case, 22 Car. p. 2, 1671.

Rey v. Wyoherly, 8 C.&P. p. 262, 1838.

Rex v. Green, 7 Howell, State Trials, p. 185–86, 1682.

Rex v. Pembroke, 6 Howell, State Trials, p. 1337–41, 1678.

Spencer v. Cowper's Case, 13 Howell, State Trials, p. 1126–35, 1699.

Chapter 4

FINGERPRINTS

Television, books, and movies have often emphasized the value of fingerprints in solving serious crimes. Until the advent of computer technology, that value was mostly mythical. Fingerprints were used to inculpate or exculpate based on a suspect group. A search of fingerprint files for the match to a fingerprint found at the scene of a crime was the subject of fiction. The classification system used in categorizing stored fingerprints, and the large number of fingerprints stored, made it impossible to manually check through a fingerprint collection looking for a match. Computers have turned art into reality. Automated fingerprint identification systems (AFIS) now allow police to do what screenwriters and movie directors have long pretended they could.

The possibilities this technology provides can only be appreciated when we consider the size of the fingerprint data base the federal government has collected. The Federal Bureau of Investigation has been receiving copies of fingerprint cards from all state and federal agencies that require employees to be fingerprinted. They have copies of all the prints of persons who have served in wars from Korea to Desert Storm. Additionally they have copies of all persons arrested, as juveniles or adults, for misdemeanors or felonies, which arrest resulted in booking the suspect. In considering the vast numbers, we can see the potential tool that has awaited technology's arrival.

Finger Individuality

No two fingers have yet been found that share identical characteristics. Fingerprint individuality is not dependent on age, size, gender, or race. The identifiable aspects of a fingerprint is called minutiae (ridge characteristics). The shape, location, and number of minutiae individualize a fingerprint. There is no agreement as to how many ridge characteristics must be present between a discovered print and that of a suspect before they can be said to be identical. After a three-year study, the International Association for Identification determined that "no valid basis exists for requiring a predetermined minimum number of friction ridge characters which must be present in two impressions in order to establish positive identification" (Saferstein, 1995). In each and every instance when identification is made between two impressions, that identification will be the product of a comparison done by an expert. The value of the expert opinion will be based upon:

1. the number of comparable ridge characteristics,
2. the knowledge of the expert,
3. the experience of the expert,
4. the ability of the expert to explain how that comparison was done, and
5. the quality of the testimony of the adverse expert.

Immutability

From birth to death, a fingerprint retains its classifiable characteristics. The hand and fingers may grow, the print will enlarge with that growth, but the ridge characteristics will remain the same. Efforts to eradicate prints are futile and the scar tissue that results from attempts to do so are as individual as were the small number of ridge characteristics that may have been destroyed. Fingerprints are a mirror image of the friction ridge skin of the palm, fingers and thumb. It is these friction ridges of skin that are reproduced by the black lines of an inked fingerprint impression.

The friction ridges of the fingers when examined under a microscope reveal a single row of pores that are ducts through which sweat is deposited. That sweat, along with body oils which have been picked up when the fingers touch other parts of the body, may be deposited upon a touched surface. This touch may result in a transfer of sweat and oils in the shape of finger friction skin ridges (fingerprint) onto the surface touched. Prints that are deposited onto a surface but invisible to the naked eye are latent prints. Only those that cannot be readily seen with the unassisted eye can be technically referred to as latent prints. Police have embraced the term latent to mean any fingerprint left at a crime scene whether visible or not.

Classifying Prints

There are three classes into which prints may fall based on general patterns. The most common class is the **loop;** about 65 percent of the population have loop patterns on at least one finger. Approximately 35 percent of the population have a **whorl** pattern on a finger or thumb, and only about 5 percent of the population have **arches.**

Loop Patterns

Loops must have one or more ridges entering from one side of the print, recurving and exiting from the same side. Loops are divided into two groups:

1. ulnar loops — those that open toward the little finger and
2. radial loops — those that open toward the thumb.

Additionally, a loop pattern must have a core and a delta. The core is the center most point of the loop at the apex of the innermost ridge of the loop. The delta is a two-sided triangular shape to one side of the loop that resembles a river delta (loop prints have only one delta per print). These two points are necessary in further classifying a print based on the number of friction ridges between the delta and the core of the loop.

Whorl Patterns

As is often the case in things technical, the classification of whorls is needlessly confusing. This confusion arises as a result of the four groupings into which a whorl pattern may fall:

1. plain whorl
2. central pocket loop whorl
3. double loop whorl
4. accidental whorl

The confusion for those unaccustomed to print classification results in using the word loop in describing a whorl pattern while at the same time having a pattern which is not a whorl called a loop. It helps to clear the fog if we remember that the two loop patterns are radial and ulnar, based on the radial and ulnar bones in the arm. The use of the descriptive terms "central pocket loop" and "double loop" can be seen as loops occurring inside a whorl, therefore central pocket loop whorl and double loop whorl. Remember that a radial and ulnar loop have but one delta.

It is a necessary element of a whorl pattern that there be a minimum of two deltas. What appears to be a loop having two deltas is a double loop whorl or a central pocket loop whorl. Any pattern that is not covered by one of the categories or is two patterns in one print is called an accidental.

Arches

The least common pattern is also the simplest to classify. Arches are either plain or tented. A plain arch is formed by friction ridges entering from one side of the print and exiting on the opposite side rising to a peak in the center of the ridge forming a hill like pattern. The tented arch instead of rising gently to the center and sloping easily away, thrusts up in the center and falls quickly away.

It is basic to fundamental understanding of fingerprint comparisons to understand the fingerprint patterns. Once prints can be compared as to pattern the individual print can be further examined for similarities in ridge numbers and configuration.

Detecting Prints

Although police use the term latent (invisible) print to describe fingerprints found at a crime scene, many of the prints discovered are visible and the word latent when applied to such prints is incorrect and misleading. Any lawyer or expert who unartfully uses the word latent to describe a visible print can expect to be challenged on competent cross examination. Such a simple point is not lost on jurors who are looking for a simple understandable reason for determining why one witness is more believable than another. There are three distinct types of prints found at a crime scene:

1. visible prints
2. plastic prints
3. latent prints

Friction skin ridges found on the finger are finger skin friction ridges. Residue left on surfaces reflecting these finger skin friction ridges are fingerprints or fingerprint impressions. Just as a photographic print is not the original scene depicted in the photo, it helps in understanding fingerprint vocabulary to remember that fingerprints are not the actual finger skin friction ridges.

Visible Prints

These prints are readily identifiable as fingerprints with the unassisted eye. Visible prints are left by fingers that have been in contact with a colored material such as toner, ink, blood, paint, oil, chocolate, or any other such substance. Once the material has soiled the fingers the material may be transferred to a surface to which ridges have come in contact. It is important that such prints be immediately photographed and can often be preserved by bagging the object upon which they were found, relegating the surface upon which they were found small enough to be bagged or they can be lifted as described below in the procedure for lifting latent prints. A dry bloody finger print on the body of a decedent can be lifted using lift tape, rather than to mutilate the body in attempting to preserve the print. Any such efforts should have been preceded by a set of photographs in case the lifting procedure was not successful.

Plastic Prints

If fingers come in contact with a soft material such as soap, wet putty, wet cement, wet plaster, dust, or other such materials, a ridge impression may be left sufficient upon which comparisons can be made. As children, most of us have left hand, foot, or finger impressions in wet cement. In Hollywood, a cultural artifact has been built around celebrities embedding their hands and feet in a wet cement paver leaving hand and foot prints. These are plastic impressions upon which a fingerprint comparison could be made. If such a celebrity were a suspect in a crime and was not forthcoming with inked impressions (prints taken by the police), there is a very good probability that a comparison could be made with the suspect print and that left in the cement in Hollywood.

Latent Prints (Invisible Prints)

Body perspiration and oils may conspire in leaving invisible residues on surfaces that if visualized would be a usable impression of the finger skin friction ridges of the finger(s) that left them. Visualizing such prints requires the use of techniques, chemicals, and powders the selection of which is based upon the type of surface upon which the latent print reposes. Developing prints from a nonabsorbent surface requires a different approach than developing prints from softer more absorbent surfaces.

Developing Prints

Fingerprints discovered on absorbent surfaces lend themselves to visualization through the application of powder. The type of powder varies depending on a number of variables.

Powders

Latent prints may be developed (visualized) by applying one of a variety of fingerprint powders available from a large number of distributors of fingerprinting equipment. These powders differ in color, consistency, density, and polarity. They may be applied by brush, magnetic wand, or blown onto the latent print. The powder will cling to the fluids that created the fingerprint. Excess powder will be removed by whirling a camel hair brush while it hovers above the print or by blowing the excess powder from the print. The technical skill arises in the selection of the appropriate powder for the print, surface composition, and surface color. Light powders for dark surfaces and dark powder for light surfaces. The method whereby the print is visualized is referred to as the development of the print (heavy hands do not a fingerprint technician make). On horizontal surfaces, once the print is developed, the technician can write in the excess powder around the impression her name, the date, crime scene location, and case number. The information written in the excess powder can be lifted at the same time as the impression, thereby creating a record that is part of the impression. If the surface is horizontal, a "tag board" (a white piece of rigid cardboard) can be propped up against the vertical surface or taped next to it, upon which the same information is recorded. Once developed and tagged, it should be photographed. This obsession with photography can best be understood after losing a print during the lift process or misplacing the print once lifted. Additionally, it will be the photograph that will allow enlargements of the suspect and latent print to be presented to the jury during expert testimony to assist the jury in understanding why this person and only this person could have left the print.

Chemical Development

The most common chemical used for developing latent prints on porus (as opposed to nonporous) surfaces such as paper and cloth is ninhydrin. Ninhydrin chemically reacts with the amino acids in sweat and renders a purple-blue colored print. The color is reminiscent of the copies teachers use to pass out to students run from a spirit master. Ninhydrin (triketohydrindene hydrate) is sprayed on the surface. The chemical is commercially available in fuming spray cans and wet wipes for ease of application. Development time of one to twenty-four hours can be hastened by heating the specimen to a temperature of 100 degrees centigrade.

Super glue fuming is gaining acceptance in technical circles for the development of fingerprints on nonporous surfaces such as formica, metal, or plastic bags. Super Glue is cyanoacrylate ester; this is the chemical that develops the print. Cyanoacrylate fumes are created when super glue is heated or placed on a piece of cotton with sodium hydroxide. The item upon which the latent is impressed must be placed along with the super glue in an air-tight container and allowed to "work." After five hours the fumes will begin to adhere to the latent print and develop that print. The hand-held cyanoacrylate wand can be used at the crime scene to develop latents in lieu of powder. The problems associated with powder development are avoided when using the fuming wand. The print is not likely to be obliterated or smeared by a heavy-handed technician.

Florescence and Alternate Light Sources

The earliest use of florescence to visualize fingerprints came with the illumination provided by argon-ion lasers. The laser was used when it was discovered that the blue-green light of the laser made sweat fluoresce (like the black light posters of the 1960s). It was later discovered that fingerprints treated with zinc chloride after ninhydrin or the application of the dye rhodamine 6G after super glue fuming caused fluorescence and sensitivity to laser light. These discoveries led to experimentation with alternate light sources as a method of visualizing fingerprints (Saferstein, 1995). Today there are numerous products that use light to visualize fingerprints and they have decreased the time and effort necessary to develop fingerprints.

The use of various powders and chemicals to develop fingerprints must be approached with a word of caution especially in the case of blood and any evidence that may be related to blood traces. All common fingerprint developers interfere with blood testing used to classify bloodstains (Duncan, 1986).

Handling and Preserving Prints

Once the latent print has been developed it, like plastic and visible prints, must be prepared and preserved for possible use in the laboratory and courtroom. As mentioned above, it cannot be stressed too strongly the necessity of photographing the visualized print before further handling. Once print photos have been obtained efforts can be made to remove the print from the crime scene. As mentioned earlier this can be done by preserving the item upon which the print lies or by "lifting" powdered prints. Specialized adhesive lifters are provided by numerous manufacturers. The lifter is a transparent tape which is placed on the powdered print with the adhesive side down. When the tape is removed, the fingerprint powder is removed with it. The lifter is provided with a black or white card upon which the transparent tape and powdered print can then be placed, adhesive side down. The colored card provides contrast to the colored powder used, which visualizes the print on the lift card. "Lift" tape comes in a variety of sizes and configurations depending on the size, number, and location of the print(s) being "lifted."

Direct Examination

Latent Crime Scene Fingerprint Expert

What follows is a sample of a direct examination of a laboratory technician who discovered and lifted a latent fingerprint at a crime scene. Bear in mind that it may require more than one witness to lay the complete predicate for a piece of evidence. For example, a homicide investigator discovers a gun at a crime scene and after proper measuring and handling turns it over to the crime scene technicians to check for latent prints. The technician discovers latent prints and manages to successfully develop, photograph, and "lift" the print. A suspect has inked fingerprint impressions taken. The latent print and the inked impression are provided to the crime laboratory for classification and comparison. It will take the testimony of four witnesses before the comparison can be admitted as evidence:

1. The investigator who discovered the weapon will identify the weapon and attest to the fact that it is the one found and testify that it has not in any way been altered since his discovery.

2. The technician who developed, photographed, and "lifted" the print will extend the custody chain, identify the weapon, identify the latent prints, describe the method whereby the print was developed and "lifted," and attest that it has not been altered.

3. The officer taking the inked impression of the suspect will identify the inked impression, identify the person from whom the impressions were taken, and attest that the card upon which the impressions have been inked and the impressions have not been altered.

4. The laboratory technician will extend the custody chain for both the inked and latent prints, identify both, and express an opinion regarding the laboratory comparison that was made.

As each witness testifies, the prosecutor will request that provisional admissibility be allowed the exhibit pending the anticipated cumulative testimony of all four witnesses. After all four witnesses have testified, the prosecutor should have overcome any objections as to the authenticity of the exhibit offered, and the court should allow the exhibit into evidence (Becker, 1995).

Q. Would you state your name please?

A. Respond with full legal name.

Q. Where do you live?

A. A completely irrelevant question that the witness may choose not to answer. This question is so commonly asked that few lawyers bother to ask what relevance it may have to the testimony about to be elicited. If a police officer prefers that her home not be a matter of public record, the prosecutor should not ask this question.

Q. What is your occupation (profession)?

A. Give specific function and organization.

Q. How long have you served in that capacity?

A. An approximation should be made and stated as such.

Q. For whom did you work prior to this position?

A. This question should begin a review of all professional employment leaving no gaps unaddressed. Approximate times and dates should suffice. The witness should describe one position at a time and wait for a prompt from the prosecutor before continuing. Keep in mind that the opposition has checked the witnesses work history and may have a better recollection of that work record than does the witness.

Q. Returning to your current employment, what is your responsibility pertaining to fingerprints and crime scenes?

A. locating, visualizing (developing), photographing, and lifting fingerprints.

Q. To perform the type of work that you do, are there any educational or training requirements?

A. Describe fully all relevant education, training, workshops, and seminars.

Q. Is there a certification process required for the type of services you provide?

A. Describe all certification requirements.

Q. Have you ever published an article pertaining to your work?

A. To be asked only if such publications exist.

Q. Describe each relevant article?

A. Title, publisher and summary.

Q. Do you belong to any professional organizations?

A. To be asked only if such membership exists and is relevant.

Q. Have you taught any seminars, workshops, or classes pertaining to your area of specialization?

A. To be asked only if such teaching has occurred.

Q. Have you testified in court before pertaining to fingerprint identification (this word may need to be replaced if objected to by the defense, possible substitutes: visualization, development, "lifting")?

A. Yes.

Q. How many times?

A. An approximation may be acceptable if the number is large and the exact number is not known. An estimate must be qualified as such.

Q. How many times have you testified on behalf of the state? (This question is optional depending on whether or not the prosecutor anticipates the defense asking the question. This question has more relevance for expert witnesses who are not employed by the state. Nonetheless, it is always better to hear any unfavorable testimony during the direct examination to reduce the impact if brought out on cross examination.)

A. An approximation will do if the specific number is not known.

Q. In the course of your employment as a fingerprint technician, approximately how many fingerprints have you discovered?

A. An approximation will do.

Q. In the course of your employment as a fingerprint technician, approximately how many fingerprints have you developed using fingerprint powder?

A. An approximation.

Q. In the course of your employment as a fingerprint technician, approximately how many fingerprints have you photographed?

A. An approximation.

Q. In the course of your employment as a fingerprint technician, approximately how many fingerprints have you "lifted"?

Although not required in most jurisdictions, this would be the point where a formal offer to the court be made of the expert as having been qualified as an expert in the field of fingerprint discovery, fingerprint development, fingerprint photography, and fingerprint "lifting." Even in jurisdictions where such offer is not required, there is no jurisdiction that prohibits the offering attorney from making such an offer. Having the court accept the witness as an expert can only help to bolster her testimony in the eyes of the jurors. Continuing the examination will require the defense to interpose a request that the defense be allowed to voir dire the witness as to her expertise. The offer of the witness will signal to the defense the opportunity to make such a request. Many defense lawyers will attempt to interrupt the offering attorney before the witness has been completely qualified. The appropriate response to such an interruption is to advise the court that you have not yet completed qualification of the witness. Expert witness qualification will go a long way in convincing the jury that this witness is to be believed, and the process should not be bypassed or shortened for anyone's convenience, except perhaps the judge's (and that done only under protest (objection)). Once the expert is qualified and withstands impeachment efforts during the defendant's voir dire, the examination can now continue and begin to focus on the evidence as opposed to the expert's qualifications.

Q. Can you tell us what a fingerprint is?

A. The pattern of the finger friction skin ridges left on a touched surface.

Q. Can you explain what you mean by finger friction skin ridges?

A. The raised ridges on the surface of the fingers and thumbs.

Q. Does everyone have such ridges?

A. Yes.

Q. Are these ridges unique to each individual?

A. To date, in the millions of fingerprints that have been taken, no two people have been found to have the identical fingerprint.

Keep in mind that simple is understandable and that simple is believable. The responsibility of a lawyer and his expert is to conspire to make the complex understandable and the difficult simple. Language should facilitate communication. Technical vocabularies enhance communication between individuals who share the same vocabulary. It can be used for purposes other than communication. It can intentionally confuse and intimidate. Unexplained technical language and jargon have no place in the courtroom. There is no technical word or combination of words that cannot be translated into understandable nontechnical communication. Often lawyers use legal words when talking to other lawyers. Law students become lawyers by using a newly learned vocabulary until it becomes a natural process. Doctors also have a very technical vocabulary that allows them to communicate effectively and efficiently. Using these vocabularies among peers is what such vocabularies were designed for. Using such vocabularies among people who do not share that faculty is self-aggrandizing and self-defeating. People may be impressed and intimidated, but they certainly do not understand what is being said, and if they do not understand it, how can they be expected to believe it? Simply put, anything that can be spoken, from foreign languages to technical languages, can be translated into words a well-educated 15-year-old can understand. If it cannot, it is either because that communication is spurious or the party communicating does not understand it. For example, a resection, externalization, and anastomosis convey considerable information from one doctor to another but have little value in describing what took place to the average patient, family, or jury. The same concepts can be conveyed by describing the removal of a part of the intestine, sewing the ends together, and leaving those ends outside the body until they heal, at which time they can be replaced inside the body. Keep it simple, keep it understandable, keep it believable.

Q. Are there different types of fingerprints that can be left at a crime scene?

A. Yes.

Q. Can you describe them for us?

A. Visual, plastic and latent.

Q. What is a visual print?

A. One that can be seen with the naked eye.

Q. Can you give the jury an example?

A. If a finger contacts oil, paint, blood, or some similar material it may leave an impression of the finger ridges.

Q. What is a plastic print?

A. The best example of a plastic print would be the impression left after a child pressed her hand onto a wet cement sidewalk (or any similar material which may be in question).

Q. What is a latent print?

A. Finger friction skin ridges have pores through which sweat is released. These friction ridges may also pick up oils as a result of hand and finger contact with the face and hair. These oils and sweat may be deposited on a surface in the pattern of the friction skin ridges of the finger or fingers that made contact with that surface.

Q. Will you describe to the jury how such an invisible fingerprint is found at a crime scene?

A. There are two general ways in which a latent print can be found:
1. random application of powder placed on various surfaces which the suspect may have touched, or
2. certain types of lights when shone upon a surface from an angle will illuminate the print so that the eye can now see it.

Q. Once you have found it, what then do you do with it?

A. If it appears on examination under a magnifying glass that the print has sufficient ridge patterns, we will develop it, photograph it and "lift" it.

It should be pointed out that this will be an area of fruitful cross examination if the number of identifiable ridge characteristics are minimal. Comparisons between the crime scene latent and the defendant's inked fingerprint impression can become more meaningful even if limited in number if a chart-sized enlargement is used for those comparisons. It is at this juncture that such demonstrative evidence can begin to be used.

Q. I hand you what has been marked as State's Exhibit Number 1 and ask you if you can identify it?

A. It is an enlargement of a fingerprint. (Any objection at this point should be overruled if the enlargement is simply being used for demonstrative purposes and not as evidence. If the enlargement is of the defendant's inked fingerprint that is going to be used for comparison purposes, it can be admitted later. Reference to this enlargement will again be made during the direct examination of the expert who is going to provide comparison testimony and it will be proven up and entered into evidence at that time. Presume that this witness will not provide comparison testimony.)

Q. Will you point out for the jurors where the finger friction skin ridges are represented?

A. Approach the enlargement and do so.

Q. Once you have discovered a latent print with sufficient ridge characteristics, what would you do with it?

A. Photograph it?

Q. Would you take the photograph?

A. Yes.

Q. What type of camera do you use to photograph the latent impression once you have found it on an object at a crime scene?

A. It is a camera specially designed for fingerprint photography.

Q. How does it work?

A. The lens tube is placed around the latent impression so that the impression is centered; the lens and camera produce a negative that is the same size as the impression. It is a 35mm, single reflex, auto focus camera operating with a set of four strobe lights.

Q. After you photograph a latent fingerprint that you have made visible, what do you do with it?

A. It is marked "lifted" and mounted.

Q. How do you mark a fingerprint?

A. There is a paper backing upon which the fingerprint after being lifted will be mounted. That paper backing has information lines for time, date, case identification number, and technician name. This information is recorded prior to "lifting" the print.

Q. What do you do with the latent print after it has been marked?

A. I "lift" the print.

Q. Will you explain to the jury what you mean when you say you "lift" the print?

A. A "lift" is a transparent tape backed by a silicon-treated piece of paper. The tape is hinged at one end of the paper to allow the transparent tape to be separated from the paper, allowing the tape to be placed over the visualized impression adhesive side down. The tape is smoothed over the impression, then lifted straight up. When done correctly, the powder, in the shape of the impression, will then stick to the adhesive side of the tape which is then placed back on top of the silicon-treated paper and smoothed out again.

Q. Once the latent impression has been photographed, marked, and "lifted," what is done with it?

A. It is submitted to the laboratory for identification, classification, and comparison.

Q. Did you do the identification, classification, and comparison?

A. The answer to this question will depend on department resources and procedure. Often the lifting technician does not provide any further services, in which case an additional witness would be required to answer the questions pertaining to classification and comparison.

Q. Have you ever been to (location of crime scene)?

A. Yes.

Q. When, specifically?

A. Provide the dates of any and all visits.

Q. Did you discover any latent prints on any of those visits?

A. A simple "yes" may be the answer to this question or it may be that other assistant technicians discovered the prints or an investigator discovered them and requested laboratory assistance. Whatever the case this technician should testify how they came to her attention for each visit and for each impression.

Q. How many?

A. Total discovered, total developed, total photographed, and the total "lifted."

Q. What did you do with the various impressions that you discovered?

A. Developed (visualized), photographed, marked, "lifted," and submitted them to the laboratory.

Q. When you first arrived on the scene, were there any other persons present?

A. Yes.

Q. Who?

A. Name all persons on the premises.

Q. Were there finger impressions found at the scene that belonged to any of these people?

A. Yes, there were impressions left by the victim and occupants of the residence as well as those of certain police personnel.

Q. How did you determine that these individuals left fingerprint impressions at the crime scene?

A. We took inked impressions of all persons whom we knew to have been on the premises.

Q. What is an inked impression?

A. Finger friction skin ridge patterns resulting from placing individual fingers and thumbs from both hands onto an inked pad then pressing those fingers and thumbs onto a piece of white cardboard. The ink transfers the finger friction skin ridge patterns onto the cardboard. These inked impressions can then be compared to the latent prints lifted at the crime scene eliminating those who had legitimate access to the premises.

Q. What type of objects did you dust for latent prints?

A. List all surfaces dusted.

Q. Referring to State's Exhibit Number 2, would you point out the location of the broken glass (item) you dusted?

A. Point out the location on the crime scene diagram of the glass dusted. (If the exhibit is placed at a distance from the witness stand it will be necessary to approach the diagram. This diagram should have been proved up by the investigating officer. For diagram predicates see the chapter on police as expert witnesses).

Q. Now, will you please mark the glass represented on the diagram you are referring to with your initials, and today's date in black ink?

A. Do so.

Q. I now hand you what has been marked as State's Exhibit Number 3 and ask you if you recognize it?

A. Yes, I recognize it.

Q. What is it?

A. It is a piece of the glass from the crime scene from which I "lifted" a number of latent prints.

Q. How do you know this is the same piece of glass?

A. I marked the glass with my initials, the case number and the date I lifted the print (or I tagged the evidence including my name, date, and case number).

Q. Has this item been changed in any way since last you saw it?

A. No.

Now offer State's Exhibit Number 3 into evidence.

Q. Would you demonstrate for the judge and jury the manner in which you dusted State's Exhibit Number 3 for development of latent impressions?

A. A very effective demonstrative method is to use an overhead projector. Placing the thumb on the glass will leave a latent print that cannot be seen until the fingerprint powder is dropped and the excess powder removed. The entire process can be projected onto a large screen and the judge and jury can actually see the print visualized as the excess powder is removed. An oral description of what is being done should be provided by the witness as she does it. Once the impression has been dusted, the technician should have written in the dust her name, crime scene location, and case identification number. These etchings can be lifted along with the print, thereby tagging and mounting the print simultaneously.

Q. I again hand you what has been labelled as State's Exhibit Number 3 and ask you where thereon you discovered latent impressions.

A. Point out from where the latents were "lifted."

Q. What did you do with the latent impressions after you visualized them?

A. I photographed them.

Q. Using the type of camera you have previously described?

A. Yes.

Q. Did you examine the camera before you used it?

A. Yes.

Q. What did you find?

A. It was in good working order.

Q. After photographing the latent impressions, will you demonstrate how you "lifted" those impressions and the writing in the excess fingerprint powder?

A. Returning to the overhead projector the witness can then demonstrate how the hinged "lift" was placed onto the print and writing, smoothed, and "lifted." Also demonstrate how the lifted materials were mounted on the silicon backed paper. A running narrative describing the procedure should be provided by the witness.

Q. Once you "lifted" the impression, what did you do with it?

A. I turned it over and printed on the back of the silicon backed paper my initials, the time, date, the location of the premises and the location within the premises where the "lift" was taken.

Q. I now hand you State's Exhibit Number 4 and ask you if you recognize it?

A. Yes.

Q. Does State's exhibit number 4 truly and accurately portray the latent impressions that you observed on the surface of the glass found at the scene of the crime on the date in question?

A. It does.

Q. At what time did you leave the crime scene with the latents represented in State's exhibit number 4?

A. Approximately, but must be substantiated by evidence logs.

Q. At what time did you arrive at the crime laboratory?

A. Approximately, but must be substantiated by evidence log.

Q. Was State's Exhibit Number 4 in your possession during that time (necessary for chain of custody purposes)?

A. Yes. If not, account for all times not in possession. Now offer the latent "lifts" as States Exhibit Number 4.

Q. I now hand you what has been marked as State's Exhibit Number 5 and ask you if you recognize it?

A. Yes.

Q. What is it?

A. A photographic negative.

Q. A photographic negative of what?

A. A photographic negative of the latent impressions on the glass found at the crime scene.

Q. A photographic negative of the latent impressions that you have previously identified as State's exhibit number 4?

A. That's correct.

Q. When was the first time you saw this photographic negative?

A. Provide the specific date and time the film was developed.

Q. Whose writing appears within the photographic negative on the card located next to the impression?

A. Mine.

Q. What does that writing say?

A. Read name, date, time, location, and case identification number.

Q. Is that from the identifying card you placed next to the prints?

A. Yes.

Q. Is it a fair and accurate representation of the latent impressions as you observed them on the surface of the glass found on the floor in the living room of the house at (address of the crime scene) which you "lifted" on (the date "lifted")?

A. Yes.

Q. Did you submit the negatives described as States Exhibit Number 5 to the identification and comparison section of the police laboratory?

A. Yes.

Q. Has it been changed in any way?

A. If any identifying information has been appended to the photographic negative, it should be described as a change.

Q. Other than what you have told us, has this photographic negative been altered in any way?

A. No.

State's Exhibit Number 5 should now be offered into evidence.

The above authentication and chain of custody predicate must be provided for each group of latent impressions "lifted" that are going to be used in evidence, less the demonstrations as to developing, lifting, and marking. If latents are discovered on fixed objects that cannot be carried into the courtroom, they should be described by locating them using cardinal directions within the crime scene and using feet and inches from recognizable points of measure, e.g., six inches below the doorknob on the bedroom door in the southeast bedroom of the premises.

Latent Fingerprint Identification Expert

Q. Would you state your name please?

A. Respond with full legal name.

Q. Where do you live?

A. Although having nothing to do with the facts in issue, background questions are designed to put the witness at ease by asking non-threatening questions that require little thought process. In this day and age, however, it may be prudent not to provide such intimate information to the defendant, friends of the defendant, or other potential assailants.

Q. What is your occupation (profession)?

A. Give specific function and organization.

Q. How long have you served in that capacity?

A. An approximation should be made and stated as such.

Q. For whom did you work prior to this position?

A. This question should begin a review of all professional employment.

Q. Returning to your current employment what is your present assignment?

A. I work with the fingerprint identification section of (name of agency).

Q. To perform the type of work that you do, are there any educational or training requirements?

A. Describe fully all relevant education, training, workshops, and seminars.

Q. Is there a certification process required for the type of services you provide?

A. Describe all certification requirements.

Q. Have you ever published an article pertaining to your work?

A. To be asked only if such publications exist.

Q. Describe each relevant article.
A. Title, publisher, and summary.
Q. Do you belong to any professional organizations?
A. To be asked only if such membership exists and is relevant.
Q. Have you taught any seminars, workshops, or classes pertaining to your area of specialization?
A. To be asked only if such teaching has occurred.
Q. Have you testified in court before pertaining to fingerprint identification?
A. Yes.
Q. How many times?
A. An approximation may be acceptable if the number is large and the exact number is not known. An estimate must be qualified as such.
Q. How many times have you testified on behalf of the state?
A. An approximation will do if the specific number is not known.
Q. In the course of your employment in fingerprint identification, approximately how many fingerprints have you identified?
A. An approximation will do.
Q. In the course of your employment in fingerprint identification, approximately how many fingerprint comparisons have you completed?
A. An approximation will do.
Q. What is the purpose of the Crime Laboratory Identification Section?
A. To maintain fingerprint files and data bases, arrest records, photographic files, and mug shots of people who have been arrested, and files of active fingerprint impressions that are part of ongoing investigations.
Q. What is the function of the latent finger print section?
A. To receive photographs, negatives, and "lifts" of latent fingerprints that have been processed by the crime laboratory technicians, to evaluate these impressions to determine if they are suitable for comparison purposes and upon request to make those comparisons.
Q. Can you tell me upon what fundamental principles the science of fingerprints is based?
A. Two basic scientific principles:
   1. UNIQUENESS—the skin that covers the inside of the fingers, the palms and the soles of the feet, are formed in about the fourth month of fetal life, and they remain unchanged through a person's life until destroyed by death and decomposition.

2. IMMUTABILITY—no given area of friction skin is ever duplicated on the body of the same person or the body of another person.

Q. In your study of the science of fingerprints and in your years of experience have you ever encountered, read about, or heard about two people who had identical fingerprints?

A. No.

Q. What is a latent fingerprint or impression?

A. The word latent means hidden from view or invisible. In the science of fingerprints only those fingerprints that cannot be seen with the unaided eye are latent prints. But as a result of police and media usage, a latent print has come to mean any fingerprint that is left at the crime scene. A fingerprint impression that has inadvertently been left on a relatively smooth surface.

Q. What is an inked impression or inked fingerprint?

A. An impression of the friction ridges on a finger or thumb as a result of applying ink to the finger or thumb and then pressing that digit onto a piece of nonabsorbent paper which is a preprinted on a fingerprint card.

Q. What is the difference between an inked impression and a latent print?

A. An inked impression is intentionally recorded and a latent print is inadvertently left.

Q. Does finger friction ridge skin form identifiable patterns?

A. Yes.

Q. Would you explain what these patterns are?

A. There are three basic types.
It would be helpful at this juncture for the witness to refer to various demonstrative exhibits depicting each of these patterns. And a brief explanation of each:
1. loop
2. whorl
3. arch

Q. Of what value is the ability to identify fingerprint pattern types?

A. It assists us in making comparisons between inked impressions and latent fingerprints.

Q. Does everyone have loops, whorls, and arch patterns?

A. No. The most common ridge characteristics are loops, about 65 percent of all fingerprints on files are loops. Whorls are found in about 35 percent of all patterns on file and arches, being the least common, comprise about 5 percent of fingerprints.

Q. Do these ridge characteristics differ from person to person?

A. No, the lines that make the ridges and patterns are common stuff; however, their location and their relationship to one another differs. We may have any combination of patterns, only loops or loops and arches, loops arches and whorls, arches and whorls, loops and whorls. Sometimes there may be more than one pattern in a print.

Q. Can you describe for the jury the procedure that you employ in comparing a latent impression with an inked impression?

A. I examine the prints by placing each under a dual lensed magnifying glass, by adjusting the focus I can examine both prints simultaneously (if a fingerprint comparator is used it needs to be described). It is readily apparent if the patterns are of the same type. If they are, a closer examination of the ridges that make up the pattern will display a similarity in length, spacing, forking, and divergence. By grouping these characteristics in one print, I should be able to readily identify if that group of characteristics is present in the other. It is not necessary that an entire pattern be recognized in order to compare two prints. Parts of a latent pattern have characteristics that can be grouped and used to compare to an inked impression. Two characteristics within a pattern will allow me to count the ridges between those characteristics and further assist in identifying the latent print.

At this point it would be helpful to demonstrate to the jury how this process is conducted. Again using an overhead projector, the expert's partial thumb print can be placed on the projector screen in full or partial display. Once developed the print should be covered with a lift but not lifted. Next to the developed partial print the expert can role a full impression of his thumb and develop it, covering the rolled impression with a lift. Now the grouping of characteristics and ridge counting can be conducted while the entire jury watches. It can be helpful to point out the core of the print, bifurcations, deltas, and other distinguishing features on both impressions. In those agencies that are computer literate there are a number of software programs that will allow the same procedure to be "captured" on computer disk. Using a computer projection panel and a screen, the entire demonstration can be prepared prior to trial. However, there is much to be gained by using the overhead projector method because it demonstrates the development techniques, thereby reinforcing their familiarity and reliability.

Q. In examining a latent fingerprint left at a crime scene, is it common to have provided you the entire finger friction ridge skin pattern of that finger?

A. No. More often than not they are fragmentary; you seldom get an entire fingerprint.

Q. How much of the finger friction skin ridge pattern of a latent print is required in order to compare that latent print with an inked impression?

A. An identification can be made from a latent print that is an eighth of the size of the same inked impression if sufficient ridge characteristics are present.

The danger here is in trying to quantify how many ridge characteristics are enough; this can only be addressed by the expert's prior experience and training. The thing to remember is that the witness is the expert and, although opinions may differ, her opinion based on her experience and training is as valid as another expert who may disagree. As questioning progresses, the use of enlargements of the latent and inked impressions in question and pointing out the comparable characteristics, the number of similarities can become irrelevant when it is apparent to the untrained eye that these prints are identical.

At this juncture the witness should be formally offered as the State's expert on fingerprint identification and offered to the opposition for voir dire.

Q. Now sir I would direct your attention to the morning of (insert appropriate date); were you working that morning?

A. Yes.

Q. How late did you stay?

A. Give departing time.

Q. I hand you what has been marked as State's Exhibit number 3 and ask you if you recognize it?

A. Yes.

Q. What is it?

A. A fingerprint that has been lifted after development or a photograph of a developed latent print.

Q. Do you know from where this "lift" (photograph) came?

A. Yes, it was provided to me by (name of lifting technician).

Q. When was that?

A. Provide time and date.

Q. What were you asked to do with this fingerprint?

A. To compare it to inked impressions.

Q. Were you provided inked impressions?

A. Yes.

Q. By whom?

A. Provide the name of the officer who took the inked impressions.

Generally, these inked impressions will be proven up (the predicated laid) by the investigating officer or the jail booking officer. If the witness has taken the inked impressions then it will be necessary to ask the following questions.

Q. I hand you what has been marked as State's Exhibit Number 6 and ask you to identify it.

A. A fingerprint card.

Q. What is on the card?

A. Inked fingerprint impressions.

Q. Who took these impressions?

A. I did.

Q. From who were these inked impressions taken?

A. The defendant (name the defendant).

Q. Is the man from whom these inked impressions in the courtroom today?

A. Yes.

Q. Would you identify him please? (having the witness "point out the defendant" is not a sufficient in court identification. The proper identification method is to give a physical description of the defendant, his clothing, hair, and position in the courtroom).

Q. Was anyone else present when these impressions were taken?

A. Yes or no.

Q. If yes, who?

A. Name all who witnessed the fingerprinting.

Q. Is this fingerprint card dated?

A. Yes.

Q. What is the date?

A. Provide the date.

Q. Is this card signed?

A. Yes.

Q. By whom?

A. It bears my signature.

Q. After you took these impressions what did you do with them?

A. I made them a part of the case file of case number (insert appropriate number).

Q. And from where did you obtain them in anticipation of your testimony here today?

A. From case file number (insert appropriate number).

Q. Has this card been altered or changed in any way since the impressions were taken?

A. No.

State's Exhibit Number 6 should now be offered to the defendant for objections then tendered to the court as exhibit number 6.

Q. Did you provide the comparison that was requested of you?

A. Yes.

Q. What did you determine from your comparison of the impression lifted from the crime scene and the inked impressions of the defendant?

A. Based on ridge characteristics, these prints are identical.

Q. How many points of comparison did you establish between the latent print and the inked impression?

A. (Hopefully, no less than) eight.

Q. I hand you what has been marked as State's Exhibit number 7 and ask you if you recognize it?

A. Yes.

Q. What is it?

A. An enlargement of the latent impression lifted at the crime scene.

Q. An enlargement of the same latent impression that has been entered as State's Exhibit Number 3?

A. Yes.

Q. Is the enlargement a fair and accurate representation of the latent as you recall it?

A. Yes.

Now offer State's Exhibit Number 7 to the defense for any objections and then tender the exhibit to the court as State's Exhibit Number 7.

Q. I hand you what has been marked as State's Exhibit Number 8 and ask you if you recognize it?

A. Yes.

Q. What is it?

A. An enlargement of one of the inked impressions from the fingerprint upon which inked impressions from the defendant were taken.

Q. An enlargement of an inked impression contained on State's Exhibit Number 6?

A. Yes.

Q. Is the enlargement a fair and accurate representation of the inked impression as you recall it?

A. Yes.

Now offer the exhibit to the defendant for any objections that may be interposed, then tender the exhibit to the court.

Q. Will you take the two enlargements and point out and explain to the jury the first point of comparisons you discerned that convinced you that these prints were identical.

A. Point one on the latent impression is an ending ridge.

Q. Point one on the inked impression?

A. An ending ridge.

Q. Point two on the latent impression?

A. Point two on the latent impression is an ending ridge.

Q. Point three on the inked impression?

A. Point three on the inked impression is an ending ridge.

Q. Point four on the latent impression?

A. Point four on the latent impression is a bifurcation.

Q. Point four on the inked impression?

A. Point four on the inked impression is a bifurcation.

Q. Point five on the latent impression?

A. Point five on the latent impression is a short ridge.

Q. Point five on the inked impression?

A. Point five on the inked impression is a short ridge.

Q. Point six on the latent impression?

A. Point six on the latent impression is an ending ridge.

Q. Point six on the inked impression?

A. Point six on the inked impression is an ending ridge.

Q. Point seven on latent impression?

A. Point seven on the latent impression is an ending ridge.

Q. Point seven on the inked impression?

A. Point seven on the inked impression is an ending ridge.

Q. Point eight on the latent impression?

A. Point eight on the latent impression is an ending ridge.

Q. Point eight on the inked impression?

A. Point eight on the inked impression is an ending ridge.

Q. How many points of comparison are required in order to positively identify a latent impression?

A. The precise number is dependent upon how clear, complete, and unusual the characteristics are. In my opinion, no less than eight. Most authors agree that in no case are more than 12 necessary to positively establish identity.

Q. Based upon your experience, education, training, and the comparisons of the latent prints and the defendants inked impressions, do you have an opinion, based on a reasonable scientific certainty, as to whether or not the same person made the latent impression and the inked impression?

A. Yes, I do.

Q. What is that opinion?

A. It is my opinion that the impression lifted at the crime scene is identical with finger number 7 from the inked fingerprint card taken from the defendant and that they therefore were made by the same person.

Q. Based on your examination of the latent print "lifted" at the crime scene, do you have an opinion, based on a reasonable scientific certainty, as to the force with which it was applied.

A. It is my opinion, from an examination of the latent impression that there was considerable force applied to the glass from which the print was lifted.

Q. How were you able to determine that?

A. The skin on the hand is pliable and the ridge structure will broaden when pressure is applied. In the latent impression, portions of the ridge structure have been broadened, narrowing the distance between ridges which suggests the application of force.

Using this predicate as a guideline, there should be no procedural obstacles to the admissibility of the prints by the prosecution. However, the expert must be prepared to defend her testimony during the defendant's cross-examination. The chain of custody may be questioned or the points of comparison may be challenged. The use of enlargements, however, should allow the jury to come to the same conclusion as the witness if that testimony was credible and not reaching. Attempting to manufacture points of comparison will be difficult to defend. Use only those points of comparison that reasonable persons would agree upon.

REFERENCES

Becker, R. 1985. *The Underwater Crime Scene: Underwater Crime Investigative Techniques.* Springfield, IL: Charles C Thomas.

Duncan, G.T. 1986. Effects of super glue, other fingerprint developing agents, and luminol on bloodstain analysis. *Journal of Association of Official Analytical Chemists.* Vol. 8, p. 63.

Safferstein, R. 1995. *Criminalistics: An Introduction to Forensic Science.* New York: Prentice Hall.

Chapter 5

MENTAL HEALTH EXPERTS

Although more attention is focused on the use of psychologists and psychiatrists in hearings and trials dealing with questions of sanity, there are three areas within which such testimony is often solicited:

    a. competency hearings
    b. sanity determinations
    c. death penalty schemes

With all the media fuss accompanying insanity pleas, it would seem the most probable place to begin. However, the less dramatic competency hearing legally and logically should be the launching point for any discussion pertaining to the services provided by psychologists and psychiatrists. In an effort to streamline the treatment of this chapter we will limit the expertise to that of psychiatrists. Any prosecutor who discloses an intent to call a psychologist as an expert will be promptly one upped by facing a psychiatric expert. The impact of the respective credentials of these two classes of experts can readily be seen by the description of two seven-year-olds in discussing what it is their fathers do.

    "My father is a doctor," says one young man.

    "Yeah, well so is mine," responds his young protagonist.

    "Oh yeah, well mine is a real doctor; he can give shots," concludes the winner of the conflict.

The testimony provided by psychologists or psychiatrists in the three areas of legal mental states would be virtually the same.

The reason that competency is legally and logically the place to begin in considering the use of psychiatric testimony is because, if a defendant is found to lack competency to stand trial, there is no present need for a sanity determination. If a defendant is insane at the time of trial, he also lacks the competency legally required to proceed.

Perhaps this is a good place to address one of the common problems associated with psychiatrists: competency and insanity. Often competency in the mind of a psychiatrist is interpreted to mean insanity. Without some appreciation for the legal niceties associated with these two pleas, the expert witness may be confused, and worse, create confusion for the jury. It is absolutely imperative that the offering attorney be certain that the expert knows the legal definition of competency and sanity and can distinguish both from the medical use of the same terms. Medical dictionaries define sanity as "soundness of mind" (*Dorland's Illustrated Medical Dictionary,* 1974:1377). The same dictionary defines competence as "the ability of an organ or part to perform adequately any function required of it (id. at 345). Neither of these definitions is very helpful from a legal perspective. Legal competency is more concerned with a defendant's ability to recognize the charges against him and his ability to assist in his defense, than his overall brain functioning. As for sanity, states vary as to the standard employed, but none are concerned with mental soundness. In the various state jurisdictions one or more of the following standards are employed:

a. the M'Naghten rule;
b. the irresistible impulse rule; and
c. the substantial capacity test.

Insanity

Doctors and lawyers often speak of the "insanity defense." A successful insanity defense is different from any other defense provided criminal defendants. In all other cases in which a successful defense is put forth, the result is acquittal and release of the defendant. The successful application of the insanity defense will generally result in the defendant's commitment to a mental institution until sanity is restored. The jury does not find the defendant "not guilty" but rather "not guilty by reason of insanity" or "guilty but mentally ill" after which commitment, either automatically or through commitment proceedings, will result.

Sensational cases often bring the insanity defense to the public's attention. The John Hinckley and Jeffery Dahmer cases are examples of the type of cases in which the insanity defense receives public attention. It is therefore not surprising that the public reaction to the possibility of such offenders avoiding the maximum the law may provide is one of outrage. Media preoccupation with sensational offenses, pretrial activities, and trials lends to the belief that the insanity defense is a common tactic employed by criminal defendants to avoid the consequences of their criminal behavior.

The M'Naghten Rule

In tracing the evolution of the insanity defense, it becomes necessary to revisit the *Daniel M'Naghten Case* decided in England, in 1843, from which our basic standard for the application of the insanity defense derives. Daniel M'Naghten was suffering under the delusion that the Prime Minister of England, Sir Robert Peel, the Jesuits and the Pope were conspiring to persecute him. In the throes of such delusion, he stepped up behind Sir Robert Peel's private secretary, Edward Drummond, and shot him. Upon inquiry of the police, M'Naghten admitted to shooting Sir Robert Peel. In his defense, M'Naghten put forth a defense of insanity, with which the jury agreed. Because of the notoriety of the individuals involved, the public was not pleased with the jury's finding. The House of Lords inquired of the Queen's Bench as to what standards were to be employed in determining insanity; the Court responded with what has come to be known as the M'Naghten rule:

> Your lordships are pleased to inquire of us . . . "What are the proper questions to be submitted to the jury, where a person alleged to be afflicted with insane delusion respecting one or more particular subjects or persons, is charged with the commission of a crime, and insanity is set up as a defense?" And . . . "In what terms ought the question to be left to the jury as to the prisoner's state of mind at the time the act was committed?" And as these two questions appear to us to be more conveniently answered together, we have to submit our opinion to be, that the jurors ought to be told in all cases that every man is to be presumed to be sane, and to possess a sufficient degree of reason to be responsible for his crimes, until the contrary be proved to their satisfaction; and that to establish a defense on the ground of insanity, it must be clearly proved that, at the time of the committing of the act, the party accused was laboring under such a defect of reason, from disease of mind, as not to know the nature and quality of the act he was doing; or, if he did know it, that he did not know he was doing what was wrong.
>
> (8 Eng. Rep. 718, 1843).

The test established in M'Naghten has been referred to as the "right-wrong" test and is currently used in 21 states (Holten & Lamar, 1991).

The Irresistible Impulse Rule

In approximately half of the states following the M'Naghten rule, that rule has been modified as the result of the murder of Bennett Parson by his wife in Alabama in 1887. Suffering from delusions, Mrs. Parson undoubtedly knew the difference between right and wrong but was unable to control herself as the result of her delusions. In finding Mrs. Parson insane, the Alabama Court added the following to the M'Naghten rule;

> 1) if by reason of the duress of such mental disease, the power to choose between right and wrong is lost and the power of free agency is lost then there is no legal responsibility (Parsons v State, 81 Ala. 577, 2 So. 854, 1887).

This modification became known as the "irresistible impulse" rule (Dix & Sharlot, 1987).

The Substantial Capacity Test

In an effort to lend conformity to a legal system that was having trouble applying various tests for insanity, a tentative draft of the Model Penal Code (1955), provided what has become known as the "substantial capacity" test, wherein:

> A person is not considered responsible for criminal conduct if at the time of such conduct as a result of mental disease or defect he lacks substantial capacity either to appreciate the criminality of his conduct or to conform his conduct to the requirements of the law.

This rule has become known as the "substantial capacity" rule and is applied in all federal courts and in 29 states (Dix & Sharlot, 1987).

When John Hinckley, Jr. attempted to assassinate President Ronald Reagan, he was found not guilty by reason of insanity. At the trial the jury charge proposed that the prosecution must prove sanity beyond a reasonable doubt once the sanity issue had been raised by the defendant. Many felt that the burden of proof in insanity pleas should be upon the defendant. The American Bar Association, and the American Psychiatric Association pushed to have the "irresistible impulse" perspective removed from the insanity defense. This outcry resulted in the Insanity Reform Act of 1984, which established that:

> a) It is an affirmative defense to prosecution if at the time of the commission of the acts, constituting the offense, the defendant, as a result of a severe mental disease or defect, was unable to appreciate the nature and quality or the wrongfulness of his acts. Mental disease or defect does not otherwise constitute a defense.
>
> b) The defendant has the burden of proving the defense of insanity by clear and convincing evidence.
>
> (18 U.S.C.A. section 20)

Asserting the Insanity Defense

Insanity pleas are rare; defendants generally choose not to plead insanity. The plea has inherent procedural obstacles and adverse consequences that deter its use in all but the most aggravated of circumstances. This reluctance is overlooked because of the belief that the insanity defense is a great benefit to the defendant, who can readily purchase the psychiatric testimony necessary to convince a jury of his insanity, thereby avoiding criminal liability.

Disadvantages of Indigency

In practice, what advantages there are to the insanity defense are lost to the defendant who cannot afford to retain private psychiatric evaluation. There is a marked overrepresentation of persons of lower socioeconomic status among defendants entering a "not guilty by reason of insanity" plea. These indigents are young, male, black, single, uneducated, unskilled, and unemployed. Among the 1,100 defendants entering the insanity plea between 1970 and 1983, most were represented by a public defender (Blau, 1992).

Indigence means, as a practical matter, that the accused typically cannot hire a privately practicing psychiatric witness but must rely upon the court to appoint what is nominally referred to as an "impartial witness" (LaFave, 1987). It is difficult, if not impossible, for an indigent defendant to obtain an independent assessment of the potential for asserting an insanity defense.

The court appointed expert is likely to be associated with the public mental hospital system and he tends to view mental illness from a different perspective than do doctors in private practice. Doctors administering state mental hospitals have had to employ a rigid selection criteria because of great demand for hospital admissions. As demand increased, so did the rigor upon which admissions were made, admitting only those who were unable to function on the outside, the grossly psychotic. Often these perceptions are carried over into the legal forum where mental illness is seen only in those individuals who manifest insanity as a debilitating condition, invading every aspect of the personality and completely immobilizing it (id. at 41).

Private practitioners have as their objective diagnosis and treatment and therefore tend to be more thorough, more deeply probing, and expend more time than the diagnostic procedures typical in a state hospital. Psychiatrists in private practice are constrained by the forty-five minute interview with a person in county jail and are reluctant to commit themselves to any diagnosis or prognosis arrived at in such a time frame. Many institutional psychiatrists, however, feel qualified to testify as to their expert opinions based on that same type of interview.

Pitfalls

In many instances the alternative of a mental commitment is not that much more attractive than the prospective penal sanction or the probability of a plea bargain (Caplan, 1992). John Hinckley would have already served his time for aggravated assault or attempted murder under the penal sanctions that existed at the time.

Lawyers and psychiatrists see many pitfalls in the use of the insanity defense, some of which include:

(1) the inevitability of an indefinite commitment if the defense is successful;
(2) the belief that psychiatric treatment at the maximum-security hospital does not exist or is ineffective;
(3) many defendants do not see themselves as insane, nor do they wish to be seen as insane; and
(4) fear that release is remote even if mental health improves (Caplan, 1992).

Procedural Obstacles to the Insanity Defense

Bifurcation

An integral part of raising the defense of insanity includes a psychiatric examination that is not protected by the Fifth Amendment. A testifying psychiatrist may divulge incriminating statements made to him by the defendant. In those jurisdictions where insanity trials are bifurcated or allowed to be bifurcated in order to first address questions of guilt, wherein the State must prove the elements of the offense alleged before questions of sanity are addressed, anything said to the psychiatrist may be used at the guilt stage of the trial (United States v. Cohen, 530 F.2d. 43 [5th. Cir. 1976]).

In those states that do not allow bifurcation, the defendant must put all his eggs in one basket and admit his guilt before the insanity plea will be accepted. Once that plea has been entered, any questions as to his factual guilt have been resolved.

Burden of Proof

The initial burden of proof to go forth with the evidence is upon the defendant. This burden is based upon the presumption that men are sane and the defendant enjoys the benefits of that presumption until some amount of evidence to the contrary is produced. The shift in burden of proof also contributes to the reluctance to assert the insanity defense. That shift has become more pronounced in light of the Insanity Reform Act of 1984 wherein the defendant now carries an affirmative burden.

Verdict

After the State and the Defense rest, the jury will receive instructions from the judge pertaining to their deliberative task. Those instructions do not generally provide jurors with the effect of a verdict of not guilty by reason of insanity or a verdict of guilty but mentally ill. Such verdicts mean that the accused will be confined in a hospital for the mentally ill until the superintendent of the hospital certifies and the court accepts that the insane person has recovered her sanity and no longer poses a threat.

No statutory limit is imposed upon the conditions or term of confinement. Limits of confinement, if any, are imposed by hospital administrators and/or the court. It could prove useful to advise jurors of the consequences of a finding of insanity. Jurors know the meaning of guilty and not guilty but have little help in understanding the legal consequence of a finding of insanity (*Commonwealth v. Maine*, 323 N.E. 2d 294, 1975).

Release

In virtually every jurisdiction, persons confined because of their insanity can only be released by legal challenge to the confining court. The burden is upon the patient to prove that sanity has been restored and that she no longer poses a threat to herself or others. Such a burden may be impossible to sustain based on the diminished resources of indigents found insane who subsequently seek release from confinement.

Public Reaction

In the wake of the John Hinckley acquittal for the attempted murder of former president Ronald Reagan, there was a rush to reform the insanity defense. The most widely demanded reform was abolition of the insanity defense. These calls for reform did not stem from an increased understanding of the purpose and appropriate limits of the insanity defense, but rather, arose from a sense of emotional outrage, and factual and attitudinal misconceptions (Roberts, 1987).

An Associated NBC (1981) news poll showed that 87 percent of the public thought that too many murderers were not sent to jail because of insanity pleas (Winslade, 1983). Of those polled, 70 percent favored elimination of the insanity defense all together (id, at 119). The public's perception is often molded by the media and the use of the insanity defense is no exception.

A *Time* (1992) magazine article reporting the Jeffery Dahmer assertion of the insanity defense said, "if convicted, Dahmer will be sentenced to life imprisonment. However, if he is found not guilty by reason of insanity, he will be sent to a mental hospital where he will be eligible for release in one year." This idea that persons found to be insane get off "Scott free" is not an uncommon one and not arrived at by accident. In the Jeffery Dahmer case, as with most serial and mass murderers who plead insanity, the jury saw these heinous acts and refused to allow abrogation of criminal responsibility. Juries are the buffer against the spurious proffer of insanity. In most instances juries feel that those who commit extraordinarily odd and evil acts must be held accountable though their behavior is incomprehensible and most logically considered to be "crazy" by the moral, reasonable citizen (Becker, 1995).

The public often confuses competency to stand trial with insanity (criminal responsibility) issues. These are legally and conceptually discreet issues referring to different points in time and different aspects of the defendant's mental condition. Mental health officials have been accused of confusing competency and criminal responsibility thereby misleading the court and the media upon which the public relies (Johnson, 1990). A defendant is generally ruled to be incompetent to stand trial if he is unable to understand the charges against him and unable to aid in his own defense. This is at the time of trial, not at the time of the alleged criminal act. People found incompetent to stand trial are institutionalized until found competent at which time they may be tried for their actions.

Psychiatric witness are called to testify pursuant to capital sentencing schemes. In many states, before a defendant can be sentenced to death, he must have committed certain enumerated aggravating circumstances and pose a continuing threat of future dangerousness to the community. In proving the element of future dangerousness, the state will most often call a psychiatrist. Certain state psychiatrists have testified so often pertaining to the potential for future dangerousness of the defendant that they have lost all credibility with the defense bar. That credibility loss may not pose a problem for the jury since they are ignorant of the expert's testimonial history; however, it is a sure bet that the testimonial history of the witness will be brought to their attention during cross-examination. The fact that such a witness is eager and willing to find that a defendant poses a future danger to the community should not be the sole criterion for qualifying an expert as a state's psychiatric witness. Frankly, it is embarrassing to all professionals when a psychiatrist consistently, with little time or effort, finds defendant after defendant posing a future danger to the community. State psychiatric witnesses do not spend the same time or effort in determining dangerousness as they do in determining competence or sanity. That disparity is irrational when considering the consequences of the proffered testimony. Again, prosecutors may be so concerned with "winning" that they prefer less than a careful, complete, and competent examination upon which future dangerousness should be determined. It is understandable that prosecutors in their competitive zeal may lose sight of justice as their goal, but it is absolutely inconceivable that a psychiatrist would willing lend himself to such motivation.

The Psychiatric Witness

In all medical fields, disease identification and classification are in constant flux. New protocols, approaches and perspectives are incorporated into an ever-evolving body of knowledge. Attempts to identify and classify mental illness have resulted in terminology and definitions that vary widely among different psychiatric schools, practitioners, and countries. The American Psychiatric Association in an effort to address these differences began a *Diagnostic and Statistical Manual of Mental Disorders*. Updates of this manual have provided specific symptoms and signs, i.e., what a interviewee says and does as indicators of what he thinks and feels upon which psychiatrists of all persuasions can rely in arriving at a diagnosis. In most instances of psychiatric testimony, the information gathered from the defendant is gleaned as the result of the initial interview (often the only interview) rather than a course of lengthy treatment sessions. The idea is to form an opinion as to an individual's ability to tell the difference from right and wrong and accordingly to conform his behavior to those notions. Lengthy diagnosis is not required. However, the process in which the initial interview of a defendant is conducted should follow the same methodology as that for a patient. During that initial interview the psychiatrist should gather enough information to be able to testify to the legal standard of sanity.

The Psychiatric Interview

Questions other than background should be solicited by asking open-ended questions. A comfortable starting point is personal history, medical history, and family history. If records of these histories are made, it must be remembered that those records will be made available to the defense upon request, therefore only relevant, credible, and decorous entries should be made. All written records should be made keeping in mind that the jury may read them. A typical format used by many psychiatrists in recording the initial interview would include:

1. psychiatric history,
2. mental status.

Psychiatric Interview Checklist

Psychiatric history:
    Identifying characteristics:
      name
      age
      gender
      race
      marital status
      occupation
    Personal history:
      birth date

education
work history
sexual maturation
marital history
Defendant's version:
  offense
date
time
participants
motivation
results
recriminations
remorse
Personality and social patterns:
  social relationships
interests
activities
predominant moods
character traits
strengths
weaknesses
coping skills
coping style
stress handling
Religious and moral standards:
  denomination
early church experience
sexual repression
fixation
value integration
Ambitions and aspirations:
  realistic
approximations
planning
Habits:
  alcohol
drugs
smoking
Family history:

Parent and sibling data—
  age
  health
  occupation
  personality
  relationship
If deceased—
  date
  cause of death

Mental status:

Appearance and behavior:
  dress (the way institutional clothing is worn)
  posture
  facial expression
  motor activity
  degree of agitation
  impulsivity
  retardation
  rapport
  trust
  empathy
Thought processes (record all conversations):
  poverty of thought
  rigidity of thought
  pace and progression of speech
  logical speech
  confusing or irrelevant speech
  flight of ideas
  obsessional qualification
  distractibility
Thought content:
  special preoccupations
  obsessional ideas
  misinterpretations
  ideas of influence
  delusions
  grandiose ideation
  personal denigration
  self aggrandizement

Thought content can be evaluated through the use of various testing vehicles including the Minnesota Multiphasic Inventory or similar device.

Perceptual abnormalities:
> auditory
> visual hallucinations
> tactile hallucinations
> depersonalization
> derealization

Affect:
> happy
> elation
> sadness
> depression
> irritability
> anger
> suspicion
> perplexity
> fear
> anxiety
> blunting
> incongruity
> lability
> reactivity
> appropriateness to context

Cognitive functions:
> orientation
> memory
>> Immediate recall can be tested by asking the subject to remember 3 unrelated items for 3 to five minutes; recent memory can be evaluated by asking the subject to describe news events and prior meals; remote memory can be tested by asking about life's firsts, e.g., first date, first car, first airplane ride, etc.; orientation in time, place, person.

Concentration:
> focus
> hyperactivity
>> a normally attentive grammar school graduate should be able to repeat 7 random digits forward and 4 in reverse order, spell

WORLD backwards and perform simple calculations (nickels in $1.75 and serial sevens), months of the year in reverse.

General information:
    name the last four presidents
    State capitals
    recent films
    current events
Intelligence:
    school performance
    work performance
    current performance
        The ability to abstract can be examined through interpretation of proverbs and analogies.
General Vocabulary:
    conversation content
    conversation context
        General vocabulary can be determined by intelligence testing
Insight:
    future plans
        Insight can be inferred through psychometric testing.
Language Function:
        The functioning of language can be determined by having the defendant name simple body parts and objects and by assessing his ability to read and write.

Upon completion of the psychiatric interview, the psychiatrist should seek outside corroboration in support of any conclusions that have been drawn as the result of the interview. Additionally, contacting people who encounter the defendant in "normal" circumstances will give the psychiatrist some insight into the defendant's "normal" behavior and demonstrate the comprehensiveness of the history-taking portion of the examination. What follows is a partial checklist of individuals who can be contacted to provide such information. Who is contacted will obviously depend upon the individual circumstances of each defendant.

Checklist:
    spouse
    children
    mother
    father
    teachers

fellow students
school principal
employers
coworkers
neighbors
arresting officer
cell mates
jailers
investigating officer

Psychological Tests

When preparing for a criminal trial, it is prudent for mental health experts to tape-record their interaction with the defendant, especially when administering projective tests such as the Rorschach, Thematic Apperception Test, or the responses to the verbal portion of intelligence tests. Once the defendant has put forth an insanity defense or when competency or future dangerousness are at issue, it is in the interests of the defendant to cooperate, and objections by the defense to video taping should be forestalled. Because of the subjective nature of test interpretation, it can prove helpful for the state to show the jury the test responses upon which the expert has based an opinion. There are two main categories of forensic tests:

1. tests of cognitive functioning
2. tests of personality

Tests of cognitive functioning include various intelligence tests and neuropsychological batteries. Personality tests are either:

1. objective (inventory)
2. projective (what do you see?)

The most common objective test is the Minnesota Multiphasic Personality Inventory and the most common projective tests are the:

1. Rorschach inkblot (six different Rorschach tests are in use)
2. Thematic Apperception Test (TAT)

The most commonly used intelligence test is the Wechsler Adult Intelligence Scale (WAIS). This test provides an index of intellectual capability in terms of an Intelligence Quotient which is broken down into three scales:

1. full scale IQ
2. verbal IQ
3. performance IQ

The Full Scale IQ is the compilation of the verbal and performance results graphically represented. The Verbal IQ is derived from six subtests which require verbal responses from the individual. Performance IQ is derived from five subtests measuring the defendant's fund of general information, common sense judgment, ability to abstract, ability to perform arithmetic calculations, memory, vocabulary, perceptual-motor functions, and the ability to comprehend social situations. The three IQ's and the subtest scores can be presented in court on a chart or computer projection panel. The defendant's performance can be compared to that of people who comprise the normal range of test results.

The best known neuropsychological battery used in assessing brain damage is the Halstead-Reitan battery. This battery consists of a number of subtests involving verbal, memory, perceptual, and motor operations. This battery also provides scoring that allows graphic representation and comparison (Merck, 1988).

Objective personality assessment devices are numerous, but none has the standardization history behind it as does the Minnesota Multiphasic Personality Inventory (MMPI). The MMPI consists of 556 statements to which a true or false response is supplied. These responses are scored on ten clinical scales and three validity scales. The clinical scales correspond roughly with various psychiatric diagnoses, such as depression, schizophrenia, or paranoia. Again, quantifiable results are obtained and the defendant's responses as reflected, on the various scales, can be graphically represented at the time of trial. The scales indicate conformance or deviance to group norms only; any correlations made to the defendant's behavior and his scores is based solely upon the subjective interpretation of the psychiatrist or psychologist. It is this absence of individuality of the MMPI that prohibits its use on predicting behavior. It is valuable in classifying people into groups.

Scoring projective tests such as the Thematic Apperception Test (TAT) or the Rorschach is based almost entirely upon the subjective interpretation of the person administering the tests. The Rorschach provides for numerical scoring which can be misleading. Such numerical scoring gives the illusion of objectivity. Conclusions result from the psychologist's clinical interpretation of the data. Scoring is not fixed on specific criteria but depends on the psychologist's judgement. Scoring the TAT is even less objective. There are, however, responses to shapes on cards that are so readily identifiable that they are called "populars." In the average records of normal individuals, six or seven "populars" appear. The presence of "populars" in a defendant's records indicates he is capable of perceiving the world as do others. The style, manner, appearance, biases, and prejudices of the examiner affect the kinds of responses or data produced in the examination, interpretation, and recollection of test data. It is apparent that much latitude must be applied when considering tests results to form opinions. Regardless of the tools available to examiners, the best information and most often neglected sources of information are people who knew, or saw the defendant at or near the time of the crime.

Once the psychiatric interview has been completed, the expert should have sufficient information upon which to base an opinion as to legal competence and/or legal sanity. Keeping in mind the questions at issue in such hearings should streamline the expert's testimony. It is imperative that attorneys calling psychiatric witnesses be familiar with the American Psychiatric Association manual of definitions before directing or cross-examining such an expert. The foundation questions for a witness testifying as to competency should differ little from those in which questions of sanity are at issue. The examination questions used in establishing a psychiatrists qualifications would be conducted as in the chapter on fingerprinting. What follows is a checklist of qualifications for a testifying psychiatrist whether testifying as to sanity or competence.

Psychiatric Qualification Checklist

    A. Education
        1. Degrees obtained
        2. Universities from which they were obtained
        3. Any academic honors
        4. Graduate assistantships, or fellowships
        5. Residency
           a. As a medical doctor
              i. Where
              ii. How long
              iii. Area of specialty

      b. As a psychiatrist
        i. Where
        ii. How long
        iii. Area of specialty

The completion of a residency is one of the eligibility requirements for taking the examination that grants board certification. Should the expert have more than one area of specialty, inquiry into residency should be made for each.

    6. Board certification
      a. Number of times test was taken (defuse the defense who will undoubtedly ask this question, it is better for any embarrassment to come from a friendly questioner—however, it may well be necessary to consider another psychiatrist especially if the defense has designated a better qualified expert).

    7. Licenses
      a. Held and the requirements for each
      b. Year received
      c. Privileges accompanying each

B. Teaching Experience
    1. Name of institutions
    2. Number of years at each institution
    3. Courses taught at each institution
    4. Academic rank
    5. Textbook and treatises used for each course of instruction

It may be advantageous not to disclose this information, however it will be information that likely will be elicited by the defense. These books can be very helpful in supporting the witnesses testimony, but they can be used along with any other book the defense proffers that the witness agrees is authoritative in the field, to impeach (cast doubt upon) the witnesses opinion. It should be kept in mind that because an author or opposing expert disagrees with a testifying expert does not necessarily cast doubt upon the witness if that witness has adequately explained her opinions and the basis for holding those opinions. Being an expert does not preclude others from having valid opinions in opposition to those embraced by the testifying expert.

C. Professional experience
  1. Internships
    a. hospital
    b. dates of internship
    c. reasons for applying to that hospital
  2. Staff positions
    a. hospitals
    b. dates of employment
  3. Private practice
    a. location
    b. date begun
  4. Hospital privileges
    a. name of hospital
    b. type of privileges
    c. duration of privileges
  5. Association with governmental agencies
    a. name of agency
    b. dates of employment
    c. responsibilities
  6. Publications
    a. papers presented
      i. date(s) of presentation
      ii. name(s) of organization(s) at which presentation was made
      iii. name(s) of paper(s)
    b. books authored
      i. name of book
      ii. description of subject matter
      iii. publisher
    c. Articles authored
      i. name of journal
      ii. title of article
      iii. description of subject matter
    d. Monograms authored
      i. name of monogram
      ii. description of subject matter
      iii. publisher
D. Psychiatric examinations
  1. Number of psychiatric examinations performed
  2. Number of competency (sanity or future dangerousness) determinations made

3. Number of times called upon to testify whether or not a defendant was sane at the time of the criminal act for which he stands accused. The number of times called upon to testify whether or not a defendant was competent to stand trial or was found to pose a future danger.

Having been duly qualified and accepted by the court as a psychiatric expert witness, having been pummeled as to qualifications and need by the defense in a voir dire, the direct examination may begin.

Direct Examination of a Psychiatric Witness

Q. Doctor, have you had the opportunity to examine the defendant?
A. Yes.
Q. How many times have you examined the defendant?
A. State the number.
Q. What was the date of the first examination?
A. Provide the date.
Q. What time on that day was the examination begun?
A. State time.
Q. What time on that day was the examination ended?
A. Provide the time.
   Each examination will be discussed and dates and times for each provided.
Q. How much time to date have you spent with the defendant?
A. Refer to time records if necessary, be as accurate as possible without splitting hairs.

The answer to this question invariably is used to undermine the opinions of the expert. It is difficult to understand how the prosecution continues to be pilloried with cross-examination questions targeted at the amount of time upon which the state's expert's opinion is based. Too often the state's witness spends a limited time with the defendant while the defendant's expert spends more time than may seem necessary. The easiest way to defuse the questions that arise from this disparity is for the state's expert to parallel the time the defense expert spends with the defendant. There is no definitive rule upon which all expert's can agree as to the minimum time necessary to determine competency or legal sanity. There are legitimate concerns about state psychiatrists who can arrive at these decisions in as little as 15 to 30 minutes. If, however, a complete psychiatric history is taken, interview conducted and necessary tests performed with the objective of arriving at a true assessment of the defendant's mental state using the same standardized information gathering procedures, there should be little conflict between defense and state experts pertaining to the amount of time spent with the defendant. It is the perennial state expert who based upon his multitude of defendant assessments believes he can make such an assessment by asking the time of day. In Texas, a psychiatrist affectionately known as Doctor Death by the defense bar can determine a defendant's future dangerousness in less than 15 minutes and has never testified in a death case to the contrary. Unfortunately, prosecutors are too intimidated by gourd rattling to question the process, or are simply seeking assessments that further prosecution—not justice.

Q. How much time elapsed between the time the crime was committed and the time of your first examination?

A. The time is basically irrelevant, but this question anticipates the cross-examination and provides a positive framework in which that question can be answered.

Q. Is it possible to make retrospective statements about a persons state of mind at a particular time in the past?

A. Yes.

Q. Would it have been helpful to have completed your examination closer in time to the commission of the crime?

A. Yes.

Q. Why did you not perform your examination at an earlier time?

A. Hopefully, the examination was performed promptly upon notice of the defendant's intention to put forth an insanity defense and the answer to this question should so state. This question should provide sufficient warning that the time frame within which the examination is conducted will become a manufactured issue.

Q. Have you arrived at any opinions pertaining to the defendants sanity (competence or future dangerousness)?

A. Yes.

Q. In arriving at your opinion did you conduct a psychiatric interview?

A. Yes.

Q. Is such an interview part of a psychiatric examination?

A. Yes.

Q. During the course of that interview, did you take a medical history?

A. Yes.

Q. What is a medical history?

A. Briefly describe what is included in a medical history (as described at the beginning of this chapter).

Q. Is a medical history the type of information upon which a psychiatrist would generally rely in formulating an opinion as to an individuals sanity (competence or future dangerousness)?

A. Yes.

Q. Did the medical history provided you by the defendant assist you in arriving at your opinions as to the sanity (competence or future dangerousness) of the defendant?

A. Yes.

Q. During the course of your psychiatric examination, did you inquire into the defendant's family history?

A. Yes.

Q. What is a family history?

A. Briefly describe the type of information included in a family history (as provided at the beginning of this chapter).

Q. Is a family history the type of information upon which a psychiatrist would generally rely in formulating an opinion as to an individual's sanity (competence or future dangerousness)?

A. Yes.

Q. Did the information provided to you by the defendant in his family history assist you in arriving at your opinion as to the defendant's sanity (competence or future dangerousness)?

A. Yes.

Q. During the course of your examination of the defendant, did you evaluate his behavior and appearance?

A. Yes.

Q. What behavior and appearance is evaluated during a psychiatric examination?

A. Briefly describe the type of information gathered during a psychiatric examination dealing with behavior and appearance (as provided at the beginning of this chapter).

Q. Are behavior and appearance the type of information upon which a psychiatrist would generally rely in formulating an opinion as to an individual's sanity (competence or future dangerousness)?

Q. Did the information gleaned from the defendant's appearance and behavior assist you in arriving at your opinion as to the defendant's sanity (competency or future dangerousness)?

A. Yes.

Q. During the course of your examination of the defendant, did you assess his thought processes?

A. Yes.

Q. Can you describe for the jury how an assessment of an individual's thought processes is made?

A. Briefly describe the aspects of the interview that allow inferences to be made about the subject's thought processes.

Q. Is a thought process assessment as part of a psychiatric examination the type of information upon which a psychiatrist would generally rely in formulating an opinion as to an individual's sanity (competence or future dangerousness)?

A. Yes.

Q. Did your assessment of the defendant's thought processes assist you in arriving at your opinion as to the defendant's sanity (competence or future dangerousness)?

A. Yes (as provided at the beginning of the chapter).

Q. During the course of the examination of defendant, were you able to assess the defendant's thought content?

A. Yes.

Q. Describe the types of things you look for in assessing an individual's thought content.

A. Briefly explain what can be revealed during a psychiatric examination that allows an assessment of thought content.

Q. Are there tests that can be used to assist in assessing thought content?

A. Describe the various tests that can be used in testing thought content, e.g., the MMPI.

Q. What is the MMPI and how is it administered?

A. A standardized written test made up of yes or no responses to a questionnaire of 550 items designed to provide scores on the most important personality traits. The test includes validating scales which evaluates the test takers truthfulness, consistency, test-taking attitude, and frankness.

Generally, such tests are administered by psychologists and it may be necessary to establish that the psychologist was under the supervision of the psychiatric witness. If the psychologist was not under the supervision of the psychiatrist, it would be necessary to prove up the MMPI by examining the administering psychologist. If the psychiatrist is not able to interpret the result of the MMPI, the psychologist will be a necessary witness.

Q. Was the MMPI administered to the defendant?

A. Yes.

Q. Is an assessment of thought content the type of information upon which a psychiatrist would generally rely in formulating an opinion as to an individual's sanity (competence or future dangerousness)?

A. Yes.

Q. Did your assessment of the thought content of the defendant assist you in arriving at your opinion as to the defendant's sanity (competence or future dangerousness)?

A. Yes.

Q. During the course of your examination of the defendant, were you able to assess the defendant's affect and mood?

A. Yes.

Q. Would you explain to the jury what affect is and how it differs from mood?

A. This difference was explained at the beginning of this chapter.

Q. Is an evaluation of affect and mood the type of information upon which a psychiatrist would generally rely in formulating an opinion as to an individual's sanity (competence or future dangerousness)?

A. Yes.

Q. Did your evaluation of the defendant's affect and mood assist you in arriving at your opinion as to the defendant's sanity (competence or future dangerousness)?

A. Yes.

Q. During the course of the examination of the defendant, did you have the opportunity to assess his cognitive functions?

A. Yes.

Q. Can you explain to the jury what cognitive functions are?

A. Cognitive functions include: memory and orientation, concentration, general awareness, and intelligence.

Q. Can you test for memory?

A. Yes.

Q. How?

A. Immediate recall can be tested by asking the subject to remember 3 unrelated items for 3 to 5 minutes; recent memory can be evaluated by asking the subject to describe news events and prior meals; remote memory can be tested by asking about life's firsts, e.g., first car, first plane ride, first kiss, etc.

Q. How do you determine if an individual is disoriented?

A. Appreciation for location, date, and time.

Q. Are there tests for evaluating concentration?

A. Yes.

Q. How would you evaluate concentration?

A. A normally attentive grammar alcohol graduate should be able to repeat 7 random digits forward and 4 in reverse order (after it was determined that people can comfortably retain up to 7 numbers the telephone company immediately went to 10 and the post office went to 9 numbers in their zip codes. Spell simple five letter words backward and perform single digit calculations (nickels in $1.75). Recite in reverse the months of the year.

A caveat is in order. Any such tests foisted upon the defendant will be put to the psychiatrist on cross-examination. A better tactic is to give an example of performance as well as to describe the test. It can prove embarrassing when the psychiatrist cannot readily and comfortably perform the tests he administers to others.

Q. How do you determine the level of general information an individual possesses?

A. Basically a current event and simple trivia inquiry. Most socially aware subjects can name the last five presidents and name some of the state capitals.

Q. Are there ways to determine levels of intelligence?

A. Yes.

Q. How?

A. The most usual method is through psychometric testing. These are tests designed to infer intelligence. Additionally, conversation can often reveal level of understanding of vocabulary, and mathematical calculations. Ascertaining the ability to read and write assists in determining the competency of an individual.

Q. During the course of your examination of the defendant, did you evaluate his cognitive functions, that is, his memory, orientation, concentration, general information, and intelligence?

A. Yes.

Q. Is an assessment of cognitive functions the type of information upon which a psychiatrist would generally rely in formulating an opinion as to an individual's sanity (competence or future dangerousness)?

A. Yes.

Generally cognitive functions will be more of an issue in competency hearings than in issues of insanity or future dangerousness.

Q. Did the information you gathered as a result of evaluating the defendant's cognitive functions assist you in arriving at your opinion as to the defendant's sanity (competency or future dangerousness)?

A. Yes.

Q. In arriving at your opinion did you talk to the defendant's coworkers?

A. Yes.

Although seldom part of the psychiatric assessment this is a question that will be probed during cross examination. If coworkers have anecdotes of outrageous outbursts it would certainly be helpful to know of such behavior. If coworkers speak of the defendant in normal terms, it can bolster the impression of sanity. Actually, the primary reason for asking this and some of the following questions is to suggest to the judge or jury that the examination performed by the witness was complete.

Q. In arriving at your opinion, did you talk to the defendant's teacher(s) (fellow students, principal, departmental chair)?

A. Yes.

Q. In arriving at your opinion, did you talk to the defendant's employer(s).

A. Yes.

Q. In arriving at your opinion, did you talk to the defendant's supervisor(s)?

A. Yes.

Q. In arriving at your opinion, did you talk to those who have had the defendant in custody since his arrest?

A. Yes.

Q. Were any psychological tests performed?

A. Yes.

Q. By who?

A. Name of person or persons administering tests.

Q. Where?

A. Name of institution or office.

Q. Have you had an opportunity to review those tests?

A. Yes.

Q. What type of tests were administered?

A. MMPI, the Porteus Maze Test, the TAT (Thematic Apperception Test), the Bender Gestalt Test, the Shipley Hartford Test, the sentence completion test, the Graham Kandall Test, and the Rorschach Test.

Q. Are psychological tests the type of information upon which a psychiatrist would generally rely in formulating an opinion as to an individuals sanity (competency or future dangerousness)?

A. Yes.

Q. Did the information provided to you by these tests assist you in arriving at your opinion as to the defendant's sanity (competence or future dangerousness)?

A. Yes.

Q. Are there examinations that can be made to assist in determining the presence of organic brain disease?

A. Yes.

Q. Were examinations conducted on the defendant to determine the presence of organic brain disease?

A. Yes.

Q. Will you describe what examinations were performed to help determine if organic brain disease was present?

A. Briefly describe each:
   a. physical examination
   b. x-ray examination
   c. neurological examination (to determine the presence of central nervous system damage)
   d. electroencephalogram (an examination of brain waves which can indicate the presence of tumor or epilepsy)
   e. pneumoencephalogram (an injection of air into the brain to allow examination of any unusual spaces in the brain)

Q. Are you aware of the facts and circumstances surrounding the crime of which the defendant stands accused?

A. Yes.

Q. From where was this information obtained?

A. From arresting officers, investigating officers, and the defendant.

Q. Is the information you received from the arresting officers, investigating officers, and the defendant the type of information upon which a psychiatrist would generally rely in formulating an opinion as to an individual's sanity (competence or future dangerousness)?

A. Yes.

Q. Did the information provided to you by the arresting officers, investigating officers, and the defendant assist you in arriving at your opinion as to the defendant's sanity (competence or future dangerousness)?

A. Yes.

Q. Doctor, based on your training, education, experience, all aspects of your psychiatric examination, and interviews, have you arrived at an opinion, based on a reasonable medical certainty, as to the sanity (competence or future dangerousness) of the defendant?

A. Yes.

Q. Doctor what is that opinion?

A. The defendant is sane (competent or poses a future danger).

At this point the prosecution may wish to go into the basis for that opinion or pass the witness and allow the defendant to go into the basis for the opinions on cross-examination. What follows is a sample of a cross-examination of a defense expert psychiatric witness. The format is based on the privilege of cross-examination, which allows the use of leading questions (questions that suggest their answer). Leading questions are ordinarily unacceptable on direct examination except in providing expert qualifications and background. The cross-examination that follows can be readily adapted by prosecutors who wish to have their experts testify as to the basis for their opinions. It should be noted that this cross-examination is being conducted of a hostile (as opposed to friendly or neutral) witness. The examination presumes that an extensive vore dire of the credentials of the witness has already been conducted. Also note that what is suggested as a vigorous cross-examination of a defendant's psychiatric expert can easily be applied to the state's psychiatric expert.

Cross-Examination of a Defense Psychiatrist

Although expensive, it is fundamental to arrange for the state's psychiatrist to be present at the time of the questioning of the defense's expert. Her assistance in fashioning rebuttal questions and "keeping the good doctor honest" are invaluable. The defense will probably have their witness attend during the state's testimony which is a great disadvantage for any surprises that may have been lurking. In most criminal trials, all witnesses are excluded from the courtroom. This exclusion reduces the likelihood of collusion among witnesses. The exceptions to this policy are family and experts.

Q. In how many criminal cases have you previously testified wherein the defendant's sanity (competence or future dangerousness) was at issue?

Q. In how many of those instances did you find the defendant to be insane (incompetent or did not pose a threat of future dangerousness)?

Another tactic is to inquire as to the first time the witness testified in a criminal trial and the opinion rendered in that trial and continue on for each successive trial. It is a time-consuming method but certainly drives home to the jury the biased nature of the witnesses' testimonial history. Of course, this tactic presumes that the inquiring attorney already knows the answer to the question. It would be foolish to embark upon this line of questioning if in fact the witness has a balanced testimonial history.

Q. You are being paid for your testimony, are you not?

This is inherently an unfair question. It is designed to reflect upon the integrity of the witness who may miss the underlying innuendo and answer the question with what she believes to be a truthful affirmation. However, the knowledgeable witness will clarify the answer by rephrasing the question to mean that she is being compensated for her time and that her testimony cannot be bought. Of course, the insidious nature of the question is that the attorney can apologize for accidentally suggesting otherwise.

Q. The defendant has had a number of preliminary court appearances prior to your appointment, has he not?

Q. How many prior preliminary hearings?

Q. How many of these preliminary hearings were had prior to the defendant's having had an opportunity to consult with his attorney?

Q. During his pretrial detention, he had visiting privileges, did he not?

Q. During his pretrial detention, he was allowed to interact with other inmates, wasn't he?

Q. Isn't it true that the insanity defense was first put forth after the defendant talked to his lawyer?

Q. You have met with the defendant's lawyer, haven't you?

Q. How many times?

Q. For how long?

It may prove that the expert has spent more time with the defense lawyer than she has with the defendant, which would better dispose her to evaluate the defense lawyer than the defendant.

Q. Did you find any evidence of organic brain damage?

Q. Has the defendant been previously hospitalized for mental illness?

Obviously, the answer to this question is no or the prosecutor would not ask it.

Q. Has the defendant been previously treated for mental disease?

An alternative method of inquiry is to pose these questions as a statement rather than a question, which is a more aggressive cross-examination method, e.g., the defendant had never been hospitalized for mental disease, had he? However, this approach requires that the inquiring attorney be certain of the answer. The straightforward examination allows for error in preparation, but also relinquishes control to the witness who may choose to ramble biased irrelevancies. The aggressive method circumscribes the response generally to a simple yes or no.

Q. There is no evidence that the defendant had ever sought treatment for a mental disease is there doctor?

Q. When you first examined the defendant, did he understand the reason for the examination?

Q. Might a man who is being confronted with the possibility of lengthy incarceration or death, if found sane, tend to exaggerate symptoms of insanity or abnormality during a psychiatric interview?

The following questions are designed to elicit from the witness the comprehensiveness of her examination and therefore the credibility of her opinions.

Q. Is there a history of mental illness in the defendant's family?

Q. Did the defendant attend school?

Q. Was he a competent student?

Q. Did he finish school?

Q. Did you talk to classmates?

Q. Did you talk to teachers?

Q. Did you talk to the principal?

Q. As a result of those conversations, did you discover anyone who described the defendant's behavior as abnormal?

You do not want to ask this question without knowing the answer. By asking this question you have opened the door to hearsay evidence. The only way to be safe in this course of questioning is to assure that all of the persons referred to have been contacted by the state's expert and a follow-up by an investigator to assure that the defense expert did not do likewise.

Q. In arriving at your opinions, did you talk to the defendant's coworkers?

Q. Did you talk to his employer?

Q. Did you talk to his supervisor?

Q. As a result of those conversations, did you discover anyone who described the defendant's behavior as abnormal?

Q. Did you check the defendant's school and work attendance record?

Q. Did the defendant attend regularly?

Q. In arriving at your opinion, did you talk to the arresting officers?

Q. In arriving at your opinion, did you talk to the investigating officer?

Q. Have you formed an opinion as to what happened on the day in question?

Q. If you haven't talked to the investigating officers or the arresting officers, would it be safe to say that you have based your opinion of what happened on the day in question primarily upon what the defendant and his attorney have told you?

Q. In arriving at your opinion, did you talk to the people who are presently supervising the defendant's custody?

Q. Those responsible for the defendant's custody have not had to treat him any differently from any other defendant awaiting trial, have they?

Q. How much time have you spent with the defendant upon which you have based your opinion?

Q. When you conducted your examination did you ask him where he was?

Q. Did he know?

Q. Did you ask him why he was being detained?

Q. Did he know?

Q. Did he know who you were?

Q. Did he know why you were there?

Q. During your examination did you ask him the day, month and year?

Q. Did he know?

Q. Did he know of what he had been charged?

Q. Did he know the possible consequences should he be found guilty?

Q. Did you test for recent memory?

Q. How?

Q. Was he able to remember recent events?

Q. How did you test for recent recall?

Q. Was his memory good for remote events?

Q. How did you test for remote recall?

Q. Did he express remorse for his crime?

Obviously, a bit of a distracting question in that if the defendant expressed remorse, he must appreciate the wrongness of his conduct, which speaks directly to the legal sanity issue.

Q. Is it not reasonable to infer that if he knows his conduct is wrong now he knew it was wrong at the time he did it?

This question will probably not receive an affirmative answer and is posed simply to fix the idea in the jury's mind. It may therefore be omitted and saved for summary argument.

The defendant has available all the medical records that the state has at its disposal, however they must ask for it. The alternative would be to have independent psychological testing performed. It may be that the defense has not relied upon anything other than an interview (more commonly a state tactic). If the defense has not done a comprehensive medical and psychological evaluation, this would be the time to bring that to the jury's attention.

Q. When do your records reflect that you first met with the defendant?

Any notes used by the defendant in preparing for her testimony can be requested at this time along with a brief recess to examine them. It should also be kept in mind that any notes being used by the witness from the witness stand can be examined by the examining attorney. Witnesses should be cautioned not to bring anything to the stand that they do not wish the opposition to have. Once referred to from the witness stand, the entire document, record, or file is now subject to examination, not just the selected parts that are being used to assist in recollection.

Q. How long after the commission of the offense in question?

Q. How long did that first meeting last?

Q. When did you next meet with the defendant?

Q. How long did that meeting last?

Continue until all meetings have been accounted for. Keep track of total time spent with the defendant. When questioning the opposition witness, refer to these sessions as meetings; when questioning your own witness, refer to them as interviews or examinations.

Q. The total time you have spent with the defendant is _____ hours?

Q. And in that time you have been able to arrive at your conclusions as to the sanity (competence or future dangerousness) of the defendant? Hopefully, there is a significant time difference between the two experts to make this line of inquiry relevant.

Q. Have you examined the medical records of the defendant?

Q. Have you examined the results of the psychological tests performed by Dr. _____?

Q. Are you aware that while the defendant has been detained, he has voluntarily subjected himself to a battery of tests?

Q. Are you aware that one of the tests that was administered to the defendant was the MMPI?

Q. Are you familiar with the MMPI test?

Q. Have you used the results of the MMPI in arriving at a medical opinion in other cases?

Q. Have you read the results of the defendant's MMPI?

Q. Have you had another MMPI test performed on the defendant?

Q. Do you think that the results of this test, had you administered it, might have had some bearing on your opinion as to the sanity (competence or future dangerousness) of the defendant?

Q. Are you aware that one of the tests that was administered to the defendant was the TAT?

Q. Are you familiar with the TAT?

Q. Have you used the results of the TAT in arriving at a medical opinion in other cases?

Q. Have you read the results of the defendant's TAT?

Q. Have you had another TAT performed on the defendant?

Q. Do you think that the results of this test, had you administered it, might have had some bearing on your opinion as to the sanity (competence or future dangerousness) of the defendant?

Q. Are you familiar with the Porteus Maze test?

Q. Have you used the results of the Porteus Maze test in arriving at a medical opinion in other cases?

Q. Have you read the results of the defendant's Porteus Maze test?

Q. Have you had another Porteus Maze test performed on the defendant?

Q. Do you think that the results of this test, had you administered it, might have had some bearing on your opinion as to the sanity (competence or future dangerousness) of the defendant?

Q. Are you aware that one of the tests that was administered to the defendant was the Bender Gestalt?

Q. Are you familiar with the Bender Gestalt test?

Q. Have you used the results of the Bender Gestalt in arriving at a medical opinion in other cases?

Q. Have you read the results of the defendant's Bender Gestalt test?

Q. Have you had another Bender Gestalt test performed on the defendant?

Q. Do you think that this test, had you administered it, might have had some bearing on your opinion as to the sanity (competence or future dangerousness) of the defendant?

Q. Are you aware that the state's psychiatrist also administered or had administered the Graham Kandall test, the Shipley Hartford Test, the Sentence Completion test, and the Rorschach test?

Q. Did you give him all of these tests before arriving at your opinion?

Q. Did you test or have tested the defendant for organic brain disease?

Q. Did you perform or have performed a physical examination?

Q. Did you perform or have performed an electroencephalogram test?

Q. Did you perform or have performed a neurological examination?

Q. Did you perform or have performed a pneumoencephalogram test?

If the witness has administered these tests, they should be consistent with those administered by the state and demonstrate no evidence of organic brain disease and the witness should not hesitate in testifying to that fact. If the witness has not administered these tests, the inference is that the examination was incomplete and the opinion based thereon is unreliable. The expert should be asked if she has talked to all the persons who have provided information to the state's expert upon which the state's expert has based her opinion of sanity. Any admissions by the defendant of remorse for his crime should be posed to the expert as a suggestion of the ability to recognize the difference between right and wrong.

If, as the foregoing questions suggest, the defense expert has arrived at her opinion as the result of a single visit with the defendant, an effort at impeaching with the use of a learned treatise can be attempted. It is a bit like hoisting the expert on her own petard.

Q. Doctor what is forensic psychiatry?

Q. Does a part of what is known as forensic psychiatry specialize in rendering opinions on legal sanity (competence or future dangerousness)?

Q. Have you heard of Dr. Bernard L. Diamond, forensic psychiatrist and author of the book *The Psychiatrist in the Courtroom?*

Add all notable qualifications of the author.

Q. Are you familiar with the portion of his textbook on the psychiatric examination of the criminal defendant?

Q. Do you regard that text as authoritative within the field of criminal forensic psychiatry?

To avoid a negative response to this question, it might be best to establish the authority of the author and the text with the state's expert. It may be necessary to call the state's expert in rebuttal if the defense expert refuses to acknowledge the authority of the text and the author.

Perhaps a better tactic is to ask these questions of the state's expert and await the closing to direct the jury's attention to the answers.

Q. Let me direct your attention to page 31 of the text and ask you to read to the jury the portion pertaining to the number of examinations a criminal defendant should be subjected to before a determination as to sanity (competence or future dangerousness) is made.

Q. Do you agree with that doctor?

Q. Let me direct your attention to page 31 of the text and ask you to read to the jury the portion pertaining to criminal suspects lying during the first psychiatric examination.

Q. Do you agree, doctor, that a criminal defendant is likely to lie to the psychiatrist during the first psychiatric examination?

If the expert declines to agree, the examining attorney can focus on that disagreement and the respective credentials of the expert when compared to the author during the attorney's closing statement. If the expert agrees, the point has been made and only needs to be mentioned during closing.

The following questions address the issue of irresistible impulse as opposed to right and wrong. Of course, this may be unnecessary if the defense is that because of mental disease the defendant did not know the difference between right and wrong.

Q. In your examination, did you uncover any evidence of the defendant having been a behavioral problem in school?

Q. In your examination, did you uncover any evidence of the defendant having been a behavioral problem at work?

Q. In your examination, did you find any evidence of the defendant having been a behavioral problem in jail awaiting trial?

Q. The defendant has been in jail for over six months and in that time has had no confrontations with other inmates or staff, he has fed himself, washed himself, dressed himself, conversed in an intelligible manner, and has demonstrated no behavioral problems. Would this be evidence that he is capable of controlling any antisocial impulses he might have?

Q. If the defendant stalked his victim, would that suggest that he had some control over his antisocial impulses?

Q. If the defendant planned his crime, would that suggest that he had some control over his antisocial impulses?

Q. If the defendant waited until his victim was alone, would that suggest that he had some control over his antisocial impulses?

Q. If the defendant waited lengthy periods of time between his offenses, would that suggest that he had some control over his antisocial impulses?

Q. If the defendant fled after commission of the crime, would that suggest he knew what he had done was wrong?

Q. If the defendant buried his victims, would that suggest that he knew that what he had done was wrong?

Q. Would the defendant have committed this offense in the presence of a police officer?

Q. Would the defendant have committed this offense in the presence of his family?

Q. You understand, doctor, that if the defendant is found insane, he may one day be freed?

Q. Are you willing to take that chance?

Q. Are you willing to testify here today, under oath, that it is your professional opinion that if the defendant were to be freed, he would not kill again?

It should go without saying that the state's expert witness must be prepared to withstand the same type of cross-examination as that suggested above. The prosecutor must be certain that the expert is not only prepared from her perspective but also from a legal perspective. If the state is not willing to subject the defendant to the exhaustive examination and testing protocol outlined here, then perhaps a voluntary commitment is the appropriate approach rather than the prostitution of a professional and a less than just outcome. It should be the objective of every lawyer to ferret out those who are incapable of the culpability required as an element of each criminal offense and provide institutionalization rather than incarceration. No one's interests are served in incarcerating those with diminished capacity, or executing those who are insane. This should be the one avenue of the criminal justice process upon which both the state and the defense can agree.

There is a consensus among trial lawyers when dealing with forensic psychologists and psychiatrists and that is that most go beyond the boundaries of validated knowledge in their field, lack an adequate classification system and are excessively influenced by biases and prejudices, perform inadequate examinations, and rely excessively on jargon and labels. Juries are reluctant to accept the conclusions of these experts, which often appear esoteric in contrast to common sense explanations. Chief Justice Warren Burger (1964) has suggested that psychology and psychiatry as sciences are at best in their infancy, and that psychologists and psychiatrists "may be claiming too much in relation to what they really understand about the human personality and human behavior." It was Chief Justice Burger's concern that psychiatric and psychological judgments were often the political or social bias of the witness (Burger, 1964).

Opinion testimony of mental health experts has been and continues to be viewed skeptically by the judiciary, the bar, and jurors. Often this lack of credibility is a product of inadequate information upon which the expert is attempting to base an opinion or the absence of any "hard data." Hard data is information gathered from employment records, medical records, psychometric testing, and witnesses of the defendant's behavior at or near the time of the crime. It may be that jurors can be impressed by arcane jargon and sophistry. But impressing a jury and convincing a jury may be two different things. The prosecutor must do more than impress the jury; she must persuade the jury. In that effort the expert witness must glean as much hard data in support of expert opinions as is available and not rely on 30-minute interviews upon which to base opinions. In that effort the prosecutor must make the common sense, factual basis of the expert's opinion as clear as possible.

REFERENCES

Becker, R. 1995. Procedural obstacles inherent in the insanity defense. *Journal of Police and Criminal Psychologists,* May.

Blau, G., McGinley, H., & Pasewark, R.A. 1992. Insanity Defense and Socioeconomic Status. *Journal of Police and Criminal Psychology,* 8:1, March.

Burger, W. 1964. Psychiatrists, Lawyers and the Courts, 28 *Federal Probation,* 3:7.

Caplan, L. 1984. *The Insanity Defense and the Trial of John W. Hinckley, Jr.* Boston: D.G.R.

Caplan, L. 1992. Not So Nutty. *The New Republic,* pp. 18–20, March.

Dix, G.E. & Sharlot, M.M. 1987. *Basic Criminal law Cases and Materials.* St. Paul, MN: West, pp. 615–664.

Dorland's Illustrated Medical Dictionary. 1974. Friel J.P. ed. 25th edition. Philadelphia: W.B. Saunders.

Holten, N.C. & Lamar, L.L. 1991. *The Criminal Courts Structures, Personnel and Processes.* New York: McGraw-Hill, pp. 263–265.

Johnson, W.G., Nicholson, R.A., & Service, N.W. 1990. The Relationship of Competency to Stand Trial and Criminal Responsibility. *Criminal Justice and Behavior,* 17:2. June.

LaFave, W.R. 1987. *Modern Criminal Law.* St. Paul, MN: West, pp. 309.

Merck Manual. 1988. R. Berkow, ed. 15th edition. Rahway, NJ: Merck.

Roberts, C.F., Golding, S.L., & Fincham, F.D. 1987. Implicit Theories of Criminal Responsibility. *Law and Behavior,* 11:3.

Toufexis, A. 1992. Do Mad Acts a Madman Make? *Time,* p. 17 (February 28).

Winslade, W.J., & Ross, J.W. 1983. *The Insanity Plea.* New York: Scribners.

Table of Cases

Commonwealth v. Mutina, 323 N.E. 2d 294, 1975.

Daniel M'Naghten's Case, 8 Eng. Rep. 718, 10 Cl. & Fin. 200 (1843).

Parsons v. State, 2 So. 854, 1887.

United States v. Cohen, 530 F.2d 43 (5th Cir. 1976).

Table of Statutes

Title 18, *United States Codes Annotated,* section 20.

Chapter 6

THE POLICE EXPERT IN CRIMINAL TRIALS

Although police are not scientists they are experts and are often granted the latitude of an expert witness in their testimony. The example that most readily comes to mind is that of a police officer testifying as to the intoxicated state of a motorist. After it has been demonstrated that the officer has had experience dealing with people who have been proven to be intoxicated, the examining attorney will often ask if in the officer's opinion the motorist was intoxicated. Prior to breath analysis and video cameras, a police officer's testimony was the only vehicle upon which intoxication could be proven. The usual litany went something like this:

Q. Was there anything notable about the defendant's speech?
A. Yes, his speech was slurred.
Q. Was there anything notable about the defendant's gait?
A. Yes, his gait was unsteady.
Q. Was there anything notable about the defendant's eyes?
A. Yes, his eyes were bloodshot.
Q. Was there anything notable about the defendant's breath?
A. Yes, the defendant's breath smelled as though he had consumed alcoholic beverages.
Q. Have you seen people who in your estimation were under the influence of alcohol?
A. Yes.
Q. On one occasion or many occasions?
A. On many occasions.
Q. Based on your observations of the defendant, have you an opinion as to whether or not he was intoxicated?
A. Yes.
Q. And what is that opinion?
A. I believe he was intoxicated.

Police testify as experts in identifying the odor of burning marijuana, caliber of gun, approximation of speed, under the influence of alcohol or drugs, and in accident investigations. They perform expert services in administering breath analysis, computing coefficients of friction (drag factors), and field testing suspected controlled substances. It should be apparent that college educations and doctoral degrees are not the only expert services that the court may require.

An investigator who intends to participate in the satisfaction of successful prosecutions must excel at two things: documentation and testifying. It serves no purpose for the best of investigators to take the witness stand without adequate documentation in support of the investigation. Trials often occur months, if not years, after the investigation has been completed. The only reliable record of the investigation is the documentation prepared by the investigator. If that documentation is sparse, inaccurate, or lacking basic composition skills, the testifying investigator is at risk in attempting to remedy those shortcomings on the witness stand.

The usual catastrophe begins by the officer testifying to facts not included in the documentation. Such testimony is a gift to the defense. If the testimony is important enough to tell the jury, then why was it not included in the original report? The inference obviously is that it would have been had it happened.

A failing memory that recovers in time for trial is also risky. If the report was made close in time to the recovery operation, would not the documentation be a more accurate rendition of the facts than an uncorroborated recollection months or years later? Obviously, a contemporaneous recording of significant events is more reliable than a recollection months or years later and any suggestion otherwise is viewed as suspect.

Good trial lawyers are not born; they learn. Competent police witnesses are not born; they too are a product of (a) potential, (b) training, (c) experience, and (d) preparation. A superb, unprepared trial lawyer will lose to an average prepared trial lawyer. Every time. That adage is applicable to any witness who enters the gladiatorial arena of the law (Becker, 1995).

Preparation is reflected in the quality of the testimony. The quality of preparation is based upon the quality of the documentation that has been completed by the investigating officers, the time spent in studying that documentation, and the sources from which that documentation stems.

A policeman who testifies well will assist the prosecutor in obtaining guilty verdicts. A policeman who can reliably testify will be seen by the prosecutor as an asset to cultivate. If the prosecutor accepts cases from an officer she has learned to have confidence in, that officer's conviction rate will soar. A sustained rate of convictions for any police officer cannot hurt career perspectives.

A testifying police investigator can be a defense lawyer's ally or worst nightmare. In selecting the jury, defense lawyers inquire into the venireperson's (prospective jurors) occupational background. Anyone with police relatives or police friends will most likely be struck from a jury. These prospective jurors will be asked if they believe that a police officer is any more believable than any other witness. They will be asked if they are of the opinion that police officers do not make mistakes. They will be asked if they are of the opinion that police officers do not lie. Anyone answering these questions favorably will be subjected to being peremptorily (without reason) struck.

Why does the defense counsel place so much emphasis on the police officer? He knows that the entire case may rest on the testimony of the police and the investigation they performed. He also knows that each officer is bestowed with an invisible "shroud of veracity" by virtue of the esteem with which police are generally held in the community.

Many people believe and want to believe that police officers are honest and lack deceit. The whole jury has anticipated, since the voir dire (jury selection) the moment the testifying officer is called by the bailiff as a witness. That officer is scrutinized the moment her foot hits the floor as she steps through the door and enters the courtroom. From head to foot. If the officer walks confidently, dressed professionally and with personal pride in her appearance, many on the jury extend the courtesy of belief. That believability cannot be damaged by anything that the defense may have done or attempts to do, but it can be stripped away by incompetent, insincere, or dishonest testimony.

The penalty for false testimony for any other witness is to be labelled a perjurer and to be forgotten. The penalty for a police officer who is incompetent or dishonest is a verdict of acquittal for the defendant and a prosecutor who may not prosecute that officers cases (Becker, 1995).

PREPARING FOR TRIAL

Habit is a tool or a vice. If from habit, all investigations are conducted with the same meticulousness, a habit aimed at success has been established. That habit is difficult to cultivate because police know that the majority of investigations leading to arrest will never go to trial. If the case is not likely to be tried, why invest time and effort writing? Presuming cases will not go to trial or that another officer will do the writing assures embarrassment or dishonesty when that presumption fails. The only foolproof way to avoid falling victim to the "plea bargain" presumption is to prepare every case as though it were going to trial. It may be tedious, but it certainly provides practice. After all, practice makes a defense lawyer's life more difficult.

The easiest way for a prosecutor to obtain a plea bargain from a knowledgeable defense lawyer is to convince the lawyer that the case is ready to try and that the prosecutor is confident of the outcome. Much of the paperwork generated as part of the investigation is discoverable by the defense. If a competent defense lawyer discovers shoddy and inaccurate data included in the police investigation, why plead out?

An officer with experience testifying will not wait until the day of trial to review the case. It would be prudent to examine the paperwork, evidence, logs, photographs, diagrams, sketches, and charts that will be admitted through the officer's testimony. Review the condition of all evidence, including markings, labels, and chain of custody.

A common area of police expert testimony is in the traffic fatality. Usually this incident stems from excessive speed or intoxication that may rise to the level of criminal conduct. Considering the workload of most police officers and the distance in time from the investigation to the trial, preparation based on a complete review of the documentation is vital. All diagrams and sketches should have been constructed with the trial in mind and lend themselves to quality enlargements that will assist the jury in understanding the testimony. Most accident investigators have been trained at the hands of accident reconstruction engineers. It is a mistake to use engineering jargon and technical presentations. The key to successful accident investigation is to keep it simple. The primary objective is to establish fault, and violation of the law.

Examination of the Accident Investigation

The Police Officer

Routine Background Questions:
Name
Occupation

Place of employment
Rank
Length of employment
Training as a police officer
   academy graduate
   weeks of training
   subjects of training
   special training in accident investigation
     type of training
     number of hours
     certification awarded
Accident Investigation Experience:
   types of accidents that require investigation
   types of accidents investigated
   number of investigations
   number of investigations involving death
   number of investigations involving serious injury
   number of times called upon to be deposed
   number of times called upon to testify
     civil cases
     criminal cases

Q. What is the usual procedure employed in investigating automobile accidents that involve fatalities?

A. To:
   Photograph fatalities
   Photograph vehicles
   Interview drivers and passengers
   Request blood specimen be taken from drivers and fatalities
   Mark points of impact on the pavement
   Photograph points of impact on the pavement
   Mark points at which the vehicles came to rest
   Photograph points at which vehicles came to rest
   Measure pavement gouges
   Photograph pavement gouges
   Measure skid marks
   Photograph skid marks
   Measure vehicular intrusion
   Test roadway surface coefficient of friction (drag factor)
   Examine autos and their contents

Examine headlamps

Examine tail lights

Examine brake lights and turning signals

Photograph all vehicular damage interior and exterior

Q. Is that the procedure that was employed in this case?

A. Yes.

Q. At what time did you receive notice of this collision?

A. The answer should be reflected on all the documentation prepared by the witness.

We have grown accustomed to referring to automobile collisions as "accidents." Accidents are considered to have occurred by chance, a product of fortune. In truth, fortune and chance have little to do with most traffic collisions. Speed, following too closely, intoxication, and failure to pay attention are the precipitating mechanisms of collisions, not fortune, chance, or fate. Evidently, if we all agree to call automobile collisions "accidents," we can avoid the mantle of irresponsibility that is worn by one or more participants in a traffic "accident." Having a "traffic accident" is a lot like dying of "complications" in a hospital or during surgery. It appears that by dying of "complications," the surgery or hospital is removed from the chain of responsibility for the death. Another apt analogy is the police euphemism "he got off on a technicality," which can usually be interpreted that the police in some fashion or another failed to do their job or failed to do it correctly. Defense lawyers, for the most part, point out and exaggerate the errors of the police and the prosecution; they seldom manufacture them.

Q. How were you notified of the collision?

A. Radio dispatch.

Q. Who notified you of the collision?

A. The police dispatcher.

Q. Does the dispatcher log the time of these calls?

A. Yes.

It may be necessary to prove up the dispatch log by using the business records exception to the hearsay rule. Time may be an issue if there is some suggestion of negligence on the part of the responding police or if intoxication is a contributing issue, the prosecution will attempt to determine what the blood alcohol level was at the time of the collision using retrograde extrapolation (an attempt to determine what blood alcohol was at the time of the collision based on a particular body type's dissipation of alcohol over time).

Q. Where were you told the collision occurred?

A. Provide a general location that could be identified on a city or county map.

It is helpful if a series of plats are constructed beginning with the city or county and incrementally focusing on the neighborhood, block, intersection, and culminating with a sketch of the collision scene.

Q. Were you able to identify the parties who were involved in the collision?

A. Yes.

Q. Identify the parties, please.

A. List the names of the parties by vehicle indicating position in the vehicle.

Q. What were the mental and physical conditions of the parties?

A. Use layman's terms, not medical terms. A police officer is not generally qualified as a medical expert.

Q. Can you describe the general appearance of the drivers?

A. This will help corroborate later testimony of intoxication if it is an issue.

Q. Did you talk to each driver?

A. Yes.

Q. Did you ask them what caused the collision?

A. Yes.

Q. What was their response?

A. Briefly and succinctly summarize the theories.

Q. Did you issue a traffic citation in this case?

A. Yes.

Q. To whom and for what?

A. State the party and violation written.

The traffic violation should be entered into evidence at this point. If speeding is the offense, then the officer should be asked what the posted speed limit was. It would also be helpful if a photograph of the sign posting the relevant speed limit be included in the file. This information and photo should be provided by the investigating officer which will be essential after crash speed has been provided by a testifying engineer. It is of little value to show the jury that the preimpact speeds were 60 mph if it has not already been shown to be an area posted for a speed no greater than 40.

Q. Did this collision occur at an intersection?

A. Yes.

Q. Where was that intersection located?

A. Give street names and city quadrant.

Q. Were there any traffic control devices?

A. Yes.

Q. What kind and where were they located?

A. Provide a description of the devices present. At this point the collision scene sketch should be entered as evidence with the officer providing a description of the sketch contents.

The following are questions that are required to enter the sketch:

I hand you what has been marked as state's exhibit.

Do you recognize state's Exhibit Number 3?

What is it?

Who drew it?

When was it drawn?

Does it fairly and accurately portray the scene as you remember it?

Has it been altered or changed in any way since you drew it?

Will you describe for the jury what this sketch depicts?

Will you explain each of the markings on the sketch?

Q. Was it possible to determine if the devices were working?

A. Yes.

Q. How was that determined?

A. Witness statements and city traffic control device maintenance logs (these logs should be obtained from the maintenance department and thoroughly examined. Devices with histories of problems may become significant upon cross-examination). Such logs should be entered as evidence at this point.

Q. Is the intersection obscured by any visual obstacles?

A. No. This should be verified by videotape footage of the various approaches to the intersection from the driver's vantage point. The tape should be made at the same time of day and under the same weather and visibility conditions as existed on the day of the collision.

Q. Is the approach to the intersection flat or graded?

A. Describe the approach to the intersection.

The author tried a case in San Antonio, Texas involving the death of two passengers as the result of an inebriated driver. The defense of the defendant was that the road dipped gradually, when approaching the intersection, below the line of vision necessary to see the traffic light. If travelling at the posted speed limit, the defendant contended that once the traffic light again became visible there was not sufficient distance in which to stop safely. A vehicle of the same make and model was used to video tape the approach to the intersection with a second camera providing a "real time" video insert of the speedometer during the approach. The video footage amply demonstrated that there was sufficient distance to stop if travelling at the speed limit.

Inquiry might also be made into:

1. curves
2. hills
3. visible distance
4. roadway surface
5. roadway lighting
6. lane widths

Nighttime collisions would warrant collection of the following information:

1. vehicle lights
   a. on
   b. off
   c. high beam
   d. low beam
   e. number of lights working

When the display of lights is in question, it will be prudent to obtain the light fixtures including the light bulbs, the fixture should be removed in its entirety to avoid damage to the bulb and the filament. It should be presumed that lights will be a question in all nighttime cases and lights should be preserved accordingly.

A forensic engineer may be able to tell by filament position, and break type, from which direction the impact was received and whether or not the light was on at the time of the accident. Tungsten lamp filaments have a high melting point, and when exposed to oxygen, the combination of tungsten and oxygen creates a telltale surface oxide coating of various colors on the metal. If the bulb breaks, the broken glass may be scattered onto the filament and a hot filament will melt the glass leaving evidence of an "on bulb" (Miller and Brown, 1990). In bulbs that are unbroken, the filaments may be distorted or broken from impact. These broken filaments may have a small melted globule at the point of separation. A distorted filament is indicative of the lamp having been "on" at the time of the impact.

Choosing to leave the light fixtures in place may be a serious mistake. By the time a forensic engineer examines the vehicle, it will probably have been moved from the collision site to the police pound. The insurance company will attempt to sell the vehicle for salvage which may entail its removal to a junk yard and having it compressed into a metal block. Even if the vehicle is moved only to the police pound, the handling during the move may result in loss of crucial evidence.

2. glare—what ground clutter may have provided a visual barrier. In order to provide this information it may be necessary for the accident investigator to drive the approach to the collision site.
3. range of visibility—at the time of the collision. It is common for drivers to overdrive their headlights. Regardless of the speed limit if a motorist is overdriving her range of visibility, she is driving too fast and is violating the law.

A crucial aspect of any collision in which alcohol or speed may be involved is the presence or absence of skid marks. If there are skid marks their location, continuity, length, width, and direction are very revelatory. If skid marks are present, then coeficients of friction (drag factors) should be obtained for the entire area over which the skid marks pass. Different agencies use different types of instruments for determining drag factors. All provide data that will allow a computation of speed; some devices are better than others. A drag sled is the most reliable method of determining drag. The sled can be pulled by hand and the friction the weighted sled is exerting upon the roadway can be read by a meter which measures drag factor. The same surface may render different drag factors because of wear and oil deposits driven into the surface material. Drag factors should be considered at various locations throughout the collision scene and an average of all measurements used in speed calculations. Another means of determining drag factor is to use drag tables. These tables are approximations and are no real substitute for on-site friction testing.

The formula used to determine speed from a known stopping distance (skids plus response time rendered to miles per hour) is 5.5 a known constant times the square root of the distance of the skid marks multiplied by the composite coefficient of friction of the roadway is:

$$S = 5.5\sqrt{D} \times f$$

For example if a vehicle left 30 ft. of skid marks and the coefficient of friction was determined to be .75, the formula would be applied in this fashion:

$$S = 5.5\sqrt{30} \times .75$$

$$S = 5.5\sqrt{22.5}$$

$S = 5.5 \times 4.7$
$S = 26.1$ mph

That figure can be converted to feet per second by multiplying miles per hour by 1.47:

$S = 38.4$ fps

In order to have a reliable speed calculation, it is also necessary to figure in an average reaction time. Three-fourths of a second is the figure usually applied to represent the average driver's reaction time. Tables have been constructed to reflect the number of feet traveled in 3/4 of a second at speeds of 5 mph increments beginning at 10 mph:

MPH	DISTANCE IN 3/4 SECOND
10	11.0
15	16.5
20	22.0
25	27.5
30	33.0
35	38.5
40	44.0
45	49.5
50	55.0
55	60.5
60	66.0
65	71.5
70	77.0
75	82.5
80	88.0
85	93.5
90	99.0
100	110.0

Most accident investigators include a sketch of the accident site (sometimes architecturally redrawn) which should show the following:

Point of impact (POI) of the vehicles—information pertaining to POI can be obtained from witnesses, pavement gouges, debris, glass remnants, and fluid deposits. It will be the responsibility of the testifying expert to explain what information assisted in determining point of impact. Obviously the POI is important because the impact point may effect speed calculations as well as right of way determinations.

landmarks—permanent physical structures, e.g., buildings, curbs, highway markers, street corners, etc.

point of contact (POI)—what part of the vehicles first came into contact. Again, significant in right-of-way determinations.

point of rest (POR)—the point at which the vehicles came to rest is also helpful in using inertia formulas in determining speed at time of impact.

depth of penetration—one vehicle may have intruded into the other, the depth of penetration is also a useful figure for impact calculations.

Often, information gathered by the accident investigator will be beyond her ability to use. In cases of serious bodily injury or death, forensic engineers may be called upon to render further assistance. By the time the forensic engineer is brought into the case, the accident scene has been cleaned up, altered because of time and traffic, or physically changed. It is therefore necessary for the forensic engineer to rely on the photographs and measurements taken by the accident investigator.

Q. Did you take photographs of the collision site?
A. Yes.
Q. Did you take photographs of the vehicles?
A. Yes.
Q. Did you take photographs of the deceased?
A. Yes.

The following questions would be required in seeking to admit collision photographs:

I hand you what have been marked as state's exhibits 3 through 30, and ask you if you recognize them?

What are they?

Do they fairly and accurately portray the scene as you remember it?

Reconstruction Expert

The preliminary questions for a reconstruction expert are generally the same as for any other expert:

Name
profession
employer

educational background
reconstruction experience
special training or courses attended
special training or courses taught
list of publications
teaching experience
professional affiliations

Q. How long have you been a forensic engineer (accident reconstructionist)?

A. Include only that time reflected in professional certification.

Q. For whom have you provided services?

A. This answer is primarily designed to suggest to the jury that the expert is objective and has worked for plaintiffs, defendants, and the state. In criminal cases, many states have professionals who are employed by the state to provide this type of testimony in which case this need not be asked.

Q. How many collisions have you reconstructed?

A. An approximation will do. From the jury's perspective, the more the better.

Q. When were you asked to investigate this collision?

A. The date should be corroborated by telephone logs or a letter of retention. This may appear to be an innocuous question, but if the retention date does not reflect ample time to examine the vehicle, the collision site, and a comprehensive evaluation of the documentation and photographs, the defense will be sure to bring that to the jury's attention.

Q. What were you asked to do?

A. The obvious answer is "to provide information upon which the defendant may be convicted." However damning the evidence or odious the defendant, it is imperative the expert relate his charge as being to simply determine what happened, what speeds were involved, and who caused the collision.

Q. What information were you provided to assist you in that endeavor?

A. List all documents, photos, evidence, and statements that were provided regardless of the fact that they may not have been used in arriving at an opinion.

Q. What materials other than the ones provided you assisted in forming your opinions in this case?

A. Any reference materials or conferences with colleagues, visits with police, witnesses, or the prosecutor should be divulged.

Q. Did you conduct an independent investigation?

A. Yes. I examined the vehicles and the site and I conducted computer analysis of various data made available from my measurements as well as the measurements provided by the police and some photogrammatically extracted from photographs.

Q. Did you take any additional photographs?

A. Yes.

Q. Of what?

A. The vehicles in question.

Q. Why?

A. To confirm make and model, to assure there were no body alterations that would effect weight data. I also took photographs of a device I placed contiguous to the auto that would allow measurement and visual appreciation for the maximum penetration that occurred as a result of the collision.

Q. Were you able to determine point of impact?

A. Point of impact determinations had to be made based on police sketches, although there were some pavement gouges consistent with police photos and sketches.

Q. Is this the type of information upon which an expert in your profession would rely in forming an opinion as to point of impact?

A. Yes.

Q. Do you have an opinion as to the location of point of impact?

A. Yes.

Q. What is that opinion?

A. The point of impact was approximately 3 meters northwest of the intersection of Wurzbach Road and Lockhill Selma Road as measured from the middle of the intersection. I also triangulated the position using three permanent landmarks near the intersection.

Q. I hand you what has been marked as state's Exhibit Number 4 and ask you if you recognize it?

A. Yes.

Q. What is it?

A. A scale drawing of the point of impact and the surrounding area at the intersection of Wurzbach and Lockhill Selma.

Q. Did you draw this document?

A. Yes. If not, then:

Q. Was it drawn by someone at your direction and under your supervision?

A. Yes.

Q. Is this an accurate representation of the intersection as you recall it?

A. Yes.

Q. Has it been changed or altered since you drew it (or had it drawn)?

A. No. If it has explain all changes and the reasons for the changes.

State's exhibit number 4 should now be offered as evidence. Once the drawing has been accepted without objection or all objections have been addressed, it should be displayed where the jury can see it and where the witness can refer to it without blocking the jury's view.

Q. Would you show the jury where the point of impact is represented on your drawing?

A. Approach the exhibit with confidence, restricting the response to the question posed.

Q. Would you point out to the jury the center of the intersection as you have it marked?

A. Do so describing it in the process.

Q. Would you point out the three landmarks you used to triangulate the point of impact?

A. Do so describing them in the process. (Sit down)

Q. Is it possible to determine which direction the vehicles were traveling prior to, at the time and after impact?

A. Yes.

Q. What engineering principles did you employ in determining direction of travel of the vehicles?

A. Force vectors—that is the direction of the movement of metal as a result of applied force. Also the location of debris found at the site as rendered in the photographs taken by the police in relationship to the at rest location of the vehicles after the collision. An analysis of the deformation of the vehicle bodies revealed a considerable amount of information upon which I base my opinion. Road gouges, skid marks, police reports, and witness statements provided a human component to my analysis which I found to be remarkably consistent with the engineering data. The head lamp and tail lamp filaments also provided some information as to direction of impact and travel at the time of impact.

Q. Is this the kind of information upon which an expert in the field of forensic engineering would rely in forming an opinion?

A. Yes.

Q. In your opinion, based on your experience, education, and training, what direction were the vehicles travelling prior to, at the time of, and after impact?

A. The car driven by the defendant was driving in the north-bound, inside lane, turning onto Wurzbach to head west. The auto driven by the decedent was travelling in the south-bound, inside lane, turning onto Wurzbach to head west. As the south-bound vehicle driven by the victims attempted to turn left, the north-bound vehicle struck it on the passenger side at the front door. Both vehicles then travelled northwest, coming to rest with the victim's vehicle travelling north of the point of impact 13 meters and the defendant's vehicle travelling northeast and coming to rest against a utility pole 25 meters northeast of the point of impact.

Q. Is the direction of travel of the vehicles before, at, and after impact shown on your drawing?

A. Yes.

Q. Would you point out to the jury the direction of travel of the defendant's vehicle before impact?

A. Do so describing it in the process.

Q. Would you point out the direction of travel of the defendant's vehicle at the time of impact?

A. Do so describing it in the process.

Q. Would you point out the direction of travel of the defendant's vehicle after the impact?

A. Do so describing it in the process.

Q. Would you point out the point of rest of the defendant's vehicle?

A. Do so describing it in the process.

Q. Would you now point out the direction of travel of the victim's vehicle prior to impact?

A. Do so describing it in the process.

Q. Would you point out the direction of travel of the victim's vehicle at the time of impact?

A. Do so describing it in the process.

Q. Would you point out the direction of travel of the victim's vehicle after impact?

A. Do so describing it in the process.

Q. Would you point out the point of rest of the victim's vehicle?

A. Do so describing it in the process.

Q. Is it possible to determine the speed of two vehicles involved in an automobile collision?

A. Yes.

Q. What engineering principles and information would be used in such a determination?

A. The most obvious measure is that of skid marks and the amount of penetration of one vehicle into another. It is also helpful to know the coefficient of friction and gradient of the roadway upon which the collision occurred. The make, model, and weight of the vehicles can also be important when using computer software in determining speed. Most auto manufacturers publish data on weight and energy absorbing characteristics of vehicles they build. That information can be obtained in hard copy or be part of a computer program such as "Ed-Crash"; there are many other similar programs available. Depending on the amount and type of information that can be gleaned from the crash site, these programs can be very effective in providing speed determinations.

Q. Did you use these types of data in arriving at an opinion as to the speed of the vehicles in this case?

A. Yes.

Q. Is this the type of information upon which an expert in the field of forensic engineering would normally rely in arriving at an opinion?

A. Yes.

Q. Do you have an opinion, based on your experience, education, and training, based on a reasonable scientific certainty as to the speed of the victim's vehicle at the time of impact?

A. Yes.

Q. What is that opinion?

A. Between 5–10 miles per hour.

Q. Do you have an opinion based on your experience, education, and training, based on a reasonable scientific certainty as to the speed of the defendant's vehicle at the time of impact?

A. Between 45–50 miles per hour.

Q. Do you have an opinion based on your experience, education and training, based on a reasonable scientific certainty as to the speed of the defendant's vehicle before the brakes were applied?

A. In excess of 70 miles per hour.

Everything testified to by the forensic engineer will be disputed on cross-examination. The weights, distances, drag factors, witness statements, offense reports, drawings, photographs, and the computer program used will be challenged. An expert will be retained by the defendant who will use the same or similar computer program using different numbers and coming up with a much slower speed.

This is one situation in which permission of the court should be sought for the state's witness to assist at the time of examination of the defense expert. There are no reasons to exclude the witness once his/her testimony has been solicited and in all likelihood the defense will request that their expert be allowed the same latitude. However, before agreeing, remember that their expert will have the opportunity to hear the state's witness testify, which is definitely an advantage. It might be well for the state to object to a testifying expert assisting in the examination of the state's expert. Often in the ever-specialized world of the trial lawyer, the opposition will not only be a criminal defense lawyer, she will also be an engineer.

Chapter 7

POLICE CIVIL LIABILITY

The number of civil suits filed against the police from 1967 to 1971 increased by 124 percent. Police are presently faced with more than 30,000 civil actions yearly (Silver, 1991:8). The good news is that out of that frightening number, only about 4 percent of suits containing allegations of police misconduct result in a verdict against the police (AELE, 1980; del Carmen, 1981). In order to view this number in context, it helps to refer to the 17,000 state and local police agencies and the 500,000 employees of those agencies (Reaves, 1992a; 1992b). When viewed in this light, the number of successful suits against police is not quite so staggering.

The costs of civil suits exceeds the awards against police and agency defendants. Not factored into the awards made by juries are the legal expenses of the defendants (including those vindicated of the allegations), the lost work time of the defendants, the substitute manpower used to replace those involved in litigation, the loss of manpower because of administrative suspensions pending litigation, and the increase in the cost of errors and omissions insurance policies. As litigation increases, the costs of insurance increases concomitantly. In many instances, the collateral costs far exceed the jury awards. Considering the tremendous number of civil suits brought that must be defended that result in a verdict favorable to the police, the collateral costs alone pose a significant burden upon taxpayers.

Insurance policies exempt intentional misconduct and punitive damage awards therefore relegating the plaintiff to a search for a pocket deeper than that of the offending police officer. That pocket is usually tapped by joining police supervisors, administrators, agencies, county commissioners, and municipalities as party defendants. Taxpayers are all too aware of who ultimately pays these verdicts.

Awards against municipalities are generally greater than awards against individual police officers. Rolando del Carmen reports that in 1982 the average jury award against municipalities was $2 million. A 1982 study reports verdicts against police departments in federal court at about $134,690 (NCW, 1985). The amount of money paid as a result of jury awards does not include the settlements entered into by municipalities in the face of potential punitive verdicts. Between 1987 and 1991, New York City paid out $44 million in settlement of police liability cases (Staff, 1992). It is not surprising that Rolando del Carman has called "suing public officials the second most popular indoor sport in the country" (del Carmen, 1986:301).

One of the fastest growing areas of police litigation stems from police pursuits. Originally, law enforcement developed traffic control units and patrol units to address the growing number of automobiles in use and in misuse in America. Autos were being driven faster and with disregard for foot, horse, and bicycle traffic as well as to flee after committing serious offenses (Cunningham, 1986). Between 50,000 and 500,000 police pursuits take place annually in the United States each year (PAS, 1968; Frennessy, 1970). The difficulty in assessing just how many pursuits take place each year can be appreciated in a recent unpublished study by the author involving Texas police agencies in metropolitan areas with populations in excess of 100,000. Seven out of the twenty-two cities responding kept pursuit data, and of those that did keep pursuit data, only two kept sufficient information upon which meaningful conclusions could be drawn. There is no central collection point for such data. Texas is not significantly different from most other states. It can be assumed that:

1. Police agencies are not aware that pursuit data is valuable.
2. Police agencies are indifferent to the value of pursuit data.
3. Police agencies do not want to know the results of their pursuit policies.

Whatever the case, those agencies not keeping pursuit data will be colored as indifferent or intentionally ignorant by defense lawyers. Alpert and Dunham found in their study of the Metro-Dade Police Department and the City of Miami Police Department, conducted from 1985 to 1987 involving 952 pursuits, that approximately one-third of those pursuits ended in accident (Dunham and Fridell, 1992). As a result of the work done by Alpert and Dunham, police agencies are beginning to collect pursuit data and seriously consider their pursuit policies in light of those data. For those agencies that are not collecting data and considering pursuit policies, the courts are balancing the need for pursuits against the risk subsumed in police pursuits. Any agency interested in what happens to agencies that ignore the tendency of court decisions to favor conservative pursuit policies can refer to the growing body of case law emanating from state negligence suits involving injury and death to innocent third parties.

Police are at a loss to explain how juries can issue verdicts against police who are involved in pursuits primarily predicated on efforts to protect the public. Perhaps it lightens the blow to know that juries reluctantly do so. But consider a continuum of pursuit culpability with the fleeing malefactor at one end and the innocent public on the other. That puts the pursuing officer and her agency between the victim and the perpetrator. It is axiomatic in trial practice that when assessing innocence of parties, he who is the least innocent pays. Obviously, the pocket of first choice is the perpetrator. More often than not the perpetrator is judgment proof and without insurance. If insurance exists, it is inapplicable to those involved in fleeing from the police. It becomes readily apparent to jurors that if the family of the deceased or the injured victim is going to be compensated, it will have to come from the police, the agency, or municipality. They are disinclined to turn the injured innocent victim away with nothing. It is difficult to imagine a pursuit wherein innocent third parties are injured wherein the police are completely without fault. That fault is being more readily assessed when juries begin to take into consideration the following.

1. The real or apparent emergency nature of the situation being responded to (Hamilton v. Town of Palo, 1976).
2. The seriousness of the offense (Gibson v. Pasadena, 1978). Jurors will no longer accept misdemeanors, and traffic violations as sufficient cause to place the public at the risk inherent in a high speed pursuit. Police will not only be held responsible for how their vehicle is being operated but also upon the decision giving rise to the need for the pursuit.
3. The speed that the pursuit reaches. The higher the speed, the greater the risk and the more serious the offense must be to warrant that increased risk. The higher the speed, the longer the duration, the greater the number of traffic control devices that might have to be disregarded, the greater the increase in the risk associated with the pursuit (Brown v. City of Pinellas Park, 1990).
4. The duration of the pursuit. The longer the pursuit continues, the greater the risk and the more difficult it is to maintain that the

pursuit was intended to encourage the party in flight to desist. It can be said that only two things can happen in a high speed pursuit and one of them is bad:

    a) voluntary termination (highly unlikely if speeds escalate and duration extends)

    b) collision (with a fixed object or another motorist).

It becomes a bit of an embarrassment when police are asked on the witness stand which of these two objectives they were pursuing;

5. The probability of apprehension (again if apprehension is not a reasonable possibility, the objective must be to promote a collision). The relative performance capabilities of the vehicles as well as traffic and road conditions will serve as a reliable index as to the feasibility of apprehension.

6. Less risky alternatives to the pursuit decision (Gibson v. Pasadena, 1978). Often traffic citations and misdemeanor offenses could be addressed by mail or in person at the vehicle owner's residence.

7. The use of emergency warning devices. All states have motor vehicle codes that govern the use of emergency equipment. That equipment must exist and be used consistent with the applicable provisions of the motor vehicle code (Fowler v. North Carolina Dept. of Crime Control, 1989).

8. The density of pedestrian and motor traffic.

9. The weather and any limitations on visibility (Bickel v. City of Downey, 1987).

10. The training officers have received, not only in pursuit driving but in risk assessment (Harris v. Canton City of Ohio 1989; West v. United States, 1985).

In Kappler's (1993) examination of over two-hundred state court appellate cases on police liability for the negligent operation of emergency vehicles, he found that the courts were more likely to support a finding of police liability where multiple factors were present.

It becomes readily apparent in the face of growing case law that high speed pursuit is a risky business. So risky that many agencies are becoming more restrictive in the discretion they are allowing police. That discretion is or should be specifically delineated in the agency Standard Operations and Procedures manual. Agencies that have one sentence or one paragraph pursuit policies requiring simply that officers apply "due care" in exercising pursuit discretion are a lawsuit awaiting a place to happen. It is not sufficient to specify the latitude granted officers in initiating, continuing, or terminating pursuits. Agency policy must also address training requirements, requalification, and certification procedures comparable to those drafted for use of force and deadly use of force policies. That training must not only include tactical training but strategic training. Why was the pursuit initiated, why was it continued, and why was it not terminated are questions that will be asked and policy manuals will be examined to assure that the answers to those questions are consistent with a policy founded in the case law surrounding high speed pursuits.

The day of the expert police witness with twenty five years experience and 150 high speed pursuits to her credit is at an end. Such experts are being viewed as police officers not with 150 pursuits on record but rather one pursuit 150 times. The policy decisions governing those pursuits is obsolete and so are the police who operated pursuant to those policies. Society is demanding more accountability from her officers and agencies. The expert witness of the future will be the departmental statistician and the administrative personnel who interpret those statistics. Testimony will focus not on the driving tactics employed by the officer, although they will be an important aspect pertaining to appropriate tactical use of the vehicle, but rather on the department's pursuit policy pertaining to initiation, continuation, and termination of a pursuit along with questions designed to determine what the annual pursuit apprehension rate, accident rate, injury rate, and death rates. A failure to collect this data will result in an impression of disinterest or callousness. For those agencies that choose to ignore the need for collecting and analyzing pursuit data, the following approach would be used in attempting to prove that the pursuit in question was reasonable. Close attention should be paid to the cross-examination.

Pursuit Expert (archaic)

Direct Examination

Q. Would you state your name please?

A. Provide name and rank.

Q. With whom are you employed?

A. If with an agency, provide that information; if retired from a police agency, also provide that information.

Q. How many years have you been employed as a police officer?

A. An approximation will do.

Q. What were your responsibilities as a patrol officer?

A. Generally describe patrol activities including high speed pursuits.

Q. Have you ever worked as a police supervisor?

A. Describe all supervisory experience emphasizing pursuit supervision.

Q. Have you worked as a police administrator?

A. Describe fully emphasizing pursuit policy making.

Q. What special training is required to perform the various positions you have filled during your law enforcement career?

A. Describe all training in detail excluding pursuit training?

Q. Have you received training in the use of police vehicles in apprehending fleeing suspects?

A. Yes.

Q. Has that training included the operation of the vehicle as well as how to assess the risk associated with the pursuit?

Hopefully, the second part of this question can be asked. Often pursuit experts are selected based on the number of successful pursuits conducted in a career lifetime. Little concern is given to the decision making involved.

A. Describe all pursuit training specifically including an approximation of the number of hours each bit of training comprised.

Q. Have you ever conducted or participated in pursuit training?

A. Describe each such instance specifically.

Q. Approximately how many pursuits have you conducted.

A. An approximation will do, if the specific total cannot be determined (be careful in exaggerating this number generally the defense will attempt to verify how many pursuits were undertaken.

Q. How many pursuits have you supervised?

A. An approximation will do.

Q. How many pursuits conducted by you resulted in apprehension of the fleeing suspect?

A. Provide the most specific answer possible.

The reality is, however, that in all likelihood, unless the expert worked for a progressive department, no statistics were kept and memory may be unreliable. It should be noted here that the defense will subpoena any and all records, accident reports, and collected data from all agencies with whom the expert worked. Any embarrassing information may result in the impeachment of the witness. It is imperative that the attorney for the department adequately check the background of the prospective expert to assure there are no skeletons in the closet that may be released at the time of trial or at deposition.

Q. How many resulted in injury?

A. A precise answer should be provided if it can be discovered.

Q. How many resulted in death?

A. Honesty is a necessity in answering these questions.

Q. Would you tell the jury what documents you have examined that have assisted you in forming any opinions you might have regarding this case?

A. Leave nothing out, any omissions may become apparent upon cross-examination.

Q. Have you talked with anyone pertaining to the events that gave rise to this lawsuit?

A. Include in your response the attorney for the department, and the defendant.

Q. Based on the documents you have described and the persons with whom you have discussed this case, will you explain to the jury the events preceding and succeeding the pursuit that is the subject of this litigation as you understand them?

A. This answer should include sufficient clarity to convince the jury that you understand what happened at least as well as they do.

Q. Based on the documents you have described and the persons with whom you have discussed this case, have you formed any opinions regarding this case?

A. Yes I have.

Q. Based on the documents you have described and the persons with whom you have discussed this case, have you formed an opinion as to the reasonableness of the pursuit that gave rise to this suit?

A. I have.

Q. What is that opinion?

A. The pursuit as conducted by officer Jones was reasonable.

Q. Will you tell the jury what specifically your opinion is based upon?

A. The pursuit, as I understand it, was consistent with departmental guidelines in the following matters:
1. speed
2. warning and emergency equipment
3. due care

(In most archaic departments, these will be the only particulars provided in the policy manual.)

4. the officer operated her vehicle in a tactically acceptable manner.

5. the vehicle that struck the plaintiff's vehicle was not that of the pursuing officer but the fleeing suspect.

Q. Do you have an opinion as to who was responsible for this collision?

A. Yes.

Q. Who?

A. The fleeing suspect.

Q. In your opinion, based on the documents examined, the person with whom you spoke, your training, and experience, was the pursuing officer in any way responsible for the collision?

A. She was not.

Cross-Examination

Q. Have you had an opportunity to read the departments "Standard Operations and Procedures Manual" (SOP)?

A. Yes.

Q. What provisions were provided in restricting the types of offenses that warrant an officer engaging in a high speed pursuit?

A. There were none.

Q. What provisions were provided in restricting the speeds to which a pursuit may reach dependent upon the seriousness of an offense?

A. There were none.

Q. What provisions were provided in restricting the length of time a pursuit may continue based upon the seriousness of the offense?

A. There were none.

Q. What provisions were there regarding the type of offenses that warrant high speed pursuits in residential areas?

A. There were none.

Q. School areas?

A. There were none.

Q. In areas of high automobile traffic density? In areas of high pedestrian traffic density?

A. There were none.

Q. In other words, an officer can pursue a shoplifter or a murderer however fast for however long through whatever neighborhood she wishes?

A. That is correct.

Q. What provisions were provided suggesting alternatives to pursuits?

A. There were none.

Q. What provisions were provided regulating pursuits in relationship to weather?

A. There were none.

Q. Visibility?

A. There were none.

Q. Lighting?

A. There were none.

Q. What provisions were provided pertaining to officer training in high speed pursuit risk assessment?

A. There were none.

Q. What provisions were provided pertaining to the use of deadly force to stop a fleeing suspect?

A. There were none.

Q. What provisions were provided pertaining to ramming a fleeing vehicle to terminate the pursuit?

A. There were none.

Q. What provisions were provided pertaining to the use of roadblocks to terminate a pursuit?

A. There were none.

Q. Without these types of provisions in an operations manual, a police officer can do pretty much what she pleases when it comes to pursuit decisions, can't she?

A. Yes.

Q. What data has this agency collected regarding the number of injuries to innocent third parties resulting from high speed pursuits?

A. None.

Q. What data has this agency collected regarding the number of injuries to fleeing suspects resulting from high speed pursuits?

A. None.

Q. What data has this agency collected regarding the number of deaths to pursuing officers resulting from high speed pursuits?

A. None.

Q. What data has this agency collected regarding the number of pursuits conducted by officers?

A. None.

Q. What data has this agency collected regarding the number of pursuits that were voluntarily terminated by the fleeing suspect?

Q. Without this data an agency cannot tell how effective or safe its pursuit policy is, can it?

A. That is correct.

Often a jury may be reluctant to find a police officer who has been charged with protecting the community negligent (although they are doing so at a greater rate and in greater numbers all the time), but a jury may readily see a faceless agency as negligent in providing adequate guidelines, supervision, equipment, or training. Keep in mind that the United States Supreme Court has held, in Harris v. Canton, City of Ohio (1989), that a single incidence of failure to provide training might be sufficient evidence of a complete indifference to the rights of a citizen and constitute a policy, custom, or practice under Civil Rights Statutes (Title 42 Section 1983).

In concluding this chapter, it might serve to remember that an agency with a discretionary pursuit policy is litigation waiting to happen. Juries have demanded, with the assistance of capable plaintiff's attorneys, that police be given specific guidelines governing their behavior in the use of deadly force. Why should anyone be surprised at the trend of juries, with the assistance of capable plaintiff's attorneys, in requiring that police be given specific guidelines governing their behavior in the use of their vehicles. Any agency ignoring the trend of cases involving police pursuit does so at its peril.

REFERENCES

Alpert, G.P., & Fridell, L.A. (1992) *Police Vehicles and Firearms: Instruments of Deadly Force.* Prospect Heights, IL: Waveland Press.

Americans for Effective Law Enforcement (1980). Lawsuits Against Police Skyrocket. San Francisco, CA: A.E.L.E.

Cunningham, C. (1986). Tactical driving: A multifaceted approach. *FBI Law Enforcement Bulletin,* 55:18–19.

del Carmen, R.V. (1986). Civil and criminal liabilities of police officers. In Barker, T. & Carter, D.L. (eds.). *Police Deviance,* Cincinnati, OH: Pilgrimage.

Frennessy, E. (1970). *A Study of the Problem of Hot Pursuit by the Police.* Harvard, CT: The Center for the Environment and Man, Inc.

N.C.W. (1985). Seeking solution on liability insurance. *Nation's Cities Weekly* (Nov. 25) National League of Cities, Washington, D.C.

Reaves, B.A. (1992a). *State and local police departments, 1990.* Bureau of Justice Statistics: U.S. Department of Justice.

———— (1992b). *Sheriffs' Departments 1990.* Bureau of Justice Statistics: U.S. Department of Justice.

Silver, I. (1991). *Police Civil Liability.* New York: Mathew Bender.

Staff, L. (1992). NYPD fails to monitor police misconduct suits. *Chief Leader,* (March 6).

Table of Cases

Harris v. City of Canton Ohio, 109 S.Ct. 1197 (1989)
Bickel v. City of Downey, 238 Cal. Rptr. 351 (Ct. App. 1987)
Brown v. City of Pinellas Park, 557 So.2d 161 (Fla. Dist. Ct. App. 1990)
Fowler v. North Carolina Dept. of Crime Control, 376 So.2d 11 (N.C. App. 1989)
Gibson v. Pasadena, 148 Cal. Rptr. 68 (Cal. App. 2nd. Dist. 1987)
Hamilton v. Town of Palo, 244 N.W. 2d 329 (Iowa, 1976)
West v. United States, 617 F.Supp. 1015 (C.D. Cal. 1985)

Chapter 8

BLOOD EVIDENCE

Police, prosecutors, and experts all want to know the answer to three things when confronted with dried blood found at a crime scene:

1. Is it blood?
2. Is it human blood?
3. How closely associated is it to that of any known or discovered suspect?

In answering the first question a variety of chemical tests are available as presumptive determinants (there are some things other than blood that will test positive, although limited in number it is a sure bet that the defense will inquire into the presumptive nature of the testing). The blood tests used fall into two categories: catalytic and crystal. The crystal tests are considered to be confirmatory and are much more sensitive than are the catalytic tests.

Presumptive Catalytic Tests

The most commonly used reagents for presumptive tests for blood are o-toluidine, phenolphthalein, luminol, and Leuco Malachite Green.

1. **Phenolphthalein test:** The most common test used in determining whether a stain is blood was the benzidine color test. Because of the carcinogenic nature of benzidine, it has been discontinued and replaced with phenolphthalein (Higaki & Philip, 1976). When a blood specimen is mixed with phenolphthalein reagent, and hydrogen peroxide, the hemoglobin in the blood will cause a deep pink color to form. This test is not conclusive because there are other substances that will cause the same reaction, but the result is strongly suggestive.

2. **Luminol test:** As the name suggests, the reaction of luminol with blood causes luminescence. The reaction causes light, not color change. Luminol is dispensed as a spray upon the surface to be examined. The sprayed objects or area must be viewed in the dark. The darker, the

greater the luminescence. This test is very sensitive and allows application to large areas.

3. **O–Toluidine test:** This reagent is a mixture of o-toluidine base and ethanol. When applied as droplets followed by droplets of 3 percent hydrogen peroxide to a suspect specimen, a rapidly developing blue color is a positive.

4. **Leuco Malachite Green test:** This is a low sensitivity reagent consisting of one gram of leuco-malachite green powder, 100 ml of glacial acetic acid, 150 ml of distilled water with the entire mixture diluted with hydrogen peroxide (Moenssens, Inbau & Starrs, 1986). The application of this reagent produces a characteristic green color in the presence of blood.

It is imperative that a control test be performed with the same reagent batch to assure that the reagent is working properly. A control test of known blood using the reagent of choice should be conducted and the results recorded and made a part of the testing documentation. In this way, any questions raised by the defense as to the viability of the reagent used will be defused.

A positive result with these tests is only a presumption and serves as a preliminary step in determining the origin of the blood stain.

Crystal Tests

Precipitin test: Once it has been satisfactorily determined that a specimen is in fact blood, the next step is to establish the species of origin. The precipitin test is based on the fact that when animals are injected with human blood, antibodies are formed that react with the invading human blood in an effort to neutralize the presence of the human blood. The antibodies can be recovered by bleeding the animal that was injected and isolating the blood serum (blood clots when fibrin in the animal's blood traps the red blood cells from the human blood; when the clotted material is removed a pale yellow liquid known as blood serum is left). The serum is known as human blood antiserum. This human antiserum will contain antibodies that will react with human antigens (Safferstein, 1990).

The test itself can be conducted in a capillary tube. The bloodstain is placed on top of the human antiserum. If the blood is human, it will react with antibodies in the antiserum and form a cloudy ring where the blood and the human antiserum meet in the capillary tube. The reaction will occur with bloodstains as old as 15 years. In a criminal trial, a precipitin test produced a positive result from bloodstains from a piece of cloth that had been immersed in salt water for over three years (Bugliosi, 1992).

Blood Typing

Antigens are chemical structures residing on the surface of each red blood cell. Blood types are determined by the kind of antigen on the surface of these cells. Although their are numerous antigens on the surface of each red blood cell the ones use for typing are: A, B, O, and Rh antigens.

Blood Types

Type A blood—Has A antigens on its surface.
Type B blood—Has B antigens on its surface.
Type AB blood—Has A and B antigens on its surface.
Type O blood—Has neither A or B antigens on their surface.
Rh positive blood—Has D antigens on its surface.
Rh negative blood—Does not have the D antigen on its surface.

For every antigen there is an antibody. Each antibody is preceded by the prefix anti- followed by the name of the antigen to which it applies. An antibody will react with its specific antigen. If serum containing anti-B is added to red blood cells carrying the antigen B, the antibody will attach itself to the cell creating a network of linked cells called agglutination.

Antibodies

Type A blood—has A antigens and anti-B antibodies
Type B blood—has B antigens and anti-A antibodies
Type AB blood—has AB antigens and neither anti-A nor anti-B antibodies
Type O blood—has neither A or B antigens and both anti-A anti-B
  antibodies.

It is this process of cell linking that allows blood to be typed. In typing blood, only two antiserums are required, anti-A and anti-B serum. Blood of type A will be agglutinated by anti-A serum; blood of type B will be agglutinated by anti-B serum; AB blood will be agglutinated by both anti-A and anti-B serum; and blood of type O will not be agglutinated by either the anti-A or anti-B serum. Both anti-A and anti-B serums are available commercially.

Red blood cells rupture upon drying, leaving nothing to agglutinate. Although agglutination can no longer be used to type the dried stain, the antigens that were present on the wet stain are still present in the dried stain and can be identified by indirect means.

The current method of typing dried bloodstains is the absorption-elution technique. This procedure involves four distinct steps:

1. antiserum is placed on the stained material
2. the antiserum is then removed by washing the bloodstained material
3. the stained material is then heated at 56° thereby breaking the antibody-antigen bond (elution)
4. either A cells or B cells are then combined with the eluted antibodies and the presence or absence of agglutination is observed

This test requires that anti-A serum, anti-B serum, and anti-H serum be added to separate stain samples. The samples are incubated overnight at 4° C. to allow the antibodies in the antiserum to combine with their specific antigens. The stain samples are then washed in a cold saline solution. To separate the antigens from the antibodies, a small amount of saline solution must be added to each sample. The samples are again incubated for 20 minutes at 56° C. The heat, by separating the antibodies from the antigens in the sample, has produced an anti-serum specific to the blood type of the stain. Known A,B, and O cells are added and the absence or presence of agglutination observed. If A cells are agglutinated, the stain was type A. If both A and B cells are agglutinated, the stain was AB. If only O cells are agglutinated, the stain was type O. If only type B cells are agglutinated, the stain was type B (Miller & Brown, 1990).

Handling Blood Evidence

In crime scenes involving violent crime, often there is a transfer of blood from victim to assailant. It is the probability of this type of transfer that focuses homicide investigators on blood and bloodstained clothing. In an effort to preserve what may become important evidence, investigators will collect all the clothing from the victim as well as samples of underlying strata upon which the body rested. Even what appears to be unstained portions of clothing may be gathered. In many cases, blood may not be visible but may still respond to appropriate laboratory testing. All bloodstains should be measured and photographed prior to handling.

Packaging of bloodstained clothing is critical. Heat and moisture can reduce the viability of antigens. Time is of the essence. Blood stains should be submitted for laboratory testing immediately. Not only does time corrupt the bloodstain, it raises serious questions about efficiency and chain of custody. Airtight containers may cause condensation of moisture within the container that can cause the growth of bacteria that can destroy blood. All bloodstained clothing should be packaged separately in paper bags. If stains are wet, they should be air dried prior to packaging. Blood deposited on surfaces that do not lend themselves to packaging should be allowed to dry and be scraped onto a clean piece of paper. A control sample must also be submitted to prove that the positive results of any testing were from the sample submitted and not something underlying the sample previously deposited on the surface.

In many investigations, the determination that a stain is human blood may be sufficient. In other investigations, blood type may assist in identifying human blood on an assailants clothing. However, it takes DNA characterization of blood to link a bloodstain to a particular individual.

Proving Up Blood Evidence

Before the serologist can testify, it may be necessary for investigators and technicians to prove up the blood as found at the crime scene and ultimately received at the crime laboratory. All photographs, sketches, and physical evidence should be admitted into evidence through the testimony of investigators and technicians before the serologist takes the witness stand.

Serologist Direct Examination

Standard qualifying questions
name
occupation
   describe what a serologist is and does
organization
years employed in that capacity
relevant work history
laboratory and testing duties

educational requirements
training requirements
certification requirements
publication record
   provide titles and dates
professional affiliations
   list any offices held
   list any awards received
teaching experience

At this point the witness may be offered to the court as an expert. The witness should be prepared to withstand scrutiny at the hands of the defense at this point. The witness and the prosecutor should have had ample prior meetings to discuss and prepare for the voir dire of the expert by the opposition. Any problem areas should have been discovered prior to this point and, if not damaging, brought out during the direct examination.

Often experts with considerable experience are left to fend for themselves during trial. This is a recipe for failure. Each crime is unique and each trial is unique. Presuming that the prosecutor knows how best to handle the expert with no input from the expert is risky. Presuming the expert knows how best to handle her testimony with no input from the attorney is foolhardy.

The expert should be aware that the opposing counsel will attempt to impeach her character, credentials, or experience and that her responses will reflect her professional objectivity. Anger is not a luxury that an expert can afford. Often when intimidated or angry, an expert will fall back on technical jargon or professional vocabulary as armor. More mileage can be made by keeping it simple and understandable. Using language as a barrier or weapon may unbalance the opposition, but it will also create distrust in the minds of the jurors. If they cannot understand what is being said, they must assume they are stupid (which revelation is not going to endear you to them) or you are hiding something (much like spelling out a word in front of a child to prevent understanding). Language should be used to communicate. If it is not communicating, it is an obstacle to communication. The side that communicates the best generally wins (so much for justice); it must be understood; it must be believed. Understanding is the crucial foundation upon which believability can be based. Most jurors would rather read the *Readers Digest* version than the *Scientific American* version.

Direct Examination

Q. In the course of your employment as a serologist, how many times have you testified on behalf of the state?

A. An approximation will do but should be qualified as approximate.

Q. In the course of your employment as a serologist, how many blood samples have you personally examined?

A. An approximation may be all that can be derived.

Q. In the course of your employment as a serologist, how many blood samples have been examined by persons under your supervision?

A. With experts of many years experience, it may prove easier to ask approximately how many examinations occur in a year and then inquire into the number of years the serologist has been working. Upon arriving at a number based on the math, seek affirmation for the approximation by the witness.

Q. Of the blood stains that you have examined, of what percentage were you asked to determine if the specimen was human?

A. Approximations are all that can be expected and precision is not the goal. These numbers will assist the jury and the judge in assessing the witnesses credentials but also bolster the prospective testimony.

Q. Of the blood stains that you have examined, what percentage were you asked to determine blood type?

A. Provide an approximation.

Q. I hand you what has been previously marked as state's Exhibit Number 5 and ask you if you recognize it?

A. Yes, I recognize it.

Q. What is it?

A. It is a piece of automobile carpeting upon which a stain has been dropped.

Q. Have you seen this exhibit before?

A. Yes.

Q. When?

A. When submitted to the laboratory for testing by detective Walsh.

Q. Have you or someone under your direction written a report pertaining to the examination and testing of state's Exhibit 3?

A. Yes.

Q. By whom was the report written?

If the report was written by someone other than the testifying expert, the report must be admitted as a business record exception to the hearsay rule. The following questions should establish that the report is a business record:

q. I hand you what has been marked for identification purposes as State's Exhibit Number 4 and ask you if you recognize it?

a. Yes.

q. What is it?

a. Information pertaining to a test performed on an auto carpet sample submitted by detective Walsh?

q. Did you or someone under your direction compile this information?

a. Yes.

q. Was the record provided by someone who had knowledge of the information contained in the document?

a. Yes.

q. Is this an original or a copy?

a. If a copy: is this a true and accurate reproduction of the original as you remember it? Has it been altered or changed in any way?

q. Is this document kept in the normal course of business operations of the crime laboratory.

The exhibit should now be offered by the prosecution as State's Exhibit Number 4.

Q. What was the date and time the auto carpet specimen was received by the laboratory?

A. Should be read from the laboratory report.

Q. How can you tell it is the same item?

A. All evidence submitted to the laboratory is tagged in the field and given an evidence inventory number. That number is transcribed onto the report from the evidence tag upon receipt of the evidence. In addition, the evidence tag has a limited number of places where it can be dated and signed to show a transfer in possession. The evidence tag shows my signature; the report bears the same evidence inventory number. To prevent any questions from arising, I always place my initials someplace on the evidence itself, if possible. If you examine the back of the carpet material you can see my initials and the date inked there.

Q. In referring to the carpet fragment marked as State's Exhibit Number 3, has it been altered in any way from the condition in which it was received?

A. Yes, the material has been altered in two ways: first, part of the carpet surface has been removed, upon which tests were conducted, and part of the surface was sprayed with luminol reagent also as a test.

Q. Were you requested to perform these tests?

A. No, I was asked to determine if the stain was blood and if so, was it human blood.

Q. Who made the request?

A. Detective Walsh.

Q. Were you able to determine whether or not the stain on the carpet remnant was blood?

A. Yes.

Q. How was that accomplished?

A. When a suspected blood sample is mixed with phenolphthalein reagent and hydrogen peroxide, the blood's hemoglobin causes the mixture to turn a deep pink color. A portion of the stain from State's Exhibit Number 3 was treated in this fashion and the resulting color was a deep pink.

Q. Does that conclusively establish the stain as blood?

A. No.

Q. Why not?

A. There are a number of other possible explanations for the reaction to the testing solution.

Q. What might they be?

A. There may have been something in the carpet material itself that caused the positive reaction.

Q. Were there any tests that you could perform that might exclude any such interference with the test results?

A. Yes, I used the phenolphthalein test on carpet material that was not stained from a different part of the auto carpet and received a negative reaction.

Q. Are there things besides blood that will cause a false positive reaction to the phenolphthalein test?

A. Yes.

Q. What kinds of things?

A. Copper, nickel, potassium ferrocynide, and sodium cobalt nitrate.

Q. How can you be sure that one of these substances did not cause the positive result to your test of State's Exhibit Number 3?

A. I also performed a luminol test that does not give a false positive to copper, nickel, potassium ferroycnide, and sodium cobalt nitrate.

Q. Can you explain to the jury how the luminol test is conducted?

A. The suspected stain is sprayed with luminol reagent and placed in the dark. Luminol reagent does not cause coloration, rather, in the presence of blood it will cause luminescence.

Q. What was the result of your luminol test?

A. The stain became luminescent.

Q. Were the results of these two tests sufficient to identify the stain as blood?

A. Perhaps, but I wanted a more conclusive result and decided to run a Leuco Malachite Green test.

Q. Would you explain to the jury how a Leuco Malachite Green test is conducted?

A. Leuco Malachite Green reagent is placed on a sample of the suspect stain and a resulting green color is a positive for blood.

Q. Did the results of this test convince you that the stain was blood?

A. By itself no. A false positive can result from the presence of manganese dioxide, red lead, iron, salts, rust, cobalt, fresh potato juice, and permanganates.

Q. Based on a reasonable scientific certainty, did your tests assist you in forming an opinion as to the identity of the stain on State's Exhibit Number 3?

A. Yes.

Q. What is that opinion?

A. A positive result in all three tests performed is indicative of blood.

Q. Does the result of these tests indicate the species of origin of the blood deposited on state's Exhibit Number 3?

A. No.

Q. Were you able to determine the species of origin of the blood deposited on State's Exhibit Number 3?

A. Yes.

Q. How was that accomplished?

A. By performing a precipitin test.

Q. Would you describe to the jury how a precipitin test is conducted?

A. In order to conduct a precipitin test, human antiserum must be obtained.

Q. How is that accomplished?

A. A commercial product is available that is drawn from rabbits that have been injected with human serum.

Q. What is human serum?

A. The solid portion of blood makes up about 45 percent of its content. When blood clots, the remaining liquid is called serum.

Q. What is an antiserum?

A. A serum that reacts against something. Human antiserum generally comes from rabbits that have been injected with human blood. When the rabbit blood is drawn, it has become sensitized to human blood. When allowed to clot, the remaining liquid is a serum that will act against human blood, therefor called human antiserum.

Q. How is the human antiserum used to determine the species of origin of the blood evidence?

A. The human antiserum is placed in a capillary tube and an extract of the bloodstain is layered on top of the antiserum. Human blood reacting with human antiserum will cause a cloudy ring of precipitate to form where the antiserum and bloodstain join. An absence of this cloudy ring indicates the bloodstain is of nonhuman origin.

Q. Based on a reasonable scientific certainty, have your tests assisted you in forming an opinion as to the species of origin of the bloodstain of State's Exhibit Number 3?

A. Yes.

Q. What is that opinion?

A. The positive result of the precipitin test performed on State's Exhibit Number 3 is indicative of human blood.

Q. Were you able to determine the blood type of the bloodstain of State's Exhibit Number 3?

A. Yes.

Q. What is blood type?

A. Blood contains antigens and antibodies to assist the body in fighting disease. When foreign bodies are introduced into the blood the antigens of the blood incite the antibodies to clump together. This clumping is very specific and can identify blood into one of four groups, A, B, AB, AND O. In determining the A–B–O- blood type, two antiserums are needed, anti-A and anti-B. Both are available commercially. Blood of type A will clump when anti-serum A is added; blood of type B will clump when anti-serum B is added; blood of type AB will clump when anti-A and anti-B serum is added; and blood of type O will not clump when anti-A and anti-B serum is added.

Q. Were you able to use this method in determining the blood type of the stain on State's Exhibit Number 3?

A. No.

Q. Why not?

A. When I received State's Exhibit Number 3 the blood stain was dried. Once blood has dried, the red blood cells rupture, leaving no cells in the stain to clump.

Q. Is it possible to type dried blood?

A. Yes, although the red blood cells have disintegrated, the antigens that were present on the surface of the blood cells are still intact and can be identified using a method called the absorption-elution technique.

Q. How is this method applied?

A. This process consists of four steps:

1. Antiserum is placed on the stained material and allowed to dry.
2. The material is washed removing any antiserum that has not reacted with the stain.
3. Now that the antigen and the antibody have combined, it is possible to break the complex apart by heating the stained material, allowing the antibody-antigen bond to break.
4. When the separated antibodies are combined with a known red blood cell, clumping can be noted and its presence or absence will reveal blood type.

Q. Did you apply this method to the bloodstained material marked as State's Exhibit Number 3?

A. Yes.

Q. Were you able to determine the blood type of the stain on the material marked as State's Exhibit Number 3?

A. Yes.

Q. What was that blood type?

A. Type O.

Q. Have you been provided with a blood sample from the defendant?

A. Yes, I have.

Q. Who drew it?

A. I did.

Q. How long was the defendant's blood sample stored before you determined its blood type?

A. I tested it immediately.

Q. I hand you what has been marked as State's Exhibit Number 4, and ask you if you recognize it?

A. Yes.

Q. What is it?

A. It is my laboratory report on the blood sample taken from the defendant.

Q. Is it signed?

A. Yes.

Q. By whom?

A. By me.

Q. Is it dated?

A. Yes.

Q. What is the date of the document?

A. Date should be read from the document.

Q. This is a copy of the original is it not?

A. Yes.

Q. Does it fairly and accurately reflect the contents of the original as you recall them?

A. Yes.

Q. Has it been altered in any way?

A. No.

Q. Does the report reflect the results of the blood type tests you performed on the defendant's blood?

A. Yes.

Offer the exhibit as State's Exhibit Number 5. Proffer to the opposition for any objections. Again, if this witness did not write the report, it may be necessary to use the business exception to hearsay predicated to prove up the document.

Q. Would you tell the jury what blood type the defendant has?

A. Type O.

Each laboratory has its own testing protocol, but there is some standardization in collecting known blood specimens. The collection tubes used by lab technicians, physicians, and nurses have a variety of purposes and additives depending on what test is being performed on a blood sample. These various purposes and additives can be identified by the color of the stopper used to plug the tube. A gray-stoppered tube is generally used to collect blood for toxicology samples. They should not be used for blood typing since they contain sodium fluoride which interferes with blood group testing. Green-stoppered tubes have heparin salts added as an anticoagulant and may interfere with blood DNA analysis. The purple stoppered tube is the one used for blood typing and has EDTA (ethylenediamineterracetic acid) added as an anticoagulant that will not effect typing or DNA analysis. A red-stoppered tube indicates that the contents are whole blood. In most instances when drawing blood for analysis, it is best to submit one tube with EDTA and one with whole blood to the laboratory. This procedure may be addressed in cross-examination.

Cross-Examination

The defense will attempt to elicit testimony that will raise questions about the handling of the evidence, the test procedure, time deterioration of the sample, and chain of custody.

False Positives: The expert witness will be asked about the possibility of false positive test results pertaining to the various tests performed. False positives may result in a phenolphthalein test from the presence of copper, nickel, potassium ferrocyanide, and sodium cobalt nitrate. It is important to test stains with more than one procedure to remove the specter of a false positive. Additionally, any stains submitted to the laboratory should be accompanied by anything in the proximity of the stain at the crime scene that could possibly have contaminated the stain being tested. The Leuco Malachite Green test will yield a false positive in the presence of manganese dioxide, red lead, iron, salts, rust, cobalt, fresh potato juice, and permanganates. Color reaction tests used in combination reduce the possibility of error from false positives.

Control Tests: The laboratory has the responsibility to assure the viability of all testing substances by using all testing reagents, antiserum, antigens, and blood cells in control tests on known whole blood, failure to do so may raise questions as to the reliability of the test results.

Collection: Blood is usually recovered in one of five conditions:

1. fresh blood
2. clotted blood
3. spatters
4. smears
5. flakes

Wet blood on clothing can be siphoned with a sterile eye dropper and placed in a clean vial (marked, dated, time etc.); the remainder of the garment can be allowed to air dry and when dried rolled in paper to prevent rubbing and placed in a paper bag. Plastic bags may allow moisture to condense onto the interior surface of the plastic, contaminating the blood stain. If several garments are involved, they should be placed in separate bags. The tagged bags and tagged vial should be submitted as soon as possible to the laboratory (that time should be reflected in the report).

Dried blood stains can be recovered by using a cotton swab dampened with distilled water. The swap is rotated upon the dried stain until the cotton turns rust colored. The swab should then be placed in a sealed vial and tagged.

Dried flakes can be scraped onto a piece of filter paper or attempted to be lifted from the surface using a fingerprint lifter (or transparent tape). The flakes and paper should be placed into a clean pill box then sealed and tagged. Each flake should be boxed separately and identified as to location at time of retrieval on the crime scene sketch. All containers in which blood is placed should be saved and available at the time of trial in case of questions pertaining to the collection and handling of the evidence.

It is important that as much of the blood as possible be preserved at the scene and at the laboratory. The defense may request of the court permission to conduct independent tests, especially if DNA testing has been performed.

Handling Evidence: Unnecessary exposure of blood to heat, moisture, and bacterial contamination will shorten the survival time of its antigens. It is important that all stained material be submitted without delay. Each moment the material in question is not delivered to the laboratory must be accounted for and explained. The importance of blood evidence is such that there should be no unnecessary delay and a delivery protocol should be devised by investigators to get blood stained material as quickly as possible to the laboratory. Such a protocol will prevent embarrassing questions on cross-examination and reduce any challenges to the efficacy of the tests performed because of a deteriorated specimen.

REFERENCES

Bugliosi, V. 1992. *And The Sea Will Tell.* New York: Ivy Books.

Higaki, R.S., & Philip, M.S. A study of the sensitivity, stability and specificity or phenolphthalein as an indicator test for blood. *The Canadian Society of Forensic Science Journal,* 9:97, 1976.

Miller, L.S., & Brown, A.M. 1990. *Criminal Evidence Laboratory Manual,* 2nd ed. Cincinnati, OH: Anderson.

Saferstein, R. 1990. *Criminalistics: An Introduction to Forensic Science.* Englewood Cliffs, NJ: Prentice Hall.

Chapter 9

BLOOD SPATTER

A major concern of every homicide crime scene investigator has been the patterns of blood resulting from the actions and activities of the victim and the assailant. Dr. Paul Jeserich, a Berlin forensic chemist, examined blood patterns at crime scenes in 1910. In France, Dr. Victor Balthazard conducted research and experiments with blood trajectories and patterns. In the United States, Dr. Paul L. Kirk of the University of California at Berkeley provided painstaking work on bloodstain pattern interpretation and became best known for his contribution to the analysis of blood patterns left at the scene of the crime in the Sam Sheppard case in Cleveland, Ohio in 1955. The importance of bloodstain interpretation is readily evident in the increased interest in the area and the availability of in-service training programs for forensic scientists, criminalists, investigators, and medical examiners. Because blood is a very common source of evidence at crime scenes, it is imperative that it be handled not only as physical evidence to be "tagged and bagged" but that every one entering that scene recognize the importance of not disturbing the patterns of blood that may reveal as much to the trained eye as the laboratory results of the blood itself. The interpretation of bloodstain patterns requires careful planned experiments utilizing surface materials comparable to those found at the crime scene. It is therefore imperative that anyone assigned the responsibility of interpreting these stains be allowed first access to the crime scene and that the blood patterns be photographed.

Herbret L. MacConell has made an in-depth study of blood pattern interpretation (1971). A summary of his study would include:

   a. Surface texture as the foundation upon which the interpretation of blood patterns is based (both figuratively and literally). The harder and less porous a surface, the more contained the pattern.

   b. When a drop of blood hits a hard smooth surface it breaks up splashing smaller droplets about it. These smaller droplets travel in the same direction as the original drop leaving a pattern that is teardrop shaped, with the pointed end pointing toward the point of origin.

c. The circular distortion of a stain on a flat surface will allow a determination of the angle of impact. The more nearly perpendicular the angle of impact the more circular the blood drop stain. As the angle increases, the stain becomes more elongated. This elongation allows trigonometric determination of the point of origin (MacDonell, 1993).

Using methods described by MacDonell and others, a computer program has been developed that greatly simplifies the data handling and computations necessary to apply the formulas. This program can be used to represent graphically, the position of the victim at the instant blood was shed, making manual reconstruction of the point of origin unnecessary. The primary focus of the program is blood spatter on floors and walls and can not reconstruct a three-dimensional point of origin from patterns on surfaces of oblique orientation (Eckert & James, 1993).

Glossary

An abbreviated glossary of terms may serve to assist in the discussion of blood spatter and in the preparation of expert testimony.

Angle of impact: the angle at which blood strikes a surface relative to the horizontal plane of that surface.

Arterial spurting: blood patterns resulting from blood exiting under pressure from a breached artery.

Backspatter: blood that is directed toward the energy source causing the spatter.

Barrel blowback (drawback): is the blood residue found in a gun barrel that can often be found as a result of large caliber contact wounds. Barrel blowback is backspatter contained in the gun barrel.

Cast-off pattern: blood that has been projected (thrown) onto a surface other than the impact site. This pattern is produced by a bloody object in motion.

Directionality: the direction a drop of blood traveled from point of origin to point of impact.

Drip pattern: blood that drips into blood creating round blood spatters around the periphery of the central bloodstain.

Forward spatter: blood that travels in the same direction of the force causing the spatter. Forward spatter is often associated with gunshot exit wounds.

High-velocity impact spatter: a pattern caused by high-velocity force travelling at a speed of 100 feet per second or greater, resulting in a mistlike dispersion which has traveled only a short distance.

Low-velocity impact spatter: a pattern produced when the blood source has been subjected to a force of 5 feet per second or less.

Medium-velocity impact spatter: a pattern produced when the blood source has been subjected to a force between 5 and 25 feet per second.

Point of convergence: a point to which a bloodstain pattern may be traced. This point can be determined by tracing the long axis of bloodstains within the pattern back to a common point.

Point of origin: the location from which the blood that produced a bloodstain originated. This is determined by projecting angles of impact of bloodstains back to an axis constructed through the point of convergence.

Satellite spatter: droplets of blood projected around a drop of blood upon impact with a surface.

Secondary splash (richochet): the deflection of large volumes of blood after impact with a target surface to a secondary target surface.

Smudge: a bloodstain that has been distorted to a degree so that further classification is not possible.

Spine: the pointed edge pattern that radiates away from a drop of blood that has impacted a target surface.

Splash (projected pattern): a pattern created by a low-velocity impact upon the surface of a 0.10 ml. or greater "pool" of blood.

Swipe (smear): the transfer of blood onto a surface not already contaminated with blood.

Target: the surface upon which blood has been deposited.

Terminal velocity: the maximum speed to which a free-falling drop of blood can accelerate in air which is approximately 25.1 feet per second.

Transfer pattern: a contact bloodstain created when a wet, bloody surface contacts a second surface. A recognizable mirror image or at least a recognizable portion of the original surface may be transferred to the second surface.

Wipe: a bloodstain pattern created when an object moves through an existing bloodstain removing blood from the original stain and altering its appearance (Eckart & James 1993).

Bloodstain Interpretation

MacDonell organized formal instruction for investigators in bloodstain interpretation through bloodstain institutes conducted throughout the United States. As a direct result of these efforts, police, investigators, forensic scientists, and laboratory technicians have become competent in the interpretation of bloodstain evidence and courts are receiving these interpretations into evidence upon proven qualifications of the testifying expert. It should be noted that police not directly involved in homicide investigations are receiving bloodstain interpretation training. Bloodstain interpretation cannot occur at a scene that has not been preserved or one upon which first responding police officers have unnecessarily trod. Dr. Henry Lee, a serologist blood spatter specialist, has been involved in training seminars throughout the United States using slides of photos taken at various crime scenes which he has observed. One of the slides offered by Dr. Lee displays what he calls the "circle the wagons" method of bloodstain interpretation. The slide shows the body of the victim and four pairs of blood smeared shoes on the feet of the investigating team. His point is obvious: it is a waste of time and resources to attempt to reconstruct a crime scene that has not been preserved with bloodstain interpretation in mind.

Bloodstain interpretation may be accomplished by direct examination of the crime scene or by careful examination of color crime scene photographs. When performed indirectly, it is also necessary to examine clothing and weapons along with any other physical evidence. Autopsy reports can also be helpful. However, interpretation should leave hospital records, postmortem examinations, autopsy reports, and autopsy photographs for last. Often these reports may contain conjectural opinions that may affect the interpretation. The interpretation, once begun, should rely on these secondary resources for corroboration rather than formulation.

Bloodstain interpretation can provide a myriad of information:

1. origin
2. impact distances

3. direction of impact
4. type of impact
5. number of blows, stabbings, or shots
6. position of the victim and the assailant at time of bloodshed
7. movement of victim and the assailant during bloodshed
8. movement of the victim and the assailant after bloodshed

The application of fluids in motion forms the basis for bloodstain interpretation of the location, shape, size, and direction of impact of bloodstains relative to the forces that produce them.

Bloodstain Mechanics

Free-Falling Blood

As a drop of blood falls, the surface tension of the drop minimizes surface area creating a spherical shape. This spherical drop will not break up until acted upon by a force other than gravity. When a free-falling drop of blood impacts a nonporous, smooth, horizontal surface, it will create a circular bloodstain. A rough-textured surface will cause the surface tension to rupture and exhibit a stain with spiny edges. The degree of distortion of the stain of a free-falling drop of blood is a product of surface texture not distance fallen (Laber, T.L., 1985). The diameter of the bloodstain produced by a free-falling drop of blood is a product of the volume of the drop, the distance fallen, and the surface texture of the impact surface.

Maximum diameters are achieved when the height of the blood source allows the blood drop to reach its terminal velocity. MacDonell (1971) has established that for a 0.05 ml drop of free-falling blood terminal velocity is 25 feet per second, which would be achieved with a falling distance of about 20 feet. Smaller drop volumes would have less terminal velocity and larger drop volumes would be higher. Blood drops in excess of 0.05 ml will produce bloodstains with a greater diameter at less falling distance. Conservative estimates should be made upon experimentation by the investigator using comparable surface textures and angles of impact. Investigators and experts today are able to recognize the types of bloodstains resulting from free-falling blood drops based on their size, shape, and distribution at a crime scene. This interpretation can include information as to velocity, possible source, and movement.

Nonhorizontal Surface Impact Angles

Free-falling blood dropping vertically, impacting on a horizontal surface at 90 degrees, will produce circular bloodstains. Blood drops falling on a nonhorizontal surface produces elongated oval shaped stains. The greater the angle, the greater the elongation. The narrowest end of the stain will point in the direction of travel and away from the point of origin. This angle can be calculated by measuring the width and length of the bloodstain. Most angle of impact calculations are being done with the help of computer software. However, it is possible to determine width to length ratio (W/L) by using the following formula: Angle of impact = arc sin W/L.

Point of Convergence

When a body is subjected to sufficient force to cause bleeding, the blood released will strike various surfaces at a variety of angles. A point of convergence is a common point to which individual bloodstains can be traced. Stains on a surface, when traced through their long axis, will come together on that surface showing the direction from which the stains came and converging at a place upon that surface indicative of the direction of travel. For example, blood stains on a floor when viewed through the long axis of blood drop stains will point back along the floor to a common point. This point on a surface is the point at which lines drawn through the center of blood drop stains on that surface would intersect.

Point of Origin

The point of convergence will assist us in determining from where the blood source came. The point of origin is a three-dimensional point or points in space, hopefully consistent with the location of the body at the time it was struck, causing bleeding and bloodstains. This is determined by projecting angles of impact of well-defined bloodstains back to an axis constructed through the established point of convergence. In other words, the point of convergence tells us the general direction the blood traveled. By examining the blood drop stains, we can see a distortion in the shape of the drop based not on surface texture but on the angle at which the blood drop hit the surface. This distortion reveals the impact angle of the blood. Strings can be projected from each measured bloodstain at its angle of impact back to an axis perpendicular to the plane on which the bloodstains are located and passing through their point of convergence. The area at which these strings come together will represent in three dimensions a point or points in space from which the bloodstains could have originated. When conclusions are drawn, a range of possible impact sites should be expressed and a range of possible flight paths should be considered that could produce the same angle of impact.

Low Velocity Impact Bloodstains

Splashed Blood

Secondary blood splashing, or ricochet, may occur as a result of the deflection of large volumes of blood after impact on a target surface to another target surface. Splashed bloodstain patterns usually have a large, central area with peripheral spatter, appearing as elongated, oval-shaped spots. These patterns are often produced when pools of blood are disturbed by objects such as a shod foot stepping into blood or by large volumes of blood falling from a source such as a victim's wound. The larger the quantity of splashed blood, the greater the spatter.

Projected Blood

When large quantities of blood are acted upon by medium and high-velocity impact, the resulting pattern is forcibly projected upon a target surface or surfaces. When blood is directed horizontally or vertically downward with more force than what gravity alone would exert, the resulting pattern has a periphery of spinelike extensions and a streaking secondary spatter. Blood released under arterial pressure will form this type of pattern and is referred to as arterial gushing or spurting. The resulting stains are characteristic and readily identified by appearance and shape. Arterial gushing is common at crime scenes where shooting or stabbing has occurred.

Cast-off Blood

In blunt trauma cases, the weapon is often repeatedly swung at the victim. These repeated blows may create a pattern of blood as blood is flung from the weapon on each successive blow. Once blood has been produced by a weapon, it will often adhere to that weapon. During the back swing away from the victim, the blood on the weapon will be thrown off and travel tangentially to the arc of the swing and will impact on nearby surfaces such as walls, ceilings, floors, and other objects in its path. The initial blood that is cast from a weapon during the back swing may strike a target surface and produce circular stains at 90 degrees. These stains often appear on walls or ceilings. As the back swing continues past its apex, the remaining blood is cast off a greater distance at a greater angle and will produce oval shaped stains. Determination of the angle of impact and convergence of these cast-off bloodstains will allow a reconstruction of the position of the victim and assailant. Numerous cast-off patterns will allow a reconstruction of the movements of the victim and assailant as well as their relative positions at the time of the cast-off patterns. Multiple cast-off patterns also allow an estimation of the minimum number of blows struck. The number of distinct patterns or trails of cast-off stains would equal the minimum number of blows struck plus one since the first blow does not produce a cast-off pattern. If more than one blow was struck on the same plane, the cast-off patterns may overlap, which is the reason only a minimum number of blows struck may be estimated (MacDonell, 1971).

Flow Patterns

Flowing blood indicates the direction of travel of blood from its source and may terminate in a pool of blood. Pooled blood behaves as does pooled water. The direction of travel of either is dependent upon gravity. Flow patterns may be seen on the body of the victim as well as the surface upon which the victim is lying. Flow patterns and blood pooling may reveal movement of a victim during or after bloodshed or alteration of the crime scene. Blood flow patterns on the victim should be consistent with the victim's injuries and subsequent pooling, any inconsistencies may suggest the injuries where not sustained at the crime scene and the victim may have been transported after injury or death.

Medium Velocity Impact Bloodstains

When a strong force impacts upon an exposed source of blood, the blood is broken up into many small droplets as a result of being subjected to this increased energy. When these droplets strike a target surface, they produce bloodstain patterns that are readily distinguishable from patterns produced by dripped, projected, splashed, and cast-off bloodstain patterns, all of which are associated with low-velocity force or impact (James & Eckert, 1993).

A blood source subjected to a force between 5 and 25 feet per second will produce medium-velocity blood spatter. The speed refers to the impacting object, not the blood speed. In order to create a medium-velocity blood pattern, the blood source must be exposed prior to impact. Medium-velocity bloodstains range between 1–4mm in diameter and are often characterized by size and a radial pattern radiating away from the area of impact, producing streaking patterns. Interrupted radial patterns suggest that the assailant's body and clothing may have intercepted part of the pattern.

High-Velocity Impact Bloodstains

Impacts on a blood source in excess of 100 feet per second will create high-velocity impact pattern. Again, it is important to remember that the speed in question is that of the impacting object and not the blood. The high-velocity impact renders a mist of showering blood which, because of low density, does not travel far. High-velocity impact is generally associated with gunshot injuries. Spatter from a gunshot is multidirectional. Backspatter may occur if the assailant and weapon are proximate to the victim upon impact. The assailant and the weapon may bear evidence of blood spatter. The amount of backspatter is affected by the type of weapon and ammunition, muzzle to target distance, position of the victim at the time of impact, and physiological aspects of the impacted area (Stephens, B.G. & Allen, T.B. 1983).

In contact wounds the barrel of the weapon may contain flesh bone and blood residue from barrel blow-back. Barrel blow-back may also cause back spatter on hands and clothing. Forward high-velocity spatter is generally a product of a gunshot exit wound. High-velocity forward spatter can assist in determining the location of the victim at the time of the wounding.

Direct Examination

Blood spatter interpretation is a unique and specific art form as well as an application of common sense and scientific principles. Any expert offered to the court must be familiar with the literature in the field, have a scientific foundation, training, and education in blood dynamics and bloodstain interpretation, and preferably be a person with considerable crime scene experience. Finding someone today with those qualifications is becoming easier, but it must be remembered that this is a new "game" and the number of qualified players is still "limited." The beauty of bloodstain interpretation is that it fits nicely into a logical model that lay people can appreciate and recognize. Most large cities have bloodstain specialists available to assist in investigations. It might still prove a good idea to assess the level of competence by inquiring into the education, training, and experience of the prospective expert. Following is a partial list of materials of which an expert should have some degree of familiarity. Any of the following may be used by the opposition as a learned treatise to challenge an expert's qualifications.

Expert's Bibliography

Bevel, T. 1983. Geometric Bloodstain Interpretation. *FBI Law Enforcement Bulletin.* Office of Congressional and Public Affairs, Vol. 52, No. 5, May.

Geberth, V.J. 1993. *Practical Homicide Investigation.* 2nd. Ed. Florida: CRC Press.

Laber, T.L., & Epstein, B.P. 1983. *Bloodstain Pattern Analysis.* Minneapolis: Callan Publishing Co.

Lee, H.C., Gaensslen, R.E., & Pagliaro, E.M. 1986. Bloodstain Volume Estimation. *I.S.B.P.A. News* Vol. 3, No. 2.

LeRoy, H.A. 1983. Bloodstain pattern interpretation. *Identification Newsletter of the Canadian Identification Society,* January.

MacDonell, H.L. 1977. Preserving bloodstain evidence at crime scenes. *Law and Order,* Vol. 25, April.

_____. 1977. Reconstruction of a homicide. *Law and Order,* Vol. 25, July.

_____. 1981. Criminalistics-bloodstain examination. *Forensic Sciences,* Vol. 3, Curil Wecht, Ed. New York: Matthew Bender.

_____. 1982. *Bloodstain Pattern Interpretation.* Laboratory of Forensic Science, Corning, New York.

MacDonell, H.L., & Bialousz, L. 1971. *Flight Characteristics and Stain Patterns of Human Blood.* United States Department of Justice, Law Enforcement Assistance Administration, Washington, D.C.

_____. 1973. *Laboratory Manual on the Geometric Interpretation of Human Bloodstain Evidence.* Laboratory of Forensic Sciences, Corning, New York.

MacDonell, H.L., & Broos, B. 1977. Detection and significance of blood in firearms. In *Legal Medicine Annual,* Curil Wecht, Ed. New York: Appleton-Century-Crofts.

MacDonell, H.L., & Panchou, C. 1979. Bloodstain pattern interpretation. *Identification News,* Vol. 29, February.

_____. 1979. Bloodstain patterns on human skin. *Journal of the Canadian Society of Forensic Science,* Vol. 12, No. 3, September.

Pena, M.S. 1990. *Practical Criminal Investigations,* 2nd. Ed. San Diego, CA: Custom Publishing

Pex, J.O., & Vaughan, C.G. 1987. Observations of high velocity blood spatter on adjacent objects. *Journal of Forensic Sciences.* Vol. 32, November.

Pizzola, P.A., Roth, S., & DeForest, P.R. 1986. Blood droplet dynamics. *Journal of Forensic Sciences,* Vol. 311, January.

White, R.B. 1986. Bloodstain patterns on fabrics—The effect of drop volume, dropping height, and impact angle, *Journal of the Canadian Society of Forensic Science,* Vol. 19, No. 1.

Wilson, F.E., & Schuessler, D. 1985. Automated geometric interpretation of human bloodstain evidence. *I.A.B.P.A. News,* Vol. 2, December.

Direct Examination

Q. I know you are a familiar face to this court doctor but, for the purposes of the record, would you state your name please.

A. Full name and title.

Q. What is your occupation?

A. Serologist, forensic scientist, or other.

Q. For whom do you work?

A. Provide the full name of the lab not using abbreviations. Hopefully the expert is employed by the state and can truthfully answer that he works for the people of the state.

Q. How long have you served in that capacity?

A. If an approximation, it should be so stated.

Q. For whom did you work prior to this position?

All professional employment should be addressed in response to this question leaving no gaps. Approximate dates should be acceptable but more concise information should be included in a current resume with a copy available for both lawyers.

There should be no fabrication in the resume.

A favorite ploy of defense lawyers is to check publications of the witness both originally authored and coauthored. It can be harmful to the witness to claim senior authorship when in fact she was the secondary author. Such an insignificant exaggeration can be embarrassing. The offering lawyer should have checked the resume and its content as meticulously as a good defense lawyer will.

Q. In your capacity as serologist (blood stain specialist), what is your responsibility pertaining to blood stains at a crime scene?

A. I may be called to the crime scene by homicide investigators in order to assess and interpret the patterns of blood stains left at the scene. In some cases, investigators may provide me with photos of blood stains and ask me to interpret the patterns as reflected in the photos.

Q. What kinds of information can blood stains at a crime scene reveal?

A. If the scene has been left intact by investigators, it is often possible to tell where the assailant and victim were standing at the inception of the attack. If a blunt instrument was the weapon used, it may be possible to determine the minimum number of blows inflicted. If the victim was killed elsewhere and deposited at the crime scene, blood patterns on the clothing may reveal this movement. If the victim at the scene moved or was moved after bloodshed, the residual stains might reveal that. It may be possible to associate the clothing worn by and assailant with the blood patterns left at a crime scene.

Q. What kind of training or education is required of someone interpreting bloodstain patterns?

A. There are no formal requirements other than an understanding of the physics involved in bloodshed and the depositing of blood on various surfaces. Most departments have specialists who have formal scientific educations with an emphasis in physics, biology, or engineering. Interpretation of bloodstain patterns is generally a product of independent research, in-service training, and professional seminars.

Q. Would you describe your educational background?

A. A complete description of all academic endeavors and degrees should be provided, including any educational honors received.

Q. Would you describe all relevant training, seminars, and workshops that have contributed to your understanding of blood stain patterns?

A. Describe fully, including length of each activity and any certification presented.

Q. Do you belong to any professional organizations dealing with blood-stain pattern analysis?

A. Hopefully, the answer is yes. Give the names of each and describe the focus of each.

Q. Have you any publications pertaining to your work?

A. Yes.

Q. Describe those for us, will you?

A. List and describe all publications.

Q. Have you taught any courses, seminars, workshops, or training sessions pertaining to bloodstain interpretation?

A. Yes.

Q. Would you tell us about each of them?

A. Spend some time in describing the content, response, and class makeup of all sessions taught. The who, what, when, and where of each class would be helpful.

Q. Have you been asked to interpret bloodstain patterns at crime scenes?

A. Yes.

Q. How many times?

A. A specific number would be helpful. Caution at this point might be advised because the defense will likely inquire into some of the specifics: How many convictions? How many acquittals?

Experts today who work for the state often accept retainers to testify on behalf of defendants. It might be well to know how many times the expert has testified on behalf of the state and on behalf of the defendant. In those instances where the expert has previously testified on behalf of a defendant, the defense will focus on the areas of disagreement between the experts and strongly suggest to the jury that bloodstain pattern interpretation is open to question.

Q. Have you been asked to interpret bloodstain patterns from crime scene photos?

A. Yes.

Q. How many times?

A. Give as accurate a response as possible.

Q. Have you testified, in court, pertaining to your interpretation of crime scene bloodstain patterns?

A. Yes.

Q. How many times?

A. If many, an approximation will do.

It would be helpful for the prosecution at this point to inquire into the number of times the witness has testified on behalf of the state and how many times the witness has testified on behalf of a defendant. In most cases state experts will not have testified in cases for the defendant and this question need not be asked.

The witness can now be offered to the court as an expert, subject to examination by the defendant. In those instances where an expert of standing reputation is used, the cross-examination may be waived, and the credentials of the expert stipulated to. Remember that a stipulation offered at the beginning of the qualification of an expert is more to the advantage of the opposition. Since the stipulation saves time and a stumbling qualification of the witness, it is often greedily accepted. A potent expert should never be qualified by stipulation. An expert's credentials go a long way in predisposing a judge and jury to believe that expert.

Q. Were you contacted in regard to this case?

A. Yes.

Q. By whom?

A. Generally the investigating officer.

Q. When?

A. Date and time (should be included in lab report).

Q. What were you asked to do?

A. Examine the blood stain patterns left at the crime scene.

Q. Did you examine the bloodstains?

A. Yes.

Q. Based on reasonable scientific certainty, do you have an opinion as to what these bloodstains mean?

A. Yes.

Q. What is that opinion?

A. That the victim (in an effort to humanize the victim, it is best to refer to he or she by name—insert the name at each point in the examination where the term victim is used) had been assaulted with a blunt object. She was struck a minimum of four times while she lie on the bed. The assailant approached her from the right side, and was standing approximately 90 degrees to her head when she was struck.

Q. How were you able to determine based on reasonable scientific certainty that she was struck with a blunt object?

A. When blood is splattered it can be distributed as the result of low impact, medium impact, or high impact. Blood from low impact wounds maintains its spherical shape and generally is deposited in a stain about the size of an aspirin. Blood stains from a medium impact are about half the size of an aspirin. Blood deposited from a high impact is distributed in a mist cloud with each droplet no bigger than the diameter of a pencil lead. Although there were low-, medium-, and high-impact blood stains on the body, bedclothes, and surrounding area, there were numerous high-velocity bloodstains on the walls and headboard. High-velocity bloodstains indicate a strong force impacted with the blood source, a strong force that is consistent with the type of force used with a blunt object.

Q. I hand you what has been marked as State's Exhibit Number 1 and ask you if you recognize it?

A. Yes.

Q. What is it?

A. A photograph.

Q. A photograph of what?

A. A photograph of the high-velocity bloodstains on the walls and headboard.

Q. Is this photograph, an accurate representation of the crime scene as you remember it?

A. Yes.

Q. Has it been altered in any way so as not to reflect the crime scene as you recall it?

A. It has not.

It is not necessary for the testifying witness to have taken the photo to be able to "prove up" the photos. All that is required is for the witness to testify as to the accuracy of the contents of the photo. The photo should then be offered for admission into evidence, unless an enlargement is to be offered, in which case the following questions should be asked, and the original photo not offered.

Q. I now hand you what has been marked as State's Exhibit Number 2 and ask you if you recognize it?

A. Yes, I recognize it.

Q. What is it?

A. It is an enlargement of the photo marked as State's Exhibit Number 1.

Q. Is this also an accurate reflection of the crime scene as you remember it?

A. Yes.

Q. Will this enlargement assist you in explaining your testimony to the jury?

A. Yes.

The enlargement may now be offered into evidence. To avoid an objection of redundancy, the original photo can be marked for identification purposes only and used to establish the predicate for the enlargement. The redundancy objection, if sustained, will prevent the enlargement from being entered into evidence. However, there is no reason why the enlargement, if not admitted, might not still be offered for demonstrative purposes and not submitted to the jury. If the enlargement would be helpful to the state's case, the photo should not be offered as evidence but used only as a link in the proof for the enlargement.

Q. Using the enlargement, will you point out for the jury the high-impact bloodstains on the bed headboard?

A. The high-velocity stains should be contrasted with low-velocity stains. It is important that the original photo had a measuring device reflected in the photo to maintain scale when enlarged.

Q. You said that you believed the victim was struck a minimum of four times. Based on reasonable scientific certainty, how were you able to determine that?

A. The ceiling above the bed was stained in a fashion that is characteristic of a weapon that has been soaked in blood and swung in an arc. When the weapon is swung in an arc, blood is cast off leaving a trail of small droplets of blood on the ceiling. Each time the weapon is brought back, it leaves a trail. By counting the trails it is possible to determine a minimum number of strikes.

Q. Why only a minimum number of strikes?

A. The first strike is performed with a blood free implement; therefore, there is no cast-off blood from the first strike. In the case of multiple strikes, it is possible for subsequent strikes to layer stains on top of previously deposited stains, obscuring the old trail. In this instance, there are four discernable trails that were deposited, leading me to believe that the victim was struck a minimum of four times.

Q. I now hand you what has been marked as State's Exhibit Number 3 and ask you if you recognize it?

A. Yes, I recognize it.

Q. What is it?

A. A photograph of the blood trails on the ceiling.

Q. Is this photo a pair an accurate representation of the crime scene as you recall it?

A. Yes.

Q. Has it been altered in any way?

A. No.

Q. I now hand you what has been marked as State's Exhibit Number 4 and ask you if you recognize it?

A. Yes, I recognize.

Q. What is it?

A. An enlargement of the photo marked State's Exhibit Number 3. State's Exhibit Number 4 should now be offered into evidence.

Q. Using State's Exhibit Number 4, will you point out to the jury the four cast off trails you have referred to?

A. Do so, pointing out each distinct trail.

Q. I believe you indicated earlier that you were able to tell that the victim was struck from the right side and that the assailant was standing 90 degrees to her head. Based on reasonable scientific certainty, how were you able to determine that?

A. In examining the blood patterns surrounding the body, there was a mist-like pattern of high impact blood radiating away from the head in a circular "halo" fashion. This halo pattern was interrupted in the area 90 degrees to the head which led me to believe that the assailant's clothing absorbed the blood spatter at that point.

Q. Have you been asked to do anything else in this case?

A. Yes.

Q. What?

A. Two days after the homicide, I was provided a pair of blue jeans and a blue jean jacket and asked to examine them.

Q. Did you?

A. Yes.

Q. And what did you discover?

A. A high-velocity pattern of blood consistent with the pattern radiating from the victim's body.

Q. I hand you what has been marked State's Exhibits 5 and 6 and ask you if you recognize them.

A. Yes, I recognize them.

Q. What are they?

A. Exhibit 5 is a pair of blue jeans and Exhibit 6 is a blue jean jacket.

Q. When did you first see them?

A. Provide the date, and hopefully it is the same as on the evidence log.

Q. Where did you get them?

A. Officer Doakes, the investigating officer in this case. This clothing will have been admitted under the investigating officer's testimony. The only problem for this witness is in establishing the chain of custody. The documentation should clearly reflect when this evidence was provided to the witness, where it came from, and when it was returned there. All testimony must be consistent with the documentation.

Cross-Examination

The defense will attempt to undermine the validity of the testing by challenging the processing of the crime scene, the handling of the evidence, and/or the chain of custody. The most fertile ground for the defense is in the security provided by first responders and the various evidence teams and investigators who have had access to the premises. Contamination of the crime scene by relatives, friends, and police officers is the greatest detriment to bloodstain interpretation. An unidentified footprint often turns out to be that of one of the police on the scene. Such contamination relegates all interpretation suspect. If bloodstain interpretation is to be successfully accomplished, the first police representative on the crime scene should be the bloodstain pattern analyst or the photographer. A crime scene log will dispel any contention by the defendant that the scene has been contaminated by police.

The second most common crime scene contaminator is medical personnel and medical examiners. There is no need to rush the removal of the body from the premises. Medical personnel will apply whatever pressure they have at their disposal to hurry the removal of the remains. The longer the body reposes so to must the medical personnel. The only thing worse than discovering that a footprint in blood is that of a police representative is to discover through the defense that it is that of the EMS.

REFERENCES

Eckert, William G., & Stuart, James H. 1993. *Interpretation of Bloodstain Evidence at Crime Scenes.* Boca Raton, FL: CRC.

Laber, T.L. 1985. Diameter of a bloodstain as a function of origin, distance fallen and volume of drop. *International Association of Blood Pattern Analysts News.* Vol. 2, No. 1, pp. 12–16.

MacDonell, H.L. 1971. Interpretation of bloodstains: Physical considerations. *Legal Medicine Annual,* Cyril Wecht, Ed. New York: Appleton-Century-Crofts.

_____. 1993. *Bloodstain Patterns.* Corning, New York: Laboratory of Forensic Science.

Stephens, B.G., & Allen, T.B. 1983. Backspatter of blood from gunshot wounds—observations and experimental simulation. *Journal of Forensic Sciences,* Vol. 23. No. 2, pp. 437–439, April.

Chapter 10

DNA EVIDENCE

DNA is the architect, foreman, and bricklayer of life. In every creature, DNA carries the coded messages of heredity, governing everything from eye color to toe length. It is present in every one of the trillions of nucleated cells in the human body. Based on the work of Sir Alec Jeffreys at the University of Leicester, a method was developed to extract DNA from a specimen of blood, semen, or other tissue; slice it into fragments; and tag the fragments with a radioactive probe so that they would expose x-ray film. The resulting pattern of stripes on the film was a DNA "fingerprint." Jeffreys and his colleagues named the process for isolating and reading DNA markers "DNA fingerprinting." One of the first experiments conducted by Sir Jeffreys using his new genetic fingerprinting was on a family group to see if the pattern of inheritance was as simple as he expected it to be. From that test, he saw clearly that half of the bands and stripes were from the mother, and the rest from the natural father (Beeler & Wiebe, 1988).

Determining whether these characteristics held true for tissues other than blood was his next task. His team took both blood and semen and found that the genetic map was constant irrespective of the kind of cells from which the material had come. To determine test sensitivity, Jeffreys' team tested small quantities of blood and semen. A drop of blood or a tiny amount of semen was sufficient.

From a laboratory perspective, he had discovered a laboratory technique that appeared irrefutable. His concern, however, was for the forensic materials that are available at a crime scene. How effective would his procedure be in identifying degraded DNA? Additional testing on three-year-old blood and semen stains were equally successful.

In March of 1985, Sir Alec Jeffreys published his first scientific report in which he estimated that the chances of two people having the same DNA fingerprint (absent identical twins) was none. "You would have to look for one part in a million, million, million, million, million before you would find one pair with the same genetic fingerprint and with a world population of only five billion, it can be categorically said that a genetic fingerprint is individually specific and that any pattern does not belong to anyone on the face of this planet who ever has been or ever will be" (Wambaugh, J. 1989 p. 94).

Shortly after publication, Jeffreys was called upon to resolve an immigration case, a complicated case involving a boy who was living in Africa with his father, but who had been born in Britain of Ghanaian parents. The boy wanted to return to Britain and live with a woman he claimed was his mother, but immigration believed the woman was his aunt and he had been denied British residency.

Jeffreys had to somehow match the genetic fingerprint of the child with that of a father who was not present to supply a DNA sample. The genetic fingerprints of the undisputed children of the woman were taken. The intent was to match those fingerprints with those of the mother thereby establishing the fingerprint of the absent father. When he compared the pattern of the boy with those of his brothers and sisters, the reasonable conclusion was that the man had fathered all of the children (Wambaugh, J. 1989 P. 95).

As researchers uncover new approaches, variations, and applications to the original technique, the term DNA typing has come to be applied to describe the forensic use of DNA comparisons. The method devised by Sir Jeffries is called restriction fragment length polymorphism (RFLP) analysis.

Original research in DNA focused on inherited diseases. Today, forensic research has developed a significant body of literature for use in criminal investigations. Growing out of paternity contests and immigration cases, DNA printing has quickly become the forensic tool of the century.

Inside each of 60 trillion cells in the human body are strands of genetic material called chromosomes. Arranged along the chromosomes, like beads on a thread, are nearly 100,000 genes. The gene is the fundamental unit of heredity. It instructs the body cells to make proteins that determine everything from hair color to our susceptibility to diseases. DNA is a polymer (a polymer is a very large molecule made by linking together a series of repeating units). In DNA, these repeating units are nucleotides. A nucleotide is composed of a sugar molecule, a phosphorous-containing group, and a nitrogen-containing molecule called a base. There are only four types of bases associated with DNA. The only arrangement possible in the double-helix configuration was the pairing of bases, that process is called base pairing. The average human chromosome has DNA containing 100 million base pairs. All the human chromosomes taken together contain about 3 billion base pairs. DNA is like a book of instruction. The alphabet used to create the book is simple: A,T,G, and C. The order in which these letters are arranged defines the role and function of a DNA molecule (Saferstein, 1995).

The basis of all DNA identification techniques rests on its unique coding mechanism, with just four kinds of chemicals called bases— G,C,A, and T- strung like beads along the DNA molecule. In the nucleus of all human cells is a ribbon of deoxyribonucleic acid. The ribbon is a twisted double strand described as a double helix, two microns wide but if uncoiled, six feet in length. Each long strand contains some three billion repeating nucleotides. Each nucleotide incorporates one of four different chemicals called bases. The four bases, each represented by a letter are: adenine (A), cytosine (C), guanine (G), and thymine (T). The twin strands are connected, like the rungs of a ladder, by pairs of bases, but because of the shapes of the structures involved, a G can only link to a C, and an A can link only to a T; the DNA of the strands is complimentary. Portions of the DNA molecule contain sequences of A,G,C, and T bases randomly repeating (tandem repeats) themselves. As with any genetic trait, these repeating sequences were inherited from the parents. The key to understanding DNA typing lies in understanding that amongst the worlds' population there are numerous possibilities for the number of times a particular sequence of base letters can repeat themselves on a DNA strain. The possibilities increase when dealing with two or more chromosomes, each containing different lengths of repeating sequences. In DNA typing, restriction enzymes are used to cut up chromosomes into hundreds of fragments, some containing repeating sequences from the DNA molecule. These fragments will be cut in different lengths, depending on the length of the repeating sequences. The process of cutting these fragments gives DNA typing its name: restriction fragment length polymorphisms (RFLPs). Restriction enzymes are available commercially to biologists and geneticists. Each enzyme recognizes a specific repeating sequence and cuts the chromosome at that location (loci) (Waye & Fourney, 1991).

Once the DNA molecules have been cut up by the restriction enzyme, the resulting fragments must be sorted out. This is accomplished by separating the fragments by electrophoresis. Electrophoresis separates materials according to their migration rates across a starch or agar gel.

When the gel is electrically charged, substances, such as DNA which possess an electrical charge, will migrate across the gel. The longer the DNA fragment, the greater the resistance to the migration. The shorter fragments move further and faster across the gel. The movement of the various-sized fragments sorts them by length.

Once the electrophoresis process is completed, the double-stranded fragments of DNA are chemically treated so that the strands separate from each other. The fragments are then transferred to a nylon membrane much the way lipstick is blotted from the lips. This transfer process is called Southern blotting, named after Edward Southern its progenitor (Saferstein, 1995).

At this juncture, the DNA fragments should have been transferred to the nylon membrane; however, they cannot be seen. In order to visualize the separated and migrated RFLPs, the nylon membrane is treated with radioactively-treated fragments containing a base sequence complementary to the cut, migrated fragments. These complementary base sequences are called probes and the process of attaching the probes to the fragments to be identified is called hybridization. If we were attempting to identify RFLPs composed of a repeating string of letters spelling T–A–G, we would use a probe segment of a complimentary letter sequence of A–T–C so that the probes will bind to the desired RFLP (keep in mind that once the double strand has been separated the single remaining strand can be hybridized).

Once the questioned DNA fragments have been hybridized, the nylon sheet is placed against x-ray film and exposed for several days. As the radioactivity of the probes decay it strikes the unexposed film. When the film is processed, bands appear where the radioactive probes stuck to the fragments on the nylon sheet. The length of each fragment is determined by running known DNA fragment lengths alongside the test specimens and comparing the distances they migrated across the gel plate (Waye & Fourney, 1991).

A typical DNA fragment pattern will show two bands (one RFLP from each chromosome). When comparing the DNA fragment patterns of two or more specimens, one looks for a match between the band sets. Individualization cannot be accomplished with a single probe, using additional DNA probes, each of which recognizes different repeating DNA segments, a high degree of discrimination, or near individualization can be achieved (Saferstein, 1995).

Legal Issues

In proving up DNA evidence, two expert witnesses will generally be required, although finding one expert with dual expertise is possible. To submit DNA evidence, it will be necessary to obtain the services of a population geneticist and a molecular biologist. DNA typing involves an unusually complex and complicated series of procedures drawn from the sciences, relying heavily on chemistry and microbiology. To combat efforts on the part of the defense to distort and confuse, it may be necessary to consult experts in a variety of fields, including population genetics, chemistry, and microbiology (Thompson & Ford, 1989).

When presented in court, testimony that two DNA samples have the same origin is corroborated by statistics on the frequency of the DNA type in the general population. These figures often encompass quantities in excess of the present population on the earth. Confrontation is most likely to occur on this front. Bear in mind that DNA evidence can be attacked only from five general perspectives:

  a. as an accepted scientific procedure
  b. scientific protocol
  c. frequency statistics
  d. sample contamination
  e. expert credentials

Acceptability

Concerns over scientific acceptability of DNA evidence and testimony revolve around three points:

  1. Acceptance by the scientific community of the technique
  2. Acceptance of the technique for use on forensic samples
  3. Acceptance of the theory itself

Acceptability hurdles must be anticipated and an assessment must be made as to the relevant fields to which DNA typing belongs. That relevant field will depend on the level of acceptability in the particular court. Acceptability is an issue raised prior to trial in a challenge to the admissibility of the technique, theory, or application of the prospective DNA procedure and expert testimony. In combating these challenges to the admissibility of DNA evidence it will be necessary to ascertain which type of expert witness or witnesses will best help the court in admitting the anticipated testimony and evidence.

Acceptance by the scientific community of the technique: If the court simply requires general acceptance of the theory and application of DNA typing, the relevant fields in question should be molecular biology and genetics. The problem with this avenue of acceptability is that molecular biologists use clean samples that have little exposure to possible contamination or age whereas forensic samples will have suffered some contamination and aging.

Since there is reason to believe that forensic typing may be less reliable than the typing performed by molecular biologists, the court may require acceptability to be based on the application of DNA typing to forensic "dirty" samples. The number of experts with experience in forensic typing is limited to those employed by companies that market the techniques and the service. These experts are susceptible to impeachment because of the financial interest the company has in convincing the scientific community and the court of the reliability of DNA typing.

Acceptance of the technique for use with forensic samples: Research scientists can tolerate a greater degree of error in their laboratory settings than can forensic labs. Scientific experiments that have community significance will be repeated in many different laboratories in an attempt to determine validity. Errors in such an experiment will be brought to the attention of the scientific community and the experiment revamped to address evident problem areas. The use of DNA typing in the forensic forum is usually limited in sample size and subject to a variety of environmental contaminants and is of concern only to the prosecutor and the defendant. The likelihood of retesting is based primarily on the prosecution's dissatisfaction with the original results. Error rates that are acceptable in research laboratories may result in the incarceration or execution of an innocent defendant as the result of forensic errors.

Instead of using research scientists as DNA experts, it may prove more expedient if the expert is drawn from a profession in which individual important decisions result from the laboratory procedure. Scientists who are using DNA typing to assist in diagnostic procedures are making important decisions that are not being submitted to or corroborated by the scientific community. These experts are placed in a situation much more similar to that of the forensic scientist. If the court should admit all aspects of DNA evidence, the same issues raised against the admissibility of DNA evidence will be revisited during cross examination.

Scientific acceptance of the underlying theory: There is nothing controversial about the theory underlying DNA typing. This theory is so well accepted that its accuracy is unlikely to be raised as an issue at inadmissibility hearings. The DNA typing tests are based on the "DNA paradigm" which has formed the basis for the advancement of contemporary medicine and biology. The theory has been repeatedly put to the test and has predicted subsequent observations.

The fundamental premise of the DNA paradigm is that all inheritable information passed from parents to offspring is contained within the DNA molecule. The DNA paradigm can be summed up in the following four points:

1. DNA is unique but unchanging. DNA does not vary from cell to cell within the same organism. DNA does not alter over time.
2. The structure of DNA is a twisted ladder linked by rungs. The sides of the ladder are composed of phosphate and sugar molecules and the rungs are known as bases. There are four different kinds of bases and these bases pair specifically.
3. The order of the base pairs is a "DNA sequence," and constitutes the genetic code. Most sections of the DNA ladder vary little from one individual to another in a given species. There are certain sections that are variable from individual to individual and this variation is called "polymorphic," meaning that the sections of DNA may take different forms in different individuals.
4. The DNA ladder can be disassembled in various ways. The longer chain of DNA molecules can be broken into fragments. The two sides of the ladder can unzip into two single strands. A single strand of the broken ladder can be paired with another broken strand of the ladder if the bases in the strands are complimentary. Using this tendency of complimentary strands to come together, scientists have been able to develop special strands of DNA molecules that when placed with a separated strand from a suspect source will come together in an identifiable way; these scientifically-created strands are called probes (Thompson & Ford, 1989).

Scientific Protocol

The standard method used in DNA testing is restriction fragment length polymorphism analysis (RFLP analysis). This analysis can be broken into seven distinct procedures, performed one after the other.

Problems arising in any one portion of the procedure has a cumulative effect that will compromise any test results. The following will describe each of the seven steps and problems inherent in each.

Step 1 DNA Extraction. Forensic evidence such as blood or semen is often submitted for analysis after having dried on a surface. The first step is to wash the biological material from the surface of the material upon which it has dried. Once removed the cells must be burst by chemical application, thereby releasing the DNA.

Problems: The DNA may be of poor quality. In old or poorly preserved specimens, the long DNA molecules may break into shorter fragments—so short as to prohibit RFLP analysis. Degraded DNA will undoubtedly become problematic not only at the testing stage but also at the testimonial stage. There should be no question as to sufficient quality upon which testing is done. Degraded DNA is only a problem if the analyst fails to recognize it.

The DNA specimen may have become contaminated when deposited so as to interfere with RFLP analysis. There is a purification step that can and should be employed. The effectiveness of the purification process will undoubtedly be an important admissibility issue. The DNA extraction techniques used in research laboratories to prove extraction reliability may not prove reliable when applied to forensic settings. Research laboratories do not have to deal with floor cleaning fluids, carpet cleansers, or washing detergents. The court and juries must be convinced that the procedure employed is reliable in light of all the potential and present contaminants inherent in forensic samples. This can only be accomplished by performing validity tests.

Step 2 Restriction Fragmentation. Once cleaned, the DNA must be cut into fragments. Cutting DNA involves the use of restriction enzymes which act like biological scissors cutting the DNA chains at specific locations and only those locations. The resulting DNA pieces varying in length are called restriction fragments. Restriction enzymes have long been used in research laboratories. Although well accepted and widely used, it is seen as a complex and very sensitive procedure which can yield erroneous results if applied in a manner that departs from the accepted and exacting protocol.

Problems: It can be presumed that the test analysis will be challenged contending that the biological specimen was contaminated thereby rendering spurious results. The specificity of the location at which DNA may be "cut" may be affected by various contaminants, thereby producing restriction fragments of the improper length and as a result, incorrect bands on the bar-like code reflecting the typing results. The only way these concerns can be addressed is to perform blind proficiency testing on the analysts who actually perform the tests in the forensic laboratory.

Step 3 Gel Electrophoresis. After the DNA has been cut at specific locations, the resulting restriction fragments are separated according to size. Using a procedure known as "gel electrophoresis," the DNA is placed on a gel with electric currents applied across the gel. The DNA fragments move across the gel sorting themselves by size (length). The use of electrophoresis as a sorting technique is widely known and accepted in the field of molecular biology.

Problems: During electrophoresis, standard DNA markers of known size are run next to laboratory samples. These markers are used for calibration when determining the size of the fragments in an unknown sample. There is some suggestion that "shift" may occur. A "shift" in the known markers may occur so that the unknown sample may be identified as a particular type of DNA when in fact it is another. The problem should be readily identified by an observant analyst, especially when the samples being compared are being run on the same gel. Obviously, this is an issue the defense will choose to pursue. The offering party will want to confer with the analyst and put to rest any concerns of possible marker "shifting." In an effort to steal the defense expert's thunder, it might prove helpful to explain "shifting" and the safeguards employed by the analyst to identify it if should it occur.

Step 4 Southern Transfer. After electrophoresis, a "copy" of the arrangement of the DNA fragments and markers on the gel is made. A membrane is placed in contact with the gel, and by "blotting," a transfer occurs moving the DNA fragments from the gel to the membrane. During this step, the double stranded DNA molecule is treated with a chemical which caused the two sides of the ladder to separate, which then is ready for rejoinder (hybridization) with a genetic probe.

Problems: The use of Southern blotting is not significantly different from its use in other areas of biology, the reliability of this procedure should not be an issue.

Step 5 Hybridization. This step assists in finding the unique DNA segments from among the DNA segments found throughout the human population. The segments selected by the cutting enzymes were specifically isolated because amongst those segments are segments of individualized and unique character. Finding key polymorphic segments among all the other DNA segments on the blot is a search for a needle in a haystack. Even a haystack is penetrable when spread out if the searcher is armed with a magnet. RFLP analysis uses a "biological magnet" called a genetic probe. The probe will lock onto *only* the polymorphic segments. The probes have been "tagged" with a radioactive marker so that, after they lock onto the polymorphic segments, their positions on the blot can be determined. Hybridization is the process by which the probe locks onto specific DNA segments. The hybridization process itself is widely used in the medical and research realms. Biological probes are used to identify genes responsible for inherited diseases, as a tool in gene splicing, to detect genetically engineered microorganisms in the environment, to identify pathogens in the food and drug industry and to aid in medical diagnosis.

Problems: Stringency of hybridization describes the conditions which are used during hybridization. Stringency is defined by a simple equation which includes the temperature at which the procedure is performed, the salt concentration, the properties of the DNA, and other chemical components of the hybridization procedure. Under conditions of high stringency, the probe will only lock onto sequences which are very similar to itself, while under lower stringency the probe can lock onto DNA segments which differ from its own.

The probes used in DNA typing differ significantly from the types of probes used in most other medical and research applications. DNA typing relies on special probes which lock onto polymorphic DNA segments, those segments which differ from individual to individual. An important issue which may arise with regard to the admissibility of RFLP analysis is whether the DNA fragments identified by these probes are truly polymorphic, that is, whether differences among individuals in the segments identified by the probes are as marked as proponents of the technique claim. There have been relatively few studies of the performance of the probes used in DNA typing. The few studies that have been conducted have been the work product of companies marketing DNA typing tests. There is a need for independent validation studies of the probes used in DNA typing. Particular attention needs to be paid to the incidence of the DNA polymorphism in the population, as well as in important subgroups, such as racial minorities.

Step 6 Autoradiography. Once DNA segments have been located by the radioactive probes, the segments can be visualized by a process known as autoradiography. The blot is placed on a piece of x-ray film.

Energy from the radioactive probes exposes the film, producing a DNA print. This print is a series of bands whose individual positions indicate the location of a polymorphic segment on the blot. The location of each segment on the blot is an indication of the length of the DNA fragment which contains the segment.

Problems: The use of autoradiography in forensic science does not differ from the way it is used in medical and biological research and should not be an admissibility issue.

Step 7 DNA Print Interpretation. In most cases, DNA prints are simply visually examined to determine if two DNA prints match. Some labs use a DNA comparator that gives a print a numerical code. These codes can then be compared to further corroborate a visual confirmation. Photographic reproduction of the two prints will allow juries and other experts to draw their own conclusions.

Problems: Software is in use and being developed that will allow computer analysis of two DNA prints. The software is designed to compensate for minor irregularities between two prints which may arise out of the typing protocol. This compensation may bring into question whether or not such alterations might not result in a coincidental match (Thompson & Ford, 1989).

There are currently no formal standards for determining what constitutes a match between two DNA prints. Whether a match is declared between two prints is a subjective judgment for the forensic expert.

Frequency Statistics

The Product Rule: To determine the probability of a coincidental match between two DNA prints produced by a fifteen band probe, Sir Alec Jeffreys made DNA prints of twenty unrelated British Caucasians. The twenty prints were laid side by side, each being compared to its neighbor. Twenty-one percent of the bands were matched by a corresponding band in an adjacent print. Jeffreys concluded that there is about a 21 percent chance that a given band in the fingerprint will be matched by a band in the print of an unrelated individual. To calculate the probability that two unrelated individuals will match all fifteen bands produced by the multi-locus probe (15 points), Jeffreys applied the "product rule" and concluded that the probability of a coincidental match on fifteen bands was one in thirty billion. This figure can only be valid if the probability match on any given band is independent of the probability of a match on every other band. The assumption of independence cannot be adequately assessed based on a band sharing study such as the one conducted by Sir Jeffreys, because of the small sample size. The assumption of independence requires that there be at least thirty billion distinguishable DNA print patterns and that no pattern be more common or likely to occur than any other pattern. This requirement cannot have been met based on a sample of twenty British Caucasians, each of whom was compared to only one or two others (Harmon, 1991).

Allele Frequency

A second approach to calculating the probability of a coincidental match is an allele frequency study. Using this approach, large-scale population studies are conducted to determine the frequency, in the population, of each band that might be observed. Allele frequency studies are the method of choice for single-locus probes, the types primarily used by commercial laboratories. Each single-locus probe produces one or two bands. The position of these bands indicates the length of the restriction fragments located by the probe. A fragment of given length is known as an allele. The fragments located by the single-locus probes used in DNA typing have thirty to eighty different alleles and therefore may produce bands in thirty to eighty different positions. The goal of an allele frequency study is to determine the frequency in the population of each of the alleles identified by the probe. For criminal identification, commercial labs use three or four proves and have six to eight bands to work with when comparing samples. If two samples match, the companies report the match and the frequency in the population of the set of alleles which the samples share. To compute the frequency of a set of alleles, commercial labs simply apply the product rule, multiplying together the frequencies of the shared alleles. The use of the product rule is based on the assumption that the alleles identified by the various probes are independent of one another. This assumption is controversial (Thompson & Ford, 1991).

Assessing Allele Independence: In assessing the independence of alleles identified by a given set of probes, three distinct issues must be addressed:

1. It must be determined if the two alleles identified by each of the probes are independent of one another. There is evidence that the inheritance of the bands produced by the probes is Mendelian, one band from each parent. When there is Mendelian inheritance, the reception of a particular band from one parent is not affected by the band received

from the other parent. This independent inheritance is referred to as Hardy-Weinberg equilibrium.

2. It must be shown that the bands produced by each probe are independent of those produced by other probes. There may be an absence of independence if the DNA segments identified by different probes are physically connected or linked (linkage disequilibrium). Linkage disequilibrium occurs where the DNA segments in question are in physical proximity. Commercial laboratories choose probes that identify widely dispersed loci reducing the possibility of linkage disequilibrium.

3. The most important of the independence issues deals with the possible common occurrence of certain bands or combinations of bands within some subpopulations. Within a given subpopulation certain bands might not occur while others occur with far greater frequency than in other subgroups. To determine whether there is subgroup variability requires extensive population studies in which members of various racial and ethnic groups and people from different geographic areas can be separated and compared (Thompson & Ford, 1991).

Sample Contamination

There is unlikely to be a crime scene that will duplicate the hygienic standards found in research and medical laboratories. Defendants are of the belief that anything less than absolute purity in body samples raises questions as to the reliability of the DNA typing process. That is the beauty of the defendant's position. The word contamination raises the specter of something unnatural or careless happening to the samples before reaching the laboratory. It is imperative to address the nature of the environment in which DNA samples are deposited and that contamination and age are an integral part of the nonsterile real world. Every testifying expert will have to concur upon examination that the sample has deteriorated, has aged, and is contaminated. The more resolutely and aggressively these matters are treated on direct examination will go a long way in diffusing the impact of such testimony on cross-examination. Preparation will also lead to successful introductions of DNA evidence. Questions to the analyst:

Q. The question is not one of contamination but rather of how much contamination, is it not?

Q. Can the contaminants be removed from the sample without altering the sample?

Q. Were the contaminants removed before the typing protocol began?

Q. Would you describe the nature of the contaminants present and the method of removal?

Q. How was the sample contaminated?

Q. Where did the contamination occur?

Q. Was the contamination a result of laboratory handling?

Q. Was the contamination a result of police handling?

Q. Was there enough of the sample to run more than one test?

Q. Were such tests run?

Q. Were the results the same?

Q. Were known samples contaminated with similar contaminants, cleaned and typed?

Q. Were those results consistent with the uncontaminated samples?

Contamination is only a problem if left to the defendant as an issue with which to obfuscate or confuse. The jury should be comfortable with the idea that all forensic DNA samples are contaminated and that nothing unique or unusual happened to the samples in question.

Expert Credentials

Obtaining experts to testify can be a trying process. Research and medical experts live in a pristine world and utilize pristine DNA samples. There is little similarity between what they generally do and forensic DNA typing. Those commercial entities that provide analysis for forensic samples are best equipped to testify as experts; unfortunately their corporate status provides the opposition with more than ample material for impeachment based on vested financial interests of the corporation for which the expert works. The majority of the research efforts on the part of commercial enterprises in the DNA business is on building faster, less expensive, and less time-consuming testing procedures rather than validating the probes, and statistical samples they use in their analysis and astronomical statistical frequencies. The good news is that more and more police crime laboratories are hiring competent forensic scientists who can apply DNA typing techniques and have the credentials and developing expertise to provide competent trial testimony.

RFLP and Artificial Results

There are a number of ways in which errors in laboratory procedure or the presence of contaminants in the samples being analyzed might compromise the results. Most of these errors would simply render an uninterpretable result or at worst to falsely exculpate a guilty suspect. A number of common errors have occurred in research laboratories that will most likely be duplicated in the forensic laboratory. Occasionally, a test will result with no bands on the DNA print. In other situations, bands may be smeared or too many bands develop.

A second category of errors might alter the pattern of a DNA print exculpating a guilty suspect. The restriction enzymes may not completely digest the DNA, causing some of the fragments to be longer than they should be. The enzymes may be contaminated and cut the DNA at the wrong sites (star activity). An analyst may use the wrong enzyme or one that has been contaminated by another enzyme. All of these problems would be virtually impossible to detect after the fact. Problems can arise with the Southern blotting transfer where bands disappear creating different patterns. DNA could be contaminated with spurious DNA giving a falsely exculpating result.

Finally, there are a few problems that theoretically might cause a false positive match between two DNA prints. First, the analyst might make an error when placing the samples on the gel for electrophoresis. Samples from the suspect and from evidentiary stains are typically placed in adjoining wells on the gel. There is a possibility that some of the suspect's DNA could splash, spill, or seep into the forensic sample. Ordinarily this problem would be detected in the produced superimposition of the bands.

Second, problems can occur during hybridization that allow the probes to lock onto the wrong DNA sequence as a result of probe degradation. If the probe identifies a common sequence instead of a polymorphic sequence, a match will result. Many probes available commercially do not identify polymorphic sequences but are designed to identify sequences that are common to everyone. If the analyst uses the wrong probe, a false positive could occur.

Third, cross-contamination can occur if a small amount of the DNA probe contaminates the samples or any of the reagents used to analyze samples. Any of the contaminated samples when contacting the DNA probe would have common bands. The probe in effect locks on to itself producing aberrant bands. Although contamination can be controlled through the use of careful laboratory procedures, the problem has proved frustratingly common in research laboratories (Thompson & Ford, p. 96, 1989).

Defense Issues

Often, defense attorneys involved in hearings relating to the conventional electrophoresis techniques have been successful in broadening the scope of the admissibility hearings by injecting issues well beyond the scope of the legal admissibility standards generally required. Some of those issues include:

Q. Has every step in the technology in use been published in a peer review publication?

Q. Has there been subsequent critical review of those published methods either concurring or refuting the earlier publication?

Q. Have there been any changes to any of the peer review published methods?

Q. Have these methods undergone this peer review process?

Q. Have contamination studies been conducted involving all potential sources of contamination?

Q. Does the lab participate in proficiency testing?

Q. What have the results been?

Q. Who made mistakes?

Q. Why?

Q. What was the nature of the error(s)?

Q. What quality control assurance methods are in place to ensure that the correct result is produced each time the methodology is used?

Q. If the courts were to exclude the use of DNA evidence permanently would this exclusion have an impact on the witness's future earning potential (Harmon, 1991)?

Future use of DNA testing will require proponents to make a better showing of the tests' reliability on forensic samples. That showing could occur either through blind proficiency studies or through expert testimony by scientists familiar with the analysis of DNA from aged or contaminated samples. If the accuracy of statistics is to be accepted, it will have to be shown most convincingly that the independent alleles examined in the DNA test are truly independent.

REFERENCES

Beeler, L., & Wiebe, W.R. 1988. DNA identification tests and the courts. *Washington Law Review*, vol. 63:903.

Harmone, R.P. General admissibility considerations for DNA typing evidence: Let's learn from the past and let the scientists decide this time around. In Farley, M.A., & Harrington, J.J. 1991. *Forensic DNA Technology,* Chelsea, England: Lewis.

Saferstein, R. 1995. *Criminalistics: An Introduction to Forensic Science.* Englewood Cliffs, NJ: Prentice-Hall.

Thompson, W.C., & Ford, S. 1991. DNA typing: Acceptance and weight of the new genetic identification tests. *Virginia Law Review,* vol. 75:45.

Wambaugh, J. 1985. *The Blooding.* New York: Bantam.

Chapter 11

DRUGS

INTRODUCTION

The Addict Myth

The United States has been engaged in a twenty-year war it has been losing and seems doomed to lose. Prison populations are overburgeoning with drug and drug-related offenders. We are a country that has been enthralled with the quest for a new and more entertaining way to alter reality. We see ourselves as victims of a lawless undersociety that resorts to violence in its efforts to corner the market on illicit drugs. Media and Hollywood have convinced us that there is an epidemic of drug abuse running amok on the streets of our cities threatening law abiding citizens. The reality is that poor people do not provide the impetus for a multibillion dollar a year drug industry. White polite society is irrevocably involved in the use of controlled substances. If addicts could be removed from our mists in the morning, there would still be a significant drug industry. When we examine the drug industry in all its facets, we recognize that a large portion of the drugs that are available are not the type generally used by the socioeconomically deprived. As Robin Williams, the actor and comedian, says, "powdered cocaine is Gods' way of telling you that you have too much discretionary income." Hallucinogens, depressants, and stimulants are also the purview of the bored or jaded. Many pharmaceuticals find their way from the pharmacists into the hands of men and women who have their doctors' permission to abuse drugs. College campuses are and have been hotbeds of experimentation for curious students looking for newer and bigger kicks.

Legislatures have passed stiff penalties for "violent" drug offenders, but invariably there are "programs" for those who qualify. Generally, qualification means white, middle class, employed, educated, and financially secure. Two tiers of drug abuse have gripped our society, two tiers of enforcement strategies address the problem, and two tiers of law attempt to sanction the problem out of existence. Our myopic view of "violent drug abusers" has encouraged citizens to view the law as less than a sanction depending on their socioeconomic status.

Drug programs should not be a method whereby individuals avoid responsibility for their illegal behavior nor should they be used in lieu of legal sanctions. If a war is to be waged, and there is no evidence that one has ever been conducted, then all persons should be subjected to the same legal process and sanction for the same offense. Attempting to focus on those who supply drugs is foolhardy, expensive, and not very effective in a society based on supply and demand. Removing a supplier only results in increased prices, more violence, and an opportunity for another to fill the created void.

Substance abuse habituation should carry "special status" only if addressed prior to arrest. Many professional organizations provide substance habituation rehabilitation without personal cost to the professional member. No stigma or loss of professional status is associated with voluntarily participation in a professional organization's substance abuse program. National funds should be made available to provide drug rehabilitation programs for persons voluntarily committing themselves for treatment prior to arrest. Any citizen should be able to seek and get the same type of treatment as that afforded by professional organizations to their members. No stigma should be attached and they should be returned to their community and their employment upon successful completion of the program.

Inmates should be given no consideration for parole, work release, or time off for participation in drug programs offered by correctional institutions. The incentives provided by institutions for participation in inmate drug programs are more a product of sustaining programs in which inmates would otherwise not participate.

As a result of youthful experimentation with drugs, many lawyers do not see recreational drug use by middle class society as a problem and attempt to differentiate the casual "social" user from the more violent pusher. Any such perspective undermines the "war effort." All drug involvement ultimately inures to the benefit of the same people. When drug offenders are presented with a panoply of legal options, it is not surprising that respect for the law and for law enforcement deteriorates.

Prosecutors and legislatures may unwittingly contribute to the discriminatory treatment of drug offenders. Much sentencing is a product of plea agreements. These agreements when entered into with drug offenders may include program participation in lieu of incarceration. This approach has in at least one state lead to an amelioration of sanction based on an admission of substance habituation that may or may not be true.

THE SUBSTANCE ABUSE DEFENSE

In 1967, the President's Commission on Law Enforcement and the Administration of Justice recommended the early identification and diversion of offenders in need of treatment (The Challenge of Crime in a Free Society, 1967). From 1970 to 1980, the Law Enforcement Assistance Administration funded over 1,200 diversion programs, most of which are now funded by state and local government (Austin and Krisberg, 1981).

A study of Galvin (1977) indicates that about 45 percent of arrests are probably divertable, and that the continued overcrowding of judicial and correctional resources makes diversion a continuing part of the American landscape.

States have adopted one of two ways in which to divert substance habituated offenders:

1. statutory diversion
2. models based on the Treatment Alternatives to Street Crime (TASC).

They differ in that statutory diversion utilizes legislative authorization to divert abusers, whereas TASC provides liaison services to the criminal justice system and private drug treatment programs.

The California System

Many states have authorized diversion and California has the best known and researched statutory diversion program. Under the California approach, the local prosecutor is responsible for the selection of candidates. Defendants statutorily excluded from California's program include:

1. Persons with a prior drug related conviction
2. Persons who have committed a crime of violence
3. Probation or parole violators

4. Formerly diverted offenders
5. Drug traffickers
6. Prior felons (Galvin, 1977).

Eligible candidates are screened by the probation department and medically evaluated to confirm substance habituation. Many states have used the California model in devising diversionary programs for drug offenders. Some states have not looked to the California model and have devised their own program for diverting drug offenders.

A Potentially Discriminatory System

The Texas system is one program that has manufactured the opportunity for the discriminatory application of drug offender diversion. The Texas legislature has provided for pretrial and posttrial diversion for substance abuse offenders. Plea bargaining is an integral part of the Texas diversion process. The author undertook a study to determine what guidelines, if any, were being employed in the diversion of substance habituated offenders by Texas prosecutors.

In Texas, judicial sentencing of drug offenders is governed by statute. Sentencing of offenders who have committed nondrug-related offenses motivated by drug or alcohol dependency, in most instances, is also governed by statute. That statute specifically provides:

> On determination by the court that alcohol or drug abuse may have contributed to the commission of the offense, the court shall direct that an evaluation be made to determine the appropriateness of and course of conduct necessary for, alcohol or drug rehabilitation for the defendant and to report that evaluation to the court. (Texas Code of Criminal Procedure, Article 42.12)

The statute uses mandatory language: "shall direct that an evaluation be made . . . "

The Texas legislature attempted to address those situations in which treatment might be considered as an option to incarceration in cases involving drug and alcohol dependent offenders. In drafting this statute, the legislature intentionally, or otherwise, allowed what appears to be a sentencing loophole to inure to the advantage of defendants contending to be substance habituated. Prosecuting attorneys can, based solely on extra-legal considerations, divert defendants into "treatment" without an "evaluation being made to determine the appropriateness of and course of conduct necessary for, alcohol or drug rehabilitation for the defendant. . . . " (id.).

The Texas legislature has provided judges with the avenues to gather the information necessary to assist them in making court-ordered therapy part of the sentencing scheme. The statute goes on to delineate those situations in which such evaluations (presentence investigations) are necessary:

  a. after arrest and before conviction, if requested by the defendant;
  b. after conviction and before sentencing if the court assesses punishment;
  c. after sentencing and before the entry of a final judgment if the jury assesses punishment; and
  d. after probation is granted if convicted of a driving while intoxicated or a driving under the influence offense (id.).

The legislature requires presentence investigations for sentencing judges or juries but did not address prosecutorial plea bargains or prosecutorial pretrial diversion. This omission created a potentially discriminatory sentencing system. The goal of the study was to determine:

  1. If prosecutors were aware of the sentencing latitude extended them as a result of the Texas Code of Criminal Procedure, Article 42.12;
  2. If prosecutors were using the sentencing latitude extended them as a result of the Texas Code of Criminal Procedure, Article 42.12;
  3. Under what circumstances did prosecutors utilize that latitude;
  4. What types of offenses preclude diversion;
  5. Did violence preclude diversion; and
  6. What type of criminal history precluded diversion.

Texas prosecutors appear to view pretrial diversion of substance habituated offenders as an opportunity to:

  a. probate or divert substance habituated property offenders—as evidenced by survey responses demonstrating the pervasive use of probation and pretrial diversion into treatment programs for nonviolent, first offense, substance habituated property offenders who do not cause injury or use a weapon.
  b. save trial and institutional resources for offenses involving serious injury or deadly weapons—as demonstrated by respondents' reluctance to consider probation and pretrial diversion in those cases of substance habituated property offenders when injury occurs or a weapon is involved.

The Texas statute is silent on many of the considerations the California legislature specifically addressed. By failing to include the constraints that a California-type statute would contain, Texas has enacted a diversion statute that is inconsistently and arbitrarily applied. If Texas prosecutors are diverting and probating substance habituated property offenders, and the survey responses indicates they are, upon what bases are such decisions being made? It is axiomatic that a prosecutor's discretion is not subject to judicial review or appeal. This discretion is necessary to control the ever-escalating case loads prosecutors are confronted with. However, the discretion prosecutors exercise should be consistent with the authority granted through the legislature. Power abhors a vacuum. The legislature neglected to require prosecutors to preclude:

1. Persons with prior drug offense convictions
2. Persons whose current offense involved injury
3. Persons previously diverted
4. Person convicted of a prior felony

By failing to require medical confirmation of habituation the Texas legislature opened the door for manipulation. Without a standardized procedure, the legislature opened the door for the inconsistent application of prosecutorial discretion. That abuse may be discrimination if:

1. diversion and probation to drug programs is dependent upon an offender's financial ability to fund his own treatment, and
2. defendants can become eligible for drug treatment diversion or probation by simply confessing their substance habituation.

Texas does not employ a standardized diversion process. There is one avenue available for those who do not understand the "value" of a "substance abuse problem" and another for those who understand (or who's lawyer understands) the "value" of "substance habituation."

Defendants with financial resources can confess their drug or alcohol habituation and agree to be involved in a drug program (in-patient or out-patient) without the benefit of a presentence investigation. Those with resources can be diverted from the system into "treatment" programs at no expense to the state. Without a comprehensive presentence investigation, there is no way for a prosecutor to ascertain whether the person confessing his habituation is in fact using alcohol or drugs, since prosecutors are not provided with any specialized training in the identification and evaluation of substance habituated subjects. The Texas statute does not require any particularized screening of diversion candidates. The Texas statute does not require medical confirmation of substance habituation prior to diversion.

The concerns raised by the Texas study can be partially addressed by the legislature promulgating standards for participation in diversion programs. Standards similar to those employed by California prosecutors may be a starting point for assuring that all those participating in substance abuse treatment programs should and need to be there. That need should be thoroughly assessed the same way for those diverted or plea-bargained, as it is for all other offenders whose substance habituation is considered by the court in sentencing, through presentence investigations and medical confirmation of dependence and susceptibility to treatment.

Glossary of Street Drug Jargon

Acid: LSD
Acid Head: a person who uses LSD
Angel Dust: phencyclidine PCP
Bennies: amphetamine sulphate (Benzedrine).
Blizzard: cocaine
Bhang: marijuana
Chipping: occasional use of addictive drugs
Cooker: device used to heat diluted narcotics for injection
Crack: almost pure cocaine that can be ignited and the fumes inhaled
Designer Drugs: substances that are chemically related to some controlled drugs and are pharmacologically very potent.
Dexies: dexedrine
Dobe: marijuana cigarette
Dujie: heroin
Ecstasy: amphetamine
Flake: cocaine
Free Base: almost pure cocaine that can be ignited and smoked purer than crack but more difficult to produce
Freeze: cocaine
Goof balls: barbiturates
Grass: marijuana
"H": heroin
Hairy: heroin

Harry: heroin
Hearts: dexedrine
Hemp: marijuana
Horse: heroin
Ice: methamphetamine
King: heroin
Ludes: methaqualone
"M": morphine
Mainline: intravenous use of narcotics
Mary Jane: marijuana
Mexican Horse: brown heroin from Mexico
Miss Emma: morphine
Muggle: marijuana
Nose Candy: cocaine
Pep Pills: amphetamine
Reds and Blues: amobarbital sodium and secobarbital sodium, Tuinal
Red Birds: secobarbital sodium, seconal
Reefer: marijuana
Rig: hypodermic needle and cooking device
Roaches: marijuana cigarette butts
Rock: crack cocaine
Scag: heroin
Skin Popping: injecting narcotics under the skin rather than into a vein
Smack: heroin
Snow: cocaine
Speed: methamphetamine or any stimulant
Speedball: heroin mixed with cocaine
Truck Drivers: amphetamines
Uppers: stimulants
Weed: marijuana
Whites: amphetamine sulfate tablets
Yellow Jackets: pentobarbital sodium, Nembutal.

Drug Analysis

Forensic chemists are confronted with an array of prospective substances in the specimens that are submitted to them for analysis. The analysis must be specific and remove any doubt as to what drug, if any, is involved. That certainty must be supportable and capable of proof at the time of trial. How does a chemist determine what drug among many a particular substance is? How does a chemist confirm that the probability of any other substance responding in an identical manner to the protocol selected is beyond any reasonable scientific certainty? A two-stage protocol is employed:

1. screening tests
2. confirmation

Screening tests

Screening tests involve subjecting the questioned substance to a series of reagents that yield a characteristic color for commonly-encountered drugs. Screening tests are used both in the lab and in the field. Ease of application makes color testing an efficient field tool for tentative, presumptive identification of a drug. Color tests are useful for screening purposes and are not conclusive identification.

There are five color test reagents commonly used:

1. Duquenois-Levine is a test for barbiturates which turns the reagent violent in color. The reagent is composed of three solutions: A which is 2% vanilla with 1% acetaldehyde in ethyl alcohol; solution B is concentrated hydrochloric acid; solution C is chloroform.
2. Marquis screens for heroin, morphine, and opium derivatives and turns purple in their presence. The reagent can also be used for amphetamines and methamphetamines in whose presence the mixture turns orange-brown. This reagent is composed of 2% formaldehyde in sulfuric acid.
3. Van Urk reagent in the presence of LSD turns blue-purple.
4. Dillie-Koppanyi is a test for barbiturates, in whose presence the reagent turns violent-blue in color.
5. Scott test in the presence of cocaine renders a blue color upon application of solution A; the blue transforms into a pink upon application of solution B; and upon addition of solution C, the blue color reappears in the chloroform layer.

Each of these tests alone is insufficient to prove the drug's identity; however, the proper protocol will encompass a combination of test results that are characteristic of only one chemical substance.

Drug identification protocols generally rely upon a combination of test types to confirm a drugs' identity. That combination may include:

color tests, microcrystalline tests, chromatography, spectrophotometry, and mass spectrometry.

Microcrystalline Tests

As a result of microscopic examination, the microcrystalline test is more specific than the use of colored response to chemical reagents. In this procedure, a small quantity of the substance in question is placed on a microscopic slide and a drop of chemical reagent is added. Color is not the response sought in this test; the chemical added causes a precipitate reaction creating characteristic crystals in size and shape. The standardization of these patterns for commonly used drugs, over time, has become reliable, distinguishable, and admissible at the time of trial. These tests can be conducted in the presence of diluents. Although the crystal structure and size may be altered by the diluents experienced examiners can make the identification despite the crystal alterations. When the appropriate color tests and microcrystalline tests are conducted pursuant to a standardized protocol, the results should be determinative for only one drug (Siegel, 1988).

Chromatography

Both thin-layer and gas chromatography lend themselves to the separation of diluents and the identification of a suspected drug. Chromatography involves a comparison of a known substance with an unknown substance. It is necessary to have some idea of what the suspected substance is before drug analysis chromatography can be conducted. Generally color and microcrystalline tests precede chromatography.

Gas Chromatography: Chromatography theory is based upon the fact that chemical substances have a tendency to partially escape into the surroundings when dissolved in a liquid or when absorbed on a solid surface. In a beaker of water covered with a bell jar and kept at a constant temperature, the water is in its liquid phase and the air above the beaker is in the gas phase. The gas molecules (oxygen and hydrogen) escaping from the water through evaporation are in their "gas phase" and those molecules remaining in the water are said to be in their "liquid phase." As the gas molecules continue to escape, they will begin to accumulate above the water. The random movement of the molecules will carry some back into the water. A point will be reached when the number of molecules escaping the water is equal to the number of molecules returning to the water; at this point the liquid phase and the gas phase are in equilibrium (Klien, Kruegle & Sobol, 1979).

The distribution of a gas between the liquid and gas phases is dependent upon the solubility of the gas: the higher the solubility the greater the tendency to remain in the liquid phase.

During a chromatographic process, one phase is kept in continuous motion in a fixed direction. When two or more gases are dissolved in water, chromatography will occur when the air is forced to move continuously in one direction over the water. The gas with less solubility will have a greater number of molecules escaping into the gas phase as compared to the other gas, and will travel faster than the more soluble gas molecules. When the movement continues sufficiently, the molecules of the two gases will become completely separated. Seen as a race, the participating substances are mixed together. As the race progresses, those materials that are move movable (moving phase) will charge ahead of those substances that prefer solubility (stationary phase) (Klein, Kruegel, & Sobol, 1979).

In gas chromatography, the moving phase is called carrier gas, which flows through a column constructed of glass. The stationary phase is a thin film of liquid contained within the column. As the carrier gas flows through the column, it carries along with it the components of a mixture that have been injected into the column. Those components having a greater affinity for the moving gas phase will travel through the column at a faster rate as compared to those having a greater affinity for the stationary liquid phase. Eventually, after the mixture has traversed the length of the column, it will emerge separated into its component parts (Saferstein, 1995).

As the constituent components emerge from the column, it passes through a detector which makes a written record as a function of time. This written record of the separation is called a chromatogram. A typical chromatogram will show a series of peaks, each corresponding to a component of the mixture. The time required for a component to emerge from the column is known as the retention time. This serves as an identifying characteristic of a material. It is possible that other substances may have comparable retention times under similar chromatographic conditions, and the results of gas chromatography can only be considered presumptive and must be confirmed by other procedures.

An additional advantage of gas chromatography is that it can yield quantitative results. The amount of a substance passing through the detector is proportional to the peak recorded. By chromatographing a known concentration of a material and comparing it to the unknown, the amount of the sample may be determined by proportion.

Thin-layer chromatography: Thin-layer chromatography (TLC) incorporates a solid stationary phase and a moving liquid phase to separate the constituents of a mixture. An absorbent plate is coated with a thin film of silica gel or aluminum oxide and is held in place with plaster of Paris. If the specimen to be examined is a solid, it must first be dissolved in a solvent. A few microliters of the solution is spotted onto the lower edge of the plate, which is then placed upright in a closed chamber that contains a selected liquid in which fluorescent dye has been added. The placement is made so that only the bottom edge of the plate is resting in the liquid (test spots may not touch the liquid). The liquid will slowly rise up the plate (by capillary action). As the liquid moves past the test spots, the components of the sample will become distributed between the plate and the rising liquid. Those components that are the least soluble will travel up the plate faster than those components that are more soluble. When the liquid has traveled 10 cm past the test spots, the development is complete and the plate removed, dried, and visualized (Klein, Kruegel, & Sobol, 1979).

The plates are placed under ultraviolet light, revealing those materials that fluoresce as bright spots on a dark background. Another method of visualization involves the use of a reagent spray that causes the separated spots to color. The questioned sample must be developed alongside a standardized sample on the same thin-layer chromatograph plate. If the standard and the test materials travel the same distances up the plate, they can tentatively be identified as being the same. Identification is not definitive and cannot be used independently to provide identification (Klein, Kruegel, & Sobol, 1979).

The distance a spot has traveled up a thin-layer plate can be assigned a numerical value known as the Rf value. This value is defined as the distance traveled by the component divided by the distance traveled by the moving liquid phase. Since the liquid phase is allowed to travel 10 cm the Rf value will be in tenths of a cm for example if the spot moved 8 cm the Rf value would be 0.8. Years of research and testing have produced much published data relating to the proper selection of the TLC conditions for separating and identifying specific classes of substances including drugs (Down & Gwyn, 1975).

Mass Spectrometry

The ability of gas chromatography to separate a complex mixture into its constituent parts, although reliable, predictable, and replicable, is still only presumptive. It does not produce a specific identification. An expert cannot unequivocally base her opinion on a chromatographic retention time. By coupling the gas chromatograph to a mass spectrometer, a definitive identification can be made.

After the mixture has been separated by the gas chromatograph, a direct connection of the chromatograph columns and the mass spectrometer then allows each component to flow into the spectrometer as it leaves the chromatograph. The material enters a high-vacuum chamber in the spectrometer where a beam of high-energy electrons is aimed at the sample molecules. The electrons collide with the molecules, causing them to lose electrons and to acquire a positive charge (ion). These ions are unstable and almost instantaneously decompose into numerous smaller fragments. The fragments are passed through an electric field, where they are separated according to their masses. Under carefully controlled conditions, no two substances produce the same fragmentation pattern. These fragmentation patterns are unique enough to be considered "fingerprints" (Yimon & Zitrin, 1977).

This technique provides specific identification of a chemical structure even in minute concentrations. The combination of the gas chromatograph and mass spectrometer is further enhanced when linked to a computer system. Accuracy, speed, and sensitivity are added to the procedure along with the capability to record and store data. The system is able to detect and identify substances present in one-millionth of a gram of suspect material. Computer comparisons can be run of unknown substances avoiding the necessity of a control specimen.

Narcotics

The source of most narcotics is opium. Narcotic drugs are analgesics that relieve pain by depressing the central nervous system. Their regular use will lead to physical dependence. Opium is extracted from the unripe pod of the poppy. The morphine content of the extracted opium is from 4 to 21 percent.

Heroin

Opium the first narcotic drug, is derived from the oriental poppy. The opium poppy will grow in a wide range of climates, but production of opium is labor-intensive. The unripe seed pod is incised lightly multiple times. The milky fluid that collects on the surface is raw opium. After several hours, a collection of semi-dried material is taken from the surface. Each pod produces only a small amount of fluid, and thousands of pods have to be incised and harvested to produce a pound of raw opium. In 1945, over 200 tons of opium were imported into the United States for legitimate medical needs, and it was estimated that several times that amount was imported for illicit drug usage. Today, in spite of extensive use of synthetic analgesics, many tons of opium are imported into the United States legally, and the drug is still produced primarily in Asia where labor is still relatively cheap. Much of the illegal opium produced today is from an area referred to as the golden triangle. Some estimate that more than 15,000 to 20,000 pounds of illegal opium products, such as heroin, are brought into the United States each year (Stephens, 1993). The word narcotic is derived from the Greek word narkotikon, which means to numb or benumbing. It refers to the principal effect of opium of producing analgesia and relieving pain. The term narcotic was originally used for referencing drugs derived from opium or other drugs producing analgesia or stupor, but, through usage and legal definitions, the term no longer refers only to drugs derived directly from opium.

In 1803, the German pharmacist Serturner isolated morphine from opium. Opium contains approximately 10 percent morphine. The compound was named morphine after morpheus, the Greek god of dreams. This was obviously a reference to the effect in man of producing sleep. Eventually, codeine, occurring in opium at levels of .5 percent, was isolated. Morphine and codeine are the principal opium derived alkaloids used today. Codeine is used as an analgesic and cough suppressant, morphine is used in several forms as an analgesic, and opium is used in preparations to treat diarrhea.

All true narcotics have shown themselves to be addicting when abused, even though several were originally introduced with the suggestion that such was not the case.

Addiction is a combination of psychological and physical dependence on a drug. As tolerance to the drug develops, the user requires more than the usual amount to experience the same euphoric effect. When tolerance and habitual use develop, a physiologic dependence also occurs, so withdrawal of the drug progresses to clinical signs such as abdominal pains, nausea, and vomiting. Agitation and a feeling of distress generally resolve in several days. These physical signs can be prevented by renewing the drug levels or by substitution of drugs like methadone. Addiction is evident when the drug user has an overpowering desire and need or compulsion to obtain and take the drug and when there is a physiologic effect when the drug is withdrawn. Applying this definition of addiction, it should be noted that all narcotic users are not addicts. There are narcotic users who mediate their dosage in quantity and frequency. These users are referred to by addicts as "chippers," people "chipping" away at a habit.

Opium is most typically taken orally (tincture such as laudanum) or smoked. Smoking vaporizes the opium, allowing morphine and other alkaloids to be absorbed from the smoke. While the amount used initially is small, as tolerance increases, large amounts are required to achieve an effect.

Much like opium, morphine and heroin enjoyed a wide over-the-counter acceptance. By 1900, some estimated that there were one million addicts in the United States. Heroin, introduced in 1898, was immediately proclaimed the most effective analgesic known. Thought to be nonaddictive, heroin was recommended specifically as treatment for addiction to other opium derivatives. It was sold as an elixir and in patent medicines until the early 1900s when the danger was recognized. In 1914, the Harrison Narcotic Act made such drugs illegal (Baden, 1980).

The concentration and nature of the heroin varies widely from region to region, as does the form. "Mexican brown" or "tar" heroin is popular on the West Coast, while powder "China white" is more popular on the East Coast. Concentrations are around 10 percent but can be higher. Cutting agents vary also from region to region, with quinine used on the East Coast and lidocaine on the West Coast. Aware of the variability of drugs and cutting agents, addicts prefer to "score" from the same source (Stephens, 1993).

Heroin is usually sold as a fine white powder in a glassine envelope or paper bundle, or it may be tar wrapped in tin foil, within a balloon, condom or in a small plastic bundle. To use, the contents of the container are emptied into a "cooker." The cooker can be a spoon or wire held bottle cap, but anything that will hold about 5ml of fluid and allow heating over a flame will do. When water is added, most of the material is not immediately dissolved. A flame, usually in the form of a match or cigarette lighter, is used to warm the solution to increase solubility. The liquid is aspirated into an insulin syringe, usually through a small piece of absorbent cotton, to remove insoluble material. The needle is inserted under the skin (skin popping) or into a vein and a small amount of solution is injected as a test dose. The addict subjectively interprets how powerful the drug is and how much will be injected. This process of injecting a small amount, withdrawing some blood to keep the lumen open, is called "registering," "fooling," and "booting."

Heroin is made by reacting morphine with anhydride or acetyl chloride. The solution is cooled and neutralized with sodium carbonate. The heroin free base is then purified by adding concentrated hydrochloric acid (Saferstein, 1995).

The "high" associated with the use of heroin is short-lived, lasting three to four hours. The impact of the body's "withdrawal" from the effects of the drug, known as "keeping the sickness off," as much as the "high" associated with the drug, accounts for the users pursuit of another "fix" (a "Jones" is the amount of money spent each day to keep the "sickness off"). Common street quality heroin is from 15 to 35 percent pure, adulterated (stepped on) each time it changes hands. Traditionally, quinine was the choice of "cut" (diluent) for heroin. Contemporary pushers use other diluents such as starch, mannitol, procaine, and lactose. Mexican heroin is brown because of the refining process used. Mexican heroin is often cut with cocoa.

Legal Problems: Syringes and cookers contain only small amounts of heroin, complicated by the low concentration of the heroin in street samples. There may not be enough in such cases to perform a complete analysis. When testing, it is best to use microcrystalline or thin-layer chromatography tests first because they use minimum material and the sample can often be recovered after testing. Obviously, gas chromatography and mass spectrometry would be the preferred choice for analysis because of the small quantities capable of testing.

Methadone

There are some narcotics that are not derived from opium. These drugs are nonetheless referred to as "opiates" because of the narcotic effect of the drugs. Methadone is a synthetic opiate used in "maintenance" programs for heroin addicts. When taking 80 to 120 milligrams a day of methadone, heroin addicts will not experience the high associated with heroin or morphine use. The intent is to avoid the effects of withdrawal and the desire to get "high" for those people attempting to "kick" a heroin habit.

Codeine

Codeine is also present in opium but is usually prepared synthetically from morphine. It is used as a cough suppressant and is only one-sixth as strong as morphine. Codeine is not a drug of choice for heroin users.

Hallucinogens

Hallucinogens are drugs that cause a distortion in thought processes and perceptions as well as changes in moods. Prolonged use can bring about permanent personality changes and loss of contact with reality.

Marijuana

Marijuana includes all parts of the plant Cannabis sativa L., whether growing or not; the seeds thereof; the resin extracted from any part of such plant; and every compound, manufacture, salt, derivative, mixture, or preparation of such plant, its seeds, or resins; but shall not include the mature stalks of such plant, fiber produced from such stalks, oil or cake made from the seeds of such plant, any other compound, manufacture, salt derivative, mixture or preparation of such mature stalks (except the resin extracted therefrom) fiber, oil, or cake, or the sterilized seed of such plant which is incapable of germination (Saferstein, 1995).

The marijuana preparation consists of crushed leaves mixed in varying proportions with the flowers ("tops") stems and seeds. Often the quality of the marijuana is determined by the number of "tops" included in the bag. Usual purchases are for:

a joint—one handrolled cigarette
a matchbox—a small paper matchbox, about four "joints"
a lid—approximately an ounce contained in a plastic baggy
a lb—a pound referred to by l and b for the abbreviation for pound, sold in paper and plastic bags
a key—a kilogram 2.5 pounds

The plant secretes a sticky resin that is known as hashish ("hash"), which is sold by the gram or in compressed one ounce bars about the size of a chocolate bar. The resinous material can also be extracted from the plant by soaking in a solvent. Hashish oil is also a resinous material in a viscous form, dark green to brown in color, and having the consistency of tar. Hashish is smoked in a "hash pipe" (a metal or wooden device with a small bowl about the size of a dime), or ceramic "chillum" (a straight stemmed pipe without a filter; a rock is placed loosely over the hole in the bowl to prevent the hash from being sucked into the stem). Hash oil is dropped onto a marijuana cigarette to increase its potency or onto a regular cigarette. Distribution of hashish appears to coincide with a lapse in the leaf marijuana market. Marijuana users prefer leaf use to the resinous hashish.

Marijuana was first introduced into the United States around 1920, most probably smuggled by Mexican laborers across the border into Texas. By 1937, 46 states and the federal government had laws prohibiting the use or possession of marijuana.

Marijuana is a weed (sometimes referred to as "weed") that grows under most climatic conditions but flourishes in hot, tropical areas. The size of the plant and the potency of the marijuana are dependent on the amount of sunlight and rain it receives. The plant grows to a height of 15 feet and is characterized by an odd number of leaflets on each leaf. Each leaf contains five to nine leaflets, all having characteristic serrated edges.

In 1964, scientists isolated the chemical substance responsible for the hallucinogenic properties of marijuana. The psychoactive ingredient in marijuana is called tetrahydrocannabinol, referred to as THC. The discovery of THC allows scientists to determine the potency of marijuana preparations and the effect these preparations have on individual users. The THC content in cannabis varies in different parts of the plant, with the resin and flowers having the greatest potency. Marijuana, as generally used, and hashish have a THC content of 3 to 4 percent. The THC-rich resin extracted from the marijuana plant in the form of hash oil may have a THC content from 20 to 65 percent (Thornton & Nakamura, 1972).

Legal Problems: There are two legal problems associated with the courts and cannabis. The first problem likely to be encountered is in the attempt by the defense to impeach the expert by demonstrating that the specie of marijuana in question is suspect. This problem arose out of the assertion by some botanists that there are numerous species of marijuana other than cannabis sativa. By establishing that the expert cannot testify as to the specific species of the marijuana in question, the allegations fail because many statutes proscribe only cannabis sativa. Most courts no longer recognize this defense, relying on congressional intent to control THC regardless of marijuana species. The prepared expert, when asked the species of the marijuana in question, will answer that she has not identified the species nor can she testify that the marijuana in question is cannabis sativa. Her testimony will focus on THC content as opposed to species.

The second problem occurs only in those jurisdictions that have separate penalties and definitions for hashish. When hashish is legally defined, it may be referred to as "a resinous extract of marijuana." The obvious question to be raised by the defense is "what is meant by resinous"? Some chemists take the position that any oily preparation or cake made from marijuana is hashish. Others define hashish as the resin that contains THC and that the presence of any plant material in an exhibit contaminates the pure resin, thereby disqualifying it as hashish. The question is rendered moot in those jurisdictions that treat hashish the same as marijuana.

Lysergic Acid Diethylamide

LSD is synthesized from a type of fungus that attacks certain grasses and grains. Albert Hoffman, a Swiss scientist, first described the hallucinogenic effects of LSD after accidentally ingesting it in 1943. The widespread use of LSD is usually associated with the late 1960s and the "protest" generation. It was manufactured in a variety of forms, each having its advocates for purity and sensation. The chemical itself is colorless and tasteless and can be distributed through a variety of shapes and forms, such as:

windowpane acid—1 by 2 mm rectangles of LSD impregnated gelatin
blotter acid—an aqueous solution of LSD poured evenly over absorbent perforated paper, usually about 1 cm square
California sunshine—yellow tablets
stamp acid—postage stamps with an aqueous solution of LSD dropped onto the adhesive surface

The drug is very potent; as little as 25 micrograms is enough to start visual hallucinations that may last up to 12 hours. The "acid trip" is one of plateaus with the maximum hallucinations occurring during the drugs greatest influence (called "peak"). The onset of the hallucinations begins from 20 to 60 minutes after ingestion. More rapid absorption results when the material is dropped into the eye or injected. Subsequent dosages must be increased to obtain the same effects when LSD is used over an extended period. The drug may produce visual and auditory hallucinations as well as mood swings, feelings of anxiety, tension, and paranoia.

Legal Problems: The small amount of LSD in the submitted samples makes analysis difficult. The most common spot test for LSD is Erlich's test, which turns purple in the presence of LSD. This spot test can be used to visualize LSD after thin-layer chromatography, thereby allowing two tests to be conducted on the same sample. In some states only LSD is proscribed and isomers of LSD, such as lysergic acid methylpropylamide (LAMPA), are not included. However, this issue is rendered moot in those jurisdictions that include LSD isomers in the proscriptive definition.

Phencyclidine

Phencyclidine, once marketed by Parke-Davis as a large-animal tranquilizer, is a synthetic substance referred to on the street as PCP. PCP has appeared on the street in pill ("peace pills") and powder form ("angel dust"). PCP, regardless of delivery system, is generically referred to today as "angel dust." The drug can be placed in solution into which marijuana cigarettes can be dipped and sold individually as "sherm." The dust can be sprinkled onto marijuana and then sold as a more potent strain of marijuana, e.g., Columbian or Panama Red. Because of the simplicity of manufacture, PCP is often sold as LSD, mescaline, or THC.

Legal problems: The chemist may be called upon to analyze material suspected of being PCP or to evaluate the manufacturing capabilities of a clandestine laboratory. A through knowledge of the chemistry of the chemicals used to manufacture PCP and any analogs of PCP will be necessary for the chemist to testify that PCP was being manufactured, or was to be manufactured. Included in this knowledge will be an ability to assess the production output of a clandestine laboratory. It may be necessary for the prosecution to change the charges from "possession" or "manufacture" to "attempted manufacture," or "conspiracy to manufacture" based on the chemists analysis of the labs' "readiness."

Depressants

Barbiturates

Because of the relaxing effects of these drugs, they are referred to on the streets generically as "downers." They act on the central nervous system and create a feeling of "well-being" and drowsiness. All barbiturates are derived from barbituric acid, first synthesized by German chemist, Adolf Von Bauer. Of the twenty-five barbiturate derivatives used in medical practice, only five are commonly used: amobarbital, secobarbital, phenobarbital, pentobarbital, and butabarbital (Saferstein, 1995).

This drug is generally taken orally in 10 to 70 milligram doses and absorbed through the small intestines. Phenobarbital is absorbed slowly and is classified as a long-acting barbiturate. Abusers prefer the faster acting barbiturates. The withdrawal from physical dependence to barbiturates is more severe than that caused by any other drug.

Legal problems: Because of the large number of barbiturate derivatives manufactured it is difficult to determine which specific derivative is in question.

Stimulants

Amphetamines

These drugs are synthetic and stimulate the central nervous system. Collectively referred to by abusers as "uppers" or "speed." Methamphetamine is called "crank." Abusers may inject the drug or take it orally. Injecting the drug provides for an immediate physiological response, called a "rush," followed by an intense feeling of pleasure. Individuals who prefer amphetamines to other drugs are called "speed freaks" and often "binge," as do cocaine users. During a binge, a user may inject 500 to 1000 mg of amphetamines every 2 to 3 hours. The binge usually continues until all the drug has been injected. Users report an increase in perception, information processing, and body function. Binging may produce hallucinations and paranoia. As the drug begins to wear off, users slip into a depression and prolonged periods of sleep.

The drug is sold in "papers," a term used for any quantity less than one gram. A paper containing one-tenth of a gram sells for between $50 to $100, one gram sells for $200 to $350, an ounce for $3,600 to $4,500, and a kilogram would market from $60,000 to $100,000.

The drug is primarily known for its upper or stimulating properties, imparting a prolonged feeling of strength and well-being. Because it increases physiologic activity, tiredness is relieved and a feeling of energy is substituted. Amphetamines were used in the 1940s to increase productivity and allow prolonged activities that would normally be very tiring or tedious. Bomber pilots during World War II, for example, were given amphetamines to help them stay alert on long flights.

Methamphetamine has garnered much attention in the media, and is known on the street as "Meth," "Crystal," "Crank," and "Speed." It is most popular on the West Coast and in the Pacific Rim countries. Most of the chemical components are regulated; many chemical syntheses leading to the same compounds are possible (Derlet & Heischober, 1990).

One form of methamphetamine has received unusual press coverage. Known as "ice," "batu," or "shabu," it has been called the most dangerous drug in existence. When volatile methamphetamine oil is allowed to crystallize slowly in a refrigerator, large crystals form. White or slightly yellow in color, they are usually the size of rock salt, about one-quarter to one-half inch.

The commonly used amphetamines can be smoked. The powder or crystals may be mixed with tobacco or marijuana, but more often it is heated to vaporize unmixed on the screen of a pipe, and the fumes inhaled. The pipe is usually a glass bulb with a hole in the top and a tube on one side for the mouthpiece. The drug is placed in the pipe, and the pipe is heated until white vapor appears as the drug melts. The finger sealing the hole on the top of the pipe is removed and the user inhales from the tube as long as possible, holding the breath to allow absorption through the lung. After inhalation, the pipe is immediately cooled with a wet cloth to condense the vaporized drug. A single crystal can be used several times before it is completely consumed, and considering the length of the high, it would seem to be more economical than cocaine. A used pipe will have carbon on the outside bottom and a coating of white to grey crystals on the inside walls. Although less physiologically addicting than the narcotics, amphetamines are habituating and true withdrawal symptoms develop in long-term users (Derlet & Heischober, 1990).

A significant problem associated with the use of amphetamines is the propensity towards paranoia, violent behavior, and a desire to carry weapons.

Legal problems: The major problem in analyzing amphetamines is in distinguishing between the various isomers of amphetamine and differentiating amphetamine from methamphetamine.

The same considerations are true in amphetamine cases that exist in PCP laboratories. The chemist must not only be able to analyze the substances submitted but may also be called upon to determine the exact status of the clandestine laboratory at the time it was seized.

Cocaine

The word "coca" comes from the Aymara "khoka," meaning "the tree" (Karch, 1993). Measurable quantities of cocaine and nicotine have been detected in 3,000-year-old Egyptian mummies (Balabanova, Parsche, Pirsig, 1992).

Boerhave favorably mentioned coca in his textbook on medicinal plants, published in 1708 (Mortimer, 1901). In 1857, Carl von Scherzer, chief scientist for a German training expedition that was being sent around the world by Archduke Ferdinand, returned with 60 pounds of coca leaves which were provided to Albert Niemann, a graduate student of Carl Wolhler the chemist (Scherzer, 1861). Niemann was given the task of isolating coca's active principle. Purification of cocaine proved relatively simple; Nieman published his Ph.D. thesis, "On a New Organic Base in the Coca Leaves," in 1860 (Niemann, 1860). A *Lancet* editorial published in 1872 stated that "There is considerable difference of opinion as to its effects upon human subject, and the published accounts are somewhat conflicting; but we think that there is a strong evidence in favor of its being a stimulant and narcotic of a peculiar kind, and of some power" (anon, 1872).

It was discovered that when alcohol and cocaine were combined, cocaethylene was formed and the end product was as psychoactive as the cocaine itself. The French capitalized on this knowledge and began manufacturing wines containing coca. In early 1880, Parke Davis and Company began marketing a fluid extract containing 0.5 mg/ml of semipurified cocaine. In the United States, John Styth Pemberton began selling a "French Wine Cola." His initial marketing efforts were not very successful. In what proved to be a wise marketing move, Pemberton dropped the wine from the product, and added a combination of cocaine and caffeine. The reformulated product was named coca-cola (Kirsch, 1993).

Two events occurred in 1884 that significantly changed the pattern of cocaine use in the United States and Europe. The first was the publication of Freud's paper, "Uber Coca" (Freud, 1884). The second was Koller's discovery that cocaine was a local anesthetic (Noyes, 1884). The availability of an effective local anesthetic had tremendous impact. Cocaine was propelled into the limelight and physicians around the world were soon experimenting with the use of cocaine in a wide range of conditions (Karch, 1993).

The first reports of cocaine toxicity appeared less than one year after Koller and Freud's papers were published. An article in the *British Medical Journal* described the toxic reactions associated with cocaine use in ophthalmologic surgery (anon, 1885). None of the negative reports appeared to have much impact. Patent medicine manufacturers continued to cash in on the popularity of coca by replacing low-concentration cocaine extracts with high concentrations of refined cocaine hydrochloride. Thousands of cocaine-containing patent medicines flooded the market (Karch, 1993).

Until the early 1900s, cocaine had been taken mainly by mouth or by injection. The fact that the first cases of septal perforation and collapse were not reported until 1904 suggests that "snorting" had only become popular a year or so earlier (Maier, 1926). The first human autopsy study was published in 1922. Bravetta and Invernizzi described a 28-year-old man who had been sniffing cocaine regularly for some months before his death. He neither drank nor used other drugs (Bravetta & Invernizzi, 1922). Between 1928 and 1973 there was only one reported fatality, and it involved a surgical misadventure. In 1977, Suarez first described the "body packer" syndrome, where death results from the rupture of cocaine-filled condoms in the smuggler's intestines (Suarez, Arango & Lester, 1977). The absence of case reports reflected a decline in use. Significant toxicity from the use of coca leaf and coca leaf extract was not a problem in the United States until purified cocaine became available. The small amounts of cocaine in patent-medicines were apparently harmless, but the huge amounts of purified cocaine that could be ingested represented a quantum leap in dosage. With the appearance of crack cocaine in 1986, another order of magnitude increase in dosage occurred (Jekel, Allen, & Podlewski, 1986). Cocaine-related deaths and injuries are a product of more people using more of the drug in a more effective manner (Karch, 1993).

Coca leaf has grown in the Andean subregion for thousands of years. Early explorers found it all along the eastern curve of the Andes, from the Straits of Magellan to the borders of the Caribbean. Coca grows best on the moist, warm, slopes of mountains ranging from 1,500 to 5,000 feet. Coca shrubs grow to heights of 6–8 feet.

Major growing areas in Bolivia share many characteristics. Yungas, which is close to La Paz, has an average annual rainfall of 45 inches and Chapare, which is close to Cochabamba, has an annual rain fall of 102 inches. The plantations in Yungas can be harvested three times a year. Each harvest yields from 1 to 1.5 tons per hectare (890 to 1,336 pounds per acre) per year. The Chapare plantations are harvested four times a year with yield of 2 to 3 tons per hectare (1,789 to 2,672 pounds per acre) per year. The average coca plantation will produce for about 20 years, but after about the tenth year, its yield steadily declines. More than 60 percent of all coca leaf is grown in Peru, with another 22 percent coming from Bolivia, and 15 percent from Columbia. During processing, 400 pounds of leaf will yield 1 to 2 kg of coca paste (Abruzzese, 1989).

Cocaine extraction is a two- or three-step process, carried out in a series of laboratories. The first steps occur on site. Immediately after harvesting, leaves are placed in a shallow pit lined with heavy plastic, and then soaked in a solution of water and lime for 3 or 4 days. Gasoline or kerosene is then added to the mixture to extract the nitrogenous alkaloids.

The extracted coca leaf is discarded and sulfuric acid is added to the extract. The gasoline or kerosene is removed and the remaining solution is made alkaline by the addition of lime, causing the more basic alkaloids to precipitate out. This crude form of cocaine, called coca paste, is allowed to dry in the sun. It takes between 100 and 150 kilograms of dry leaf to produce 1 kilogram of "pasta" (Brewer & Allen, 1991).

The site where the initial steps occur is referred to as "pasta lab." Laborers, called pisacoca, keep the alkali-coca leaf mulch mixed by stirring it with their hands and feet. The fluid is very corrosive and causes ulcers. The picacocas tolerate the ulcers only because they are given a constant supply of coca paste to smoke (Weatherford, 1988).

Once the pasta is prepared, the clandestine manufacturer has two options. The pasta may be further purified at a base lab, or the producer may go directly to a crystal lab. At base labs, pasta is dissolved in dilute sulfuric acid. Potassium permanganate is added until the solution turns pink, thereby destroying the cinnamoyl-cocaine isomers present as impurities in the pasta. The reddish-pink solution is allowed to stand, then it is filtered and the filtrate is made basic with ammonia. Cocaine base precipitates out. The precipitate is filtered, washed with water, then dried. Finally, it is dissolved in diethyl ether or acetone. After filtering, concentrated hydrochloric acid and acetone are added, causing purified cocaine hydrochloride to precipitate out (Plowman & Rivier, 1983). This final step may be done on site or the semipurified cocaine may be transported to a "crystal lab," usually located in one of the larger Colombian cities. As much as 50 kg may be processed at one time. The semipurified cocaine is dissolved in a solvent, often ether. Hydrochloric acid is added, along with acetone, and white crystals precipitate out. The crystals are collected by filtration. Traces of the solvent remain and their presence can sometimes be used to identify the origin of cocaine samples. In producing countries there is a significant market for the semipurified paste itself. Paste is smoked rolled up in pieces of newspaper or packed into cigarettes (Paly, Van Dyke, Jatlow & Byck, 1980).

The purity of confiscated cocaine is considered to be a good general indicator of availability. At wholesale levels, kilogram quantities that had been averaging 80 percent during 1990 increased to 87 percent purity during 1991. At the retail level, ounce specimens, which had been only 58 percent pure in 1990, had increased to 70 percent purity by 1991. The purity of the gram-sized samples sold on the street has increased by only 2 percent during the same period. From 1990 through the first nine months of 1991, the price in the United States for kilogram quantities ranged from $11,000 to $40,000 (Karch, 1993).

Crack Cocaine

In the early 1970s, the organized production of cocaine lowered its street cost and increased its availability just as a wave of increased drug acceptance spread across the United States. Availability, coupled with social acceptance of drug use in general, led to a resurgence of cocaine use (Musto, 1991). As an acid or hydrochloride salt, the drug could be snorted or injected but not smoked. From the user's point of view, it was still expensive, compared to heroin, and the pleasurable effects did not last as long. Crack cocaine, on the other hand, can be smoked. Rather than chemically decomposing, crack cocaine melts at 98° C and vaporizes. The vapor is absorbed by all mucous membranes and the lungs, rapidly producing a euphoric sensation which may last as long as 30 minutes. For many people, this effect is so overwhelming that they will sell or do anything to get more of the drug. The euphoric effect depends on the release of dopamine, and other neurotransmitters, especially in the pleasure centers of the brain. Drug abusers state that using the drug induces a feeling of power, self-esteem, sensual well-being or sexual prowess, although higher levels or prolonged use have an adverse effect on sexuality (Stephens, 1993).

Cocaine hydrochloride has been snorted or injected for years. However, by mixing it with ammonium hydroxide and then extracting the cocaine with ethyl ether it could be changed into basic form and smoked. Smoking imparted a faster high, a more powerful onset of the drug's effect, and a longer-lasting high than the hydrochloride salt given by injection. Inexperienced or intoxicated persons handling flammable solvents and open flames as they heated the extracted crystals of base on a pipe to vaporize and inhale the fumes suffered severe burns when the flammable solvent caught fire (Stephens, 1993).

As the amount of available cocaine became greater, prices dropped. A safer way to manufacture base cocaine, using household chemicals, was developed. Mixing the alkaline solution of cocaine with common sodium bicarbonate and heating the combination results in an opaque mass which is broken into chunks or rocks. Stoves were used to drive off the water and fix the base to the cocaine molecules, but microwave ovens are now commonly used for that purpose.

Using Cocaine

Snorting involves making a "line" on a flat surface such as glass or a mirror. The thin 2–3 inch-long strip (the width of a match stick) of cocaine powder is inhaled (snorted). Single-edged razor blades are used to finely chop the cocaine powder and to construct the "line" for snorting. A rolled dollar bill (the denomination of the bill is status related), soda straw, glass, silver or gold tube, or miniature spoon may be used for snorting. Regular users may grow the fingernail on the little finger of the dominant hand for use as an ersatz spoon for "tooting" cocaine.

The typical intravenous user injects with an insulin syringe, leaving a pin prick size puncture site. Since cutting agents are usually soluble, the skin reaction, granulomas, and needle tracks seen with other drugs are not common in the case of cocaine.

Crack cocaine can be smoked in any manner that results in vaporizing the drug. It may be mixed with tobacco in a cigarette, in a regular pipe, in a pipe with a screen to hold the tobacco and drug, or in a special crack pipe. Used by itself, the drug can be heated with a propane torch. Propane is preferred because other fuels are thought to impart an unpleasant taste to the vapors.

It is dangerous to taste any powder found at a crime scene, regardless of the media's common portrayal of police tasting suspected drug substances.

Legal problems: No other controlled substance has been subjected to as many different types of scientific and legal attacks in court as has cocaine. The reasons for this include the existence of numerous isomers of cocaine and the need to eliminate them analytically, the classification of cocaine as a narcotic for legal purposes, the perception by the public of cocaine as being among the more dangerous drugs, and the relatively high income level of cocaine abusers, who have the resources to mount vigorous court defenses. The result has been increased awareness on the part of drug chemists of the potential problems in cocaine analysis and consequently, an increase in the number of tests performed on routine cocaine cases. This, in turn, has caused increases in the cost of cocaine analyses through greater time expenditures in the laboratory and in court and increased cost for instrumentation and supplies.

In some jurisdictions, most or all of these legal and scientific problems have been rendered moot through court decisions, changes in the wording of the cocaine laws, and increased levels of analysis. In other places, the arguments are alive and well.

The major technical defenses in cocaine cases can be grouped into the following categories:

1. isomers defense 1: diasteroisomers
2. isomers defense 2: enanitomers
3. classification of cocaine as a narcotic
4. the issue of aggregate weight

Isomer Defense 1: Diastereoisomers

Diastereoisomers are chemical compounds with the same chemical formula (isomers), having the same atomic bond arrangement, but differ in the orientation of the molecules in three dimensional space (stereo-isomers). These isomers are not mirror images (mirror image isomers are enantiomers). In general, diastereoisomers differ from one another in both physical and chemical properties. The diastereoisomers are not available commercially so that the chemist has nothing with which to compare a sample of alleged cocaine to positively eliminate the diastereo-isomers. It is not enough that an analytical scheme yield results that are consistent with cocaine. The scheme must also be inconsistent with all other substances, especially cocaine's isomers. Even with the increased knowledge of the chemical and physical behavior of the disastereoisomers of cocaine, there are many chemists who are still vulnerable to this challenge because they have not kept up with the literature or because they are not knowledgeable enough to grasp the concept of stereochemistry.

Some state legislatures have responded to this chemical defense argument by changing the wording of the cocaine laws. In Michigan, for example, cocaine and all its stereoisomers are now controlled within Schedule II.

Isomers Defense 2: Enantiomers

Since cocaine laws describe cocaine as a derivative of coca leaves and only l-cocaine is a coca leaf derivative, this challenge was based on the failure of the chemist to eliminate enantiomeric d-cocaine (mirror image). The most common response of the laboratories that were affected by the challenge was to add at least one test to the analytical scheme which would be able to eliminate d-cocaine from consideration.

Classification of Cocaine as a Narcotic

The legal classification of cocaine, a central nervous system stimulant, as a narcotic by some jurisdictions is improper from a medical standpoint. The term "narcotic" has had a legal connotation for many years as a catch-all term for dangerous drugs. There is no indication that any legislature meant to imply by this designation that cocaine is a narcotic medically. The argument of the misclassification is based on the fact that cocaine, classified as a narcotic in the criminal code, is therefore treated as a narcotic for punishment purposes. Opponents of this misclassification claim that it is unfair to treat cocaine in this manner, since it is not, in their opinion, as dangerous a drug as heroin and the other narcotics. The argument has had only very limited success in the courts. Most courts have ruled that the legislature has every right to label cocaine as a narcotic for sanctioning purposes as long as there is no medical intent to classify cocaine as narcotic.

The Aggregate Weight Issue

Some states have passed laws linking the penalty for possession or distribution of the drugs to the amount present in the case. The laws are written in such a fashion that the crucial weight is that of the whole exhibit, not the weight of the controlled substance. Under this sentencing scheme, 100 g of an exhibit of 1 percent cocaine would carry the same penalty as 100 g of pure cocaine. Another issue surrounding weight has to do with those sentencing schemes that enhance the penalty based on weight. The forensic chemist will be asked to testify in cases where the aggregate weight is near the borderline between the two classes. Since the weighing operation is the responsibility of the laboratory, it is certain that there will be challenges to the accuracy of the balances used to weigh the exhibits.

Drug Regulation

Federal law establishes five schedules of classification for dangerous substances on the basis of a drug's potential for abuse, potential for physical and psychological dependence and medical value. The criminal penalties for the manufacture, sale, or possession of controlled dangerous substances are related to the schedule as well. The most severe penalties are associated with drugs listed in schedules I and II.

Schedule I. Schedule I drugs are deemed to have a high potential for abuse, no accepted medical use, and lack accepted safe protocols for use in treatment under medical supervision. Drugs controlled under this schedule include heroin, methaqualone, and LSD.

Schedule II. Schedule II drugs have a high potential for abuse but have a current acceptable medical use. These drugs have a significant potential for severe psychological or physical dependence. Schedule II drugs include opium and its derivatives not listed in schedule I, cocaine, methadone, phencyclidine, most amphetamine preparations, and most barbiturate preparations containing amobarbital, secobarbital, and pentobarbital. Dronabinol, the synthetic equivalent of the active ingredient in marijuana, has been placed in schedule II in recognition of its growing medical uses in treating glaucoma and chemotherapy patients (Saferstein, R 1993).

Schedule III. Schedule III drugs have a potential for abuse less than those in schedules I and II, and have a currently accepted medical use.

These drugs have a potential for a low to moderate physical dependence or high psychological dependence. Schedule III controls all barbiturate preparations not covered under schedule II and certain codeine reparations. Anabolic steroids were added to the schedule in 1991.

Schedule IV. Schedule IV drugs have a low potential for abuse and have a current medical use. The abuse of these drugs may lead to limited dependence relative to schedule III drugs. Drugs controlled in this schedule include proposyphene (Darvon®), phenobarbital, and tranquilizers such as meprobamate (Miltown®), diazepam (Valium®), and chlordiazepoxide (Librium®).

Schedule V. Schedule V drugs have low abuse potential, have medical use, and have less potential for producing dependence than schedule IV drugs. Schedule V controls certain opiate drug mixtures that contain nonnarcotic medicinal ingredients.

The Controlled Substance Act includes a provision stipulating that an offense involving a controlled substance analog, a chemical substance substantially similar in chemical structure to a controlled substance, shall trigger penalties as if it were a controlled substance listed in schedule I. This section is designed to combat the proliferation of so-called designer drugs. Designer drugs are substances that are chemically related to some controlled drugs and are pharmacologically very potent. These substances are manufactured by skilled individuals in clandestine laboratories, with the knowledge that their products will not be covered by the schedules of the Controlled Substances Act.

Recent changes in the Controlled Substances Act reflect an effort to decrease the prevalence of clandestine drug laboratories designed to manufacture controlled substances. The act now regulates the manufacture and distribution of precursors, the chemical compounds used by clandestine drug laboratories to synthesize drugs of abuse.

Examination of the Forensic Chemist

    college degree or on the job training
    post graduate work
    number of university chemistry hours
Q. Number of prior court appearances
Q. For who?
Q. Have any of the following courses been attended
    drug assay
    spectroscopy

botany

organic qualitative analysis

Q. Have you had any specific analytical chemical education for abused drugs?

Q. Do you or does your laboratory have a general protocol that it employs in the analysis of drugs?

Hopefully a general protocol similar to the following is prescribed:

1. Visual examination of the exhibit is the first test, followed by examination under low-power microscope. Gross and net weight is determined.

2. Examination proceeds from the general to the specific. Each test narrows down the number of possible substances which the drug could be. The progression from general to specific is known as the "general unknown" analysis and consists of the following:

   a. preliminary visual examination of all exhibits

   b. weighing of all exhibits

   c. selection of representative samples

   d. screening tests (usually spot tests)

   e. separation tests

   f. confirmatory tests

   g. quantitative analysis

3. Analytical schemes and tests conform to those already in general practice in the field. Courts and juries will put more weight on the results obtained from an analytical scheme if other chemists in other laboratories are doing substantially the same tests. The defense will attempt to present evidence of other tests and examinations that could have been performed; it is the responsibility of the testifying chemists to know which tests are being generally used.

4. Whenever possible, at least one test should be specific for the drug in question. Such a confirmatory test should be an analytically different type of test from those used in the presumptive and separation phases of the examination. In most cases in drug analysis, the confirmatory tests of choice are infrared spectrophotometry and gas chromatography-mass spectroscopy. The presence of a confirmatory test in an analytical scheme is more reliable and easier to defend in court than is a scheme that is a collection of presumptive tests.

5. Some attention must be paid to conserving the drugs present in an exhibit.

6. If there is not sufficient material present to subject the drug to a complete analysis, nondestructive tests should be performed in preference to destructive ones.

7. Tests should do double duty. Tests that are used for quantitative analysis such as gas chromatography are also good qualitative tests if run properly (Saferstein, 1988).

Q. Does your laboratory have a uniform set of tests which must be performed by all chemists before a suspected sample is reported as an illegal drug?

Q. Did you conduct gross morphological analysis on the suspected controlled substance, and if so, what information was yielded?

A. The conclusions reached by the analyst must be consistent with the analysts training and experience. In particular, the results should include mention of diluents, plant fragments, or dirt being in the sample.

Q. Did the analyst record her observations in a notebook?

A. If so, that notebook is discoverable by the defendant and the witness may be examined pertaining to any notations in the notebook?

Q. Did you conduct microscopic analysis on the suspected controlled substance, and if so, what information was yielded by this analysis?

A. What specifically did the analyst see? If marijuana was examined, were cystolith hairs seen? Many plants have cystolith hairs. Often the analyst will make the identification of a drug based on nonspecific spot tests with no confirmation. Horse urine will test positive on the Duquenois-Levine test and other noncannabis plants have cystolith hairs.

Q. Did you conduct a thin-layer chromatography on the suspected controlled substance, and if so, what information did this test reveal?

A. TLC is a method of separation; absent a standard run simultaneously, identification is presumptive. Many chemicals have the same Rf (retention time).

Q. Did you make a photocopy of the chromatographic plate?

A. Obviously, such a photocopy will go a long way in defusing defense arguments.

Q. Did you conduct a spectrophotometric analysis on the suspected controlled substance and what information was yielded by this analysis?

A. Two questions often asked by the defense are: if mass spectroscopy was the analysis performed, was the observed spectrum from the defendant's sample, or could it have been from a trace residue in the injector? Was a background spectrum obtained?

Q. How many different samples have you tested during your career?

A. The answer to this question will serve to bolster the witnesses testimony. However, the defense will use the answer to this question to the witnesses disadvantage. If the number is great the defense will ask how it is possible, absent laboratory notes, to recollect all observations about the sample in question. The point will be made to the jury that confusing test results may be possible considering the large number of tests performed without referring to solid lab notes. If the prudent analyst has kept lab notes, those notes are discoverable and will be provided to the expert for the defense. Often new errors in testing can be discovered and in many cases the lab notes do not substantiate the analyst's recollection, or identification. Either as a result of incomplete or poorly kept records or poorly conducted tests.

The defense will also inquire of you:

a. the number of analyses which you performed in which you were unable to identify the suspected controlled substance, and

b. the number of identifications that were the result of false positives.

Q. Who prepared each of the reagents used?

Q. Where were they from the time of preparation to the time of use?

Q. Were each of the reagents tested on a control sample to assure viability?

Q. Did you attempt to identify any other or all substances in the sample other than the suspected controlled substance?

A. State the identity of each such substance.

Q. How was identification of these contaminants made?

Q. Could contaminants effect analysis results?

Q. State the date and time you received the suspected controlled substance.

Q. Describe the condition of the sample upon receipt.

A. The description should remove any question as to tampering, cross contamination, and sufficiency of sample.

Q. From who did you receive the substances?

Q. Were you told the suspected identity of the substances, before or during your analysis?

A. Defendants believe that analysts "find what they are looking for" that is why a "general unknown" protocol is applied and explained to investigators, prosecutors, and defendants.

Q. Did you preserve the substance upon which you conducted your procedures, if so where are they?

A. The defense will most likely have already filed motions to be present at the time of testing, to restrict destructive testing, and to have defense experts conduct their own tests. However, the request may be reserved until the time of trial as a delaying mechanism.

Q. To who did you transfer these substances?

Q. When did you transfer these substances?

Q. What was the condition of the sample when it was transferred?

Q. Where was each substance stored while in your custody?

Q. Who had access to the substances while in your custody?

Q. What records reflect the storage and access to these substances?

A. All these questions deal with chain of custody issues.

Q. When did you tell the prosecutor of your results?

A. The prosecutor has a responsibility to use due diligence in advising the defendant of testing and test results. This question can be use by the defense to establish less than due diligence on the part of the prosecutor.

The identification of the suspected controlled substances must be based on a "reasonable scientific certainty," and that language should be used when framing the response to the prosecutor's question pertaining to an expert opinion as to the identification of the suspected controlled substance.

Defense lawyers are convinced that forensic analysts seem to be more intent on proving their point than ensuring accurate identification. The media sensationalizes those cases where incompetent analysis does occur. From a defendant's perspective it would be legal malpractice to uncritically accept the results of a forensic expert. The expert can expect to have her educational background thoroughly investigated, including less than favorable comments solicited from former professors, classmates, and coworkers. On the stand, the expert can expect to be thoroughly examined as to prosecutorial bias; personal bias; the knowledge of the basis for the results put forth; the data suggesting the unreliability of many tests; and data suggesting that even when the proper test procedure is selected, there is significant error in the performance and analysis of the results of the test procedures.

REFERENCES

Abruzzese, R. 1989. Coca-leaf production in the countries of the Andean subregion. *Bulletin of Narcotics,* 41:95.

Anon (1872). Coca. *Lancet,* May 25, p. 746.

Anon (1885). Toxic action of cucaine. *British Medical Journal,* November 21, p. 983.

Austin, J., & Krisberg, B. W. 1981. Stronger and different nets: The dialectics of criminal justice reform. *Journal of Research on Crime and Delinquency,* p. 170.

Baden, M.M. 1980. Investigation of deaths from drug abuse. In Spitz, Werner U., & Fisher, R.S. eds. *Medicolegal Investigation of Death,* 2nd. ed. Springfield, IL: Charles C Thomas, p. 544.

Balbanova, S. Parsche, F., & Pirsig, W. 1992. First identification of drugs in Egyptian mummies. *Naturwissenschaften,* 79:358.

Bravata, E., & Invernizzi, G. 1922. Cocainismo. Osservazione cliniche ricerche sperimentali en anatomo-patoligiche. *Note Riv Psichiatr,* 10:543.

Brewer, L., & Allen, A. 1991. N-formyl cocaine: a study of cocaine comparison parameters. *Journal of Forensic Science,* 36:697.

Derlet, R.W., & Heischober, B. 1990. Methamphetamine-stimulant of the 1990s? *Western Journal of Medicine,* 153(6):625.

Down, G.J., & Gwyn, S.A. 1975. Investigation of direct thin-layer chromatography-mass spectrometry as a drug analysis technique. *Journal of Chromatography,* 103:208.

Freud, S. 1884. Uber coca. *Wien Centralblatt fur die ges therapie,* 2:289.

Collins, J. 1982. *Criminal Justice Clients in Drug Treatment.* Research Triangle Park, NC: Research Triangle Institute. pp. 92, 93.

Finn, P. 1989. Decriminalization of Public Drunkenness: Response of the Healthcare System. *Journal of Studies on Alcohol,* 46(1) p. 7.

Galvin, J.J. 1977. *Alternatives to Prosecution: Instead of Jail.* Washington, D.C.: U.S. Government Printing Office, vol. 3, p. 42.

Hayes & Associates, Inc. 1987. *TASC Annual Evaluation Report.* Winston Salem, N.C.

Karch, S.B. 1993. *The Pathology of Drug Abuse.* Boca Raton, FL: CRC.

Klein, M., Kruegel, A. V., & Sobol, S.P. 1979. *Instrumental Applications in Forensic Drug Chemistry.* Washington, D.C.: U.S. Government Printing Office.

Lemert, E.M. 1981. Diversion in juvenile justice: What hath been wrought. *Journal of Research in Crime and Delinquency,* 14:40.

Leonard, R. 1972. Deferred prosecution program. *The Prosecutor,* 8(4), p. 36.

Maier, H.W. 1926. *Der Kokainismus* (O.J. Kalant from the German 1926 edition, Trans.) Toronto: Addiction Research Foundation.

Mortimer, W.G. 1901. Peru: The history and regulation of a dangerous drug. *Cornell Law Review,* 58:537.

Mullen, J. 1974. *The Dilemma of Diversion.* Washington, D.C.: U.S. Government Printing Office, pp. 91, 92.

Musto, D.F. 1973. *The American Disease—Origins of Narcotic Control.* New Haven, CT: Yale.

Musto, D.F. 1991. Opium, cocaine and marijuana in American history. *Scientific American,* 265(1):40–47.

Nieman, A. 1860. *Uber eine neue organische Base in den Cocablattern.* Gottingen: E.A. Huth, Inaug-diss.

Nimmer, R. 1974. *Diversion: The Search for Alternative Forms of Prosecution.* Chicago: American Bar Foundation, p. 76.

Noyes, H. 1884. Muriate of cocaine as a local anaesthetic to the cornea; The ophthalmological Congress in Heidelberg. *Medical Record,* October 11, 17:418.

Plowman, T., & Rivier, L. 1983. Cocaine and cinnamoylcocaine of Erythroxylum species. *Ann Botany,* 51:641.

President's Commission on Law Enforcement and Administration of Justice. *The Challenge of Crime in a Free Society.* Washington, D.C.: U.S. Government Printing Office, p. 134.

Saferstein, R. 1988. *Forensic Science Handbook II.* Englewood Cliffs, NJ: Prentice Hall.

Saferstein, R. 1995. *Criminalistics: An Introduction to Forensic Science.* Englewood Cliffs, NJ: Prentice Hall.

Scherzer, K. 1861. *Narrative of the circumnavigation of the globe by the Austrian Frigate Novara.* London, Saunders, Otley.

Siegel, J.S. 1988. Forensic identification of controlled substances, in *Forensic Science Handbook,* Vol. 2, Saferstein, R., ed. Englewood Cliffs, NJ: Prentice Hall.

Suarez, C., Arango, A., & Lester, J. 1977. Cocaine-condom ingestion. *JAMA,* 238:1391.

Thornton, J.I., & Nakamura, G.R. 1972. The identification of marijuana. *Journal of Forensic Science Society,* 14:461.

Vernon's Annotated Texas Statutes, *Code of Criminal Procedure,* Article 42.12 (1994).

Weatherford, J. 1988. Indian givers. *The Drug Connection,* p. 198. New York: Crown.

Yinon, J., & Zitrin, S. 1977. Processing and interpreting mass spectral data in forensic identification of drugs and explosives. *Journal of Forensic Science,* 22(4):741.

Chapter 12

FIREARMS

Firearms Identification

Identification of firearms is often incorrectly referred to as ballistics. Ballistics is the study of projectiles in motion. Ballistics studies involve four specific and discreet regimes:

Interior ballistics — the study of the motion of projectiles in the gun barrel and the conversion of chemical energy of the cartridge propellant to the kinetic energy of the projectile.

Exterior ballistics — deals with projectile flight from the muzzle end to the target considering air resistance, gravity, windage and elevation.

Terminal ballistics — is the study of the interaction of the projectile with the target.

Transitional ballistics — deals with the passage of the projectile from interior ballistics to exterior ballistics.

Firearms identification is primarily concerned with the identification of firearms from their fired bullets and cartridges with only tangential reference to ballistics (Rowe, 1988).

Firearm Types

The firearm examiner generally comes into contact with five types of firearms:

Pistols — handheld firearms designed to be fired with one hand. Pistols are either single shot, single action revolvers, double action revolvers, or self-loading pistols commonly referred to as "automatic" pistols. If a pistol was fully automatic, it would continue to fire as long as the trigger was depressed and ammunition was still available. Pistols that are called "automatics" are incorrectly identified and should be referred to as semiautomatic or self-loading. Some self-loading or semiautomatic pistols store the recoil energy of the barrel in coiled springs, then use this energy to extract the expended cartridge casing from the firing chamber, eject it from the weapon, cock the firing mechanism preparatory to firing the next round, and load a live round into the pistol's firing chamber. Self-loading pistols may also work on a blowback principle. In blowback-operated pistols, the bolt and barrel are held together only by the inertia of the bolt and the pressure of the recoil spring. The recoil of the cartridge provides the energy for extraction, ejection, cocking, and loading (Wilbur, 1977). Revolvers may be either single or double action. Single-action revolvers must be manually cocked before each firing. Double-action revolvers are cocked by the pull of the trigger. There is a high-powered hunting pistol that fires a single high velocity rifle cartridge. This weapon is a synthesis of the power of a rifle with the portability of a handgun. It is breech-loaded with a single cartridge and must be "broken" open to eject each round and to load each new round.

Rifles — shoulder mounted weapons designed to be used with two hands fired from the shoulder position. There are single-shot rifles, lever-action rifles (feed by magazine), bolt-operated rifles (feed by clip or magazine), semiautomatic rifles (feed by clip or magazine), and automatic rifles (feed by clip or belt). Lever-action and bolt-action rifles use the manual manipulation of a lever or turnbolt to extract and eject expended cartridges, cock the firing mechanism, and load a live round into the firing chamber. Semiautomatic and automatic rifles are blowback, recoil, or gas-operated. Gas-operated rifles use a portion of the hot propellant gases tapped from the barrel by a gas piston to extract, cock, and load. Automatic rifles use limited-capacity magazines, while light machine guns generally fire belted ammunition.

Assault Rifles — During the two decades following World War II, the world's armies replaced their bolt-action and semiautomatic rifles with assault rifles.

Machine Guns — Submachine guns and machine guns are fully automatic weapons. Machine guns load their ammunition from magazines or from belts. Because of the recoil, machine guns are fired from a tripod or bipod (unless you are John Wayne or Rambo). Submachine guns are automatic weapons to be fired while being held in the hands. Submachine guns fire pistol cartridges (Hogg, 1977).

All the types of weapons discussed to this point are rifled firearms. Their barrels have a set of spiraling lands and grooves within them. The lands of the rifling are the raised ridges that bite into the surface of the bullet and give it a rotational motion as it moves down the barrel; the grooves of the rifling are the recessed areas between the lands. The rifling grips the fired bullet and engraves its surface with land and groove impressions. The microscopic imperfections of the rifling produce patterns of parallel scratches called striations or striae in these land and groove impressions.

Rifled firearms may be characterized by their caliber or bore diameter. The bore diameter of a rifled barrel is the diameter measured from the tops of opposing lands. Caliber and bore diameters of American and British weapons are normally given in inches, while those of other weapons are given millimeters. Many manufactures and users express caliber in both inches and millimeters.

Shotguns — Like rifles, these weapons are designed to fire from the shoulder, but they are a smooth-bore weapon which has no lands or grooves in the barrel. Unless firing a "slug" round, shotguns fire multiple projectiles, called pellets. Shotguns may have single or double barrels. Single-barrel shotguns may be single-shot weapons or repeaters. Repeating shotguns have magazines from which rounds are loaded into the weapon either manually with a pump action or semiautomatically (Hatcher, Jury, & Weller, 1977).

Shotguns are characterized by bore diameter. These diameters are expressed in "gauge" measurements. When all firearms fired spherical lead balls, their bore diameters or gauges were expressed as the number of such lead balls that could be made from 1 pound of lead, e.g., 10 lead balls having the same diameter as the interior of the barrel of a 10-gauge shotgun should weigh 1 pound. The exception to this measurement scheme is the 410-gauge shotgun which has a bore diameter of .410 inches (Nonte 1973).

Making Firearms

Currently there are three methods of mass producing firearm barrels:

Broaching — This process begins with a piece of round steel bar which is drilled through its length. The drilling diameter of the drill bits is increased until the diameter of the hole is of the desired diameter (remember the caliber is based on the diameter between the lands). The grooves are now cut with a tool called a gang broach. The metal in the grooves is removed as the teeth of the gang broach is forced by hydraulic pressure through the barrel. Successive cutting disks have teeth that project outward increasing distances until the desired groove depth is reached.

Button Rifling — This process also begins with the round piece of steel bar drilled through its length. The diameter of the hole drilled, however, is smaller that the desired final caliber. The barrel is rifled by forcing a very hard rifling button made of tungsten carbide, bearing a negative impression of the lands and grooves of the rifling through. It is simultaneously rifled and expanded to its final caliber (Nonte, 1973).

Hammer Forging — Again, the process is begun by drilling out a piece of round steel bar stock. The diameter of the hole is greater than the desired finished diameter. The barrel is slipped over a mandrel having the desired rifling characteristics and then hammered down over the mandrel to produce the rifling and the final bore diameter (Nonte, 1973).

The firearms examiner needs to know how certain components of a firearm's firing mechanisms are manufactured. The breechblock is the part of a firearm's action that supports the base of the cartridge in the chamber when it is fired. The firing pin is the part of the firearm's action that strikes the cartridge primer in order to fire it. Breechblocks may be finished with an end mill or turned on a lathe. They may be finished by hand filing. The breechblocks of semiautomatic pistols are usually finished by filing vertically down through the ejector slot in the slide. This gives a characteristic direction to the striations imparted to the soft metal of the primer caps of fired cartridges. Firing pins are turned on lathes or filed flat by hand (Hatcher, Jury, & Weller, 1977).

Ammunition

The three most commonly used bullets in rifled firearms are: lead alloy, semijacketed, and fully jacketed. Lead-alloy bullets are harder than pure lead bullets and less likely to produce lead fouling of the rifling. Pure lead .22 caliber bullets may be coated with a very thin film of copper. This film has a tendency to flake off the surface of the bullet, removing the striations produced by the rifling (Mathews, 1962).

Jacketed bullets consist of a lead core surrounded by a jacket of harder material. Jackets are commonly made of a copper-nickel alloy or mild steel. Semiautomatic pistols use fully-jacketed bullets because the noses of the bullets must slide up a ramp as rounds are chambered (Nonte, 1973).

Semijacketed bullets have a copper-alloy or aluminum jacket that covers only part of the bullets' surface. The jacket covers the side of the bullet, leaving the nose exposed. Semijacketed bullets are designed to mushroom on impact, so that most of their kinetic energy is expended in the target. Hollow-point bullets have a hollow in the exposed lead core at the nose of the bullet. Soft-point bullets are semijacketed bullets with a soft metal plug inserted in their noses. Both the soft metal insert and the thinner jacket facilitate bullet expansion.

Another approach to obtaining proper expansion of a semijacketed bullet is to place a hard metal insert in the nose of the bullet. Bronze-point bullets are special bullets intended for hunting. Upon impact the bronze point is forced back into the bullet's core, causing it to mushroom.

Frangible bullets are composed of powdered iron or powdered iron with an organic binder (Graham, Petty, Flohr, & Peterson, 1966). These bullets are used in shooting galleries, and in urban law enforcement, they disintegrate on impact without the danger of a ricochet or penetration through thin walls. Steel-jacketed, armor-piercing bullets have an extremely hard steel jacket surrounding a tungsten carbide core. The hardness of the jacket generally precludes the rifling of the weapon firing such ammunition from marking it extensively (Rowe, 1988). A special purpose bullet, called an "accelerator cartridge," has been developed by Remington. The projectile is a normal .223 caliber, soft-point bullet pressed into a .30 caliber plastic grommet (sabot). Upon firing, the bullet and the sabot exit the barrel. At some distance from the muzzle, the bullet separates from the sabot and continues along its trajectory as the sabot falls away. There would be no identifiable rifling marks on such a bullet.

Bullets may have round noses, pointed noses, or flat noses. Their bases may be flat or boattailed. The shape of a bullet is dictated by a number of considerations, including aerodynamics. Boattailed bullets are designed to reduce turbulence in the wake of the bullet thereby reducing bullet drag.

Propellants

Smokeless powders are classified as degressive burning, neutral burning, or progressive burning. Degressive-burning powder grains burn from the outside in; the surface area consequently decreases and along with it the burning rate of the grain. Solid, uncoated powder grains burn in a degressive manner. Neutral-burning powders have perforations so that the burning of the outside of the grains is balanced by the burning on the interiors of the perforations; the net effect is that the surface area remains relatively constant, as does the burning rate. Progressive-burning powders are coated with a deterrent material that slows down the initial burning of the powder grains; once the deterrent coating is burned off, the burning rate goes up (O'Connor, 1965).

The manipulation of powder burning rates through variations in grain size, shape, and coating is necessary because of the variations in caliber, barrel length, and chamber size among firearms. When a weapon is fired, the propellant begins to burn, generating hot gases. These gases expand, forcing the bullet from the cartridge casing into the barrel. Once the bullet begins to move, the volume available to the gases generated by the burning propellant increases. If the production of gases stopped immediately after the unseating of the bullet into the barrel, further travel of the bullet down the barrel would cause the pressure behind it to fall. At the point where the pressure exerted on the bullet is balanced by the frictional force acting between the bullet and the barrel, the bullet would come to a stop. To prevent this, the powder must continue to burn as the bullet proceeds down the barrel. Burning of powder after the bullet exits the barrel wastes energy because none of the energy released after the bullet exits the barrel can be converted into kinetic energy. The weight (amount), grain size, and burning rate of a cartridge's propellant must be adapted to the type of firearm intended to fire it.

Primers

The centerfire cartridge was a nineteenth century development. Eventually, it supplanted rimfire cartridges in all but the smallest calibers. Centerfire ammunition manufactured in the United States uses the Boxer primer (named for its inventor, E.M. Boxer, a colonel in the British army). This primer consists of a metal cup in which a small amount of primer material is placed between the metal cup and a small metal anvil. When the weapon is fired, its firing pin crushes the primer material between the metal of the primer cap and its anvil; the flame from the primer's explosion reaches their propellant through a large flash hole in the base of the cartridge. Centerfire cartridges manufactured outside the United States use the Berdan primer (named after its inventor, Hiram Berdan, a colonel in the Union Army during the American Civil War). Cartridge cases that accept the Berdan primer have a conical anvil as an integral part of their bases. The primer cap is simply a small metal cup containing a pellet of primer compound. Two or three small holes spaced evenly around the anvil communicate the flash of the primer through the base of the casing to the propellant (Tarassuk & Blair, 1979).

Beginning in 1900, primers based on potassium chlorate began to appear as replacements for mercury fulminate primers. The residue from chlorate primers proved as corrosive as the potassium chlorate primers. Modern primers are exclusively nonmercurial and noncorrosive. A typical centerfire primer cap produced today will contain lead styphnate, antimony sulfide, barium nitrate, and tetracene (O'Connor, 1965).

Cartridge Cases

Cartridge cases are available in a wide variety of shapes and sizes. Differently-shaped cases are intended for use in different types of firearms. Revolvers fire straight rimmed cartridges, the rim prevents the cartridge from falling through the revolver's cylinder. Self-loading pistols fire straight rimless cartridges; being clip fed there is no need for a rim. Cartridge cases may have cannelures rolled into them near their mouths; these cannelures prevent the bullet from being inadvertently pushed back into the case. Bullets may also be held in place by crimping the mouth of the cartridge onto the surface of the bullet (Rowe, 1988).

The heads of cartridges frequently bear stampings that provide information about the maker of the cartridges. For instance, the letters "R–P" on the head of a cartridge case indicates that it was made by Remington-Peters. Cartridges may also carry markings identifying the nominal caliber of its bullet.

Shotshells

Most shotgun ammunition contains pellets, some commercially available shotshells have either a single round ball or a rifled slug. Shotgun pellets come in a variety of sizes, from 000 buckshot (0.36 inches in diameter) down to Number 12 birdshot (0.05 inches in diameter). The larger the shot number the smaller the shot. The number of pellets of each size comprising the load of a shotshell depends on its gauge; for example, 12-gauge, Number 1 buckshot cartridges generally contain sixteen pellets, while a 16-gauge Number 1 buckshot cartridge generally contains 12 pellets. Shotgun pellets may be lead, lead alloy, or soft steel. Environmental concerns of water fowl eating toxic lead pellets has started a movement to replace all lead-based shot with the more environmentally sound, nontoxic, soft steel shot.

At one time, shot shells were made completely of brass. These brass shells have disappeared and have been replaced by shells with brass bases and paper or plastic sides. The pellets in the shot shell are separated from the propellant by one or more overpowder wads. These wads are used to separate the propellant gases from the shot and to cushion the pellets during their acceleration up the barrel. Wadding is made of cardboard, felt, or plastic. In modern shotshells, the pellets are held in a plastic sup that prevents their deformation by contact with the interior of the shotgun barrel. The plastic cup in some applications also serves as a wad (Rowe, 1988).

Cartridge Comparisons

The history of contemporary firearms examinations may have begun with the work of Dr. Albert Llewellyn Hall, a practicing physician in Buffalo, New York. In 1900, Dr. Hall published a paper in the *Buffalo Medical Journal* entitled "The Missile and the Weapon" (Hall, 1931). This paper concerned the possibility of matching fired bullets to the weapon that fired them based on microscopic examination of the striations on the bullets.

The first firearms case in the United States should have established the precedent for the admissibility of firearm comparison testimony. In Commonwealth v. Best (1902), the Supreme Judicial Court of the Commonwealth of Massachusetts permitted the introduction of the results of comparative examinations of markings on bullets. The case was ignored until it was rediscovered in the 1930s. The widespread acceptance of comparisons of bullet markings took nearly a quarter of a century. Courts seemed willing to allow the introduction of case comparisons but extremely reluctant to allow the admission of testimony pertaining to comparison of bullets, firing-pin impressions, or extractor marks. The first use of firing-pin impressions and extractor marks was during the investigation of the Brownsville Massacre. On the night of August 13, 1906, unknown persons shot up downtown Brownsville, Texas, killing a local barkeeper. Local civilian witnesses claimed that the shooting was carried out by black soldiers. During the ensuing Senate investigation, an Army officer and a civilian technician from the U.S. Arsenal at Springfield, Massachusetts, examined the firing impressions and extractor marks on cartridges found in the streets of Brownsville the day after the shooting. These examiners found that most of the cartridges had been fired from rifles of B Company, 25th Infantry. Being unable to fix blame on a specific soldier and believing that a conspiracy of silence existed among the personnel of the 25th Infantry, the War Department dishonorably discharged all 167 enlisted men in the battalion (Lane, 1971).

The readiness of courts to accept comparisons of marks on cartridges but not rifling marks on bullets may have been due to the greater visibility of the marks on cartridges and to the absence of a comparison microscope.

In 1929, Calvin Goddard was called to Chicago to examine the fired bullets and cartridges in the St. Valentine's Day Massacre. He was able to determine that the victims of the gangland execution had been killed with two different Thompson submachine guns, one with a 20-round magazine and the other with a 50-round drum magazine (Goddard, 1930). Goddard's impressive performance led to the establishment of a private forensic laboratory in Chicago under Goddard's direction. This laboratory later became the Chicago Police Department Crime Laboratory. 1929 was the same year that found Goddard testifying in the trial of Evans v. Commonwealth (1929). This case became the precedent-setting case for the admissibility of comparisons of rifling marks.

Examination of Firearms

As an examination protocol test-firing is not necessarily the first step. There is a possibility that the weapon was last used in a homicide involving a contact wound. If the barrel was in contact with the body upon firing, there may be blood and tissue in the barrel as a result of barrel blow-back. The weapons bore may also have fibers from its owner's pockets (Rowe, 1988). The examiner should examine the weapon for such trace evidence before further handling. There is also a possibility that the weapon, its components, and ammunition may retain fingerprints. Once the firearm has been processed for fingerprints a complete identification of the weapon should be made. The identification should include:

make or manufacturer
type (revolver, pistol, etc.)
caliber
serial number
model
number of shots
barrel length

The make, manufacturer, and model are determined from names, trademarks, and proof marks placed on various components of the weapon. The caliber of the weapon may be indicated by the name or trademark information. Weapons may be modified by fitting a different caliber barrel to the frame of a weapon.

The National Firearms Act of 1968 requires retailers to record the serial number of a weapon and the name of its purchaser. Because of the importance of the serial number to tracing a firearm's owners, criminals may remove the stamped serial numbers by grinding. If the grinding does not go deep enough into the metal, a stamped serial number may still be recovered by chemical etching, electrochemical etching, or ultrasonic cavitation. Many firearms have parts of the serial number stamped into internal components. Handguns often have the serial number stamped at different locations on the frame.

Before test-firing a weapon, the firearms examiner should test the functioning of the weapon's action and the operation of any safeties. The examiner may find that the weapon cannot be fired or cannot be fired safely. The laboratory's firearm collection may be used to find parts to render the weapon serviceable. The functioning of the weapon's safeties may be particularly important if a defendant in a shooting case later alleges that the weapon accidentally discharged.

In those cases involving accidental firings or firings that "accidentally" occur during a fight, trigger pull may be important. How much force is required to pull the trigger? The trigger pull may be measured by hanging successively increasing weight from the weapon's trigger while held vertically with the mechanism cocked. The measurement should be made with the actuating force applied to the trigger at the same place that a finger of a person firing the weapon would be placed (Rowe, 1988).

Examination of Bullets and Cartridges

In the absence of a suspect weapon, examinations are confined to the determination of class characteristics such as: caliber, direction of twist of the rifling, degree of twist, number of lands and grooves, and the widths of the lands and grooves. With these data, the firearms examiner may be able to determine the make and model of the firearm that fired the bullets. If there are two or more fired bullets that exhibit the same class characteristics, they are then examined under a comparison microscope to determine if the bullets were fired by the same weapon (Rowe, 1988).

Before class characteristics of bullets are determined, the bullets should be examined for the presence of trace evidence such as blood, hairs, fibers, wood splinters, glass particles, paint, concrete, or soil particles. Blood, hairs, and fibers may be picked up by a bullet as it passes through a shooting victim. Trace evidence such as wood splinters or glass particles embedded in a bullet indicates that the bullet may have passed through an intermediate target such as a door, wall, or window. Paint, concrete, or soil particles may be found if a bullet ricochets from a hard surface.

Determination of Caliber: The caliber of an undeformed fired bullet may be measured with a micrometer. The diameter of interest is the diameter across the land impressions (which on the expended bullet will be indentations made by the barrel lands). Allowance must be made for the fact that firearm calibers are merely nominal indications of the true bore diameters. A group of Colt pistols, all with a nominal .38 caliber, were found to have bore diameters ranging from 0.348 to 0.395 inches.

The caliber of an intact but badly deformed bullet may be estimated from its weight. Determination of caliber by weight will rarely allow the examiner to specify a particular caliber for the bullet, but certain calibers may be eliminated as possibilities. When the bullet is fragmented, an accurate weight can no longer be obtained. In such a case, the caliber of the bullet may be estimated by measuring the widths of a land impression and an adjacent groove impression (Mathews, 1962).

Counting Lands and Grooves: In bullets recovered intact, the number of lands and grooves can be determined by counting them. In cases where bullets are badly deformed, measurements of the widths of the land and groove impressions may be combined with a knowledge of the caliber of the bullet to calculate the number of lands and grooves. Because manufacturers use a specific number of grooves in their firearms and this number is generally constant for a given make and model, the number of lands and grooves is an important class characteristic (Mathews, 1962).

Rifling Twists: The direction of twist of the rifling may be determined by inspection of the fired bullet if it is not badly deformed. The rifling may spiral either to the left or to the right. Left-hand twist rifling is often referred to as Colt-type rifling, and right-hand twist rifling is often referred to as Smith and Wesson-type rifling.

Land and Groove Widths: The widths of the land and groove impression may also be measured using a filar micrometer, traveling microscope, or toolmaker's microscope. Measurements are made perpendicular to the axis of the bullet. Observing that the land impressions on a bullet are wider than the groove impression allows the firearms examiner to eliminate certain makes and models of firearms as possibly having fired the bullet. Land and groove impressions that are of markedly different width compared to the other impressions on the bullet may reflect a defect in manufacture that is sufficiently rare as to be almost unique (Mathews, 1962).

Bullet Comparison: Bullet comparisons are made using a comparison microscope. A comparison microscope consists of two compound microscopes, each with its own objectives, stage, and focusing adjustments. The microscopes are joined by a comparison bridge, a system of prism mirrors that brings the images of the two microscopes together so that they may be compared side by side through a single ocular. The images of the two microscopes may be superimposed or they may be viewed side by side with the field of view divided equally between the two microscopes. The bullets to be compared are attached to short cylindrical bullet holders. The bullet holders slip onto the shafts of the bullet manipulating mechanisms, which in turn are attached to the microscope stages. The bullet manipulating mechanisms are provided with universal joints so that the bullets may be oriented at any desired angle. Once the bullets are mounted, the examiner begins the search for matching patterns of striations. The limited expansion of jacketed bullets leads to only occasional contacts with the bottoms of the grooves; it may be that only the base is upset sufficiently to seat well in the barrel's rifling. The initial examination is most likely to render a pattern of striations near the base of the bullet. A land impression on a test-fired bullet is compared successively to each land impression on the suspect bullet until a match is obtained or it is determined that no match is possible. Once a match has been made with a pair of land impressions, the bullets are rotated synchronously to see if other matching striation patterns may be observed. If both bullets were fired from the same barrel, numerous matching patterns will be readily evident.

Marks other than land and groove striations may be observed:

1. *Skid Marks* — these marks are caused by the bullet sliding over the beginnings of the lands at the breech end of the barrel.
2. *Shaving Marks* — when a revolver bullet is not perfectly lined up through the cylinder to the barrel, the bullet will strike the edge

of the forcing cone (the flared opening in the revolver's frame in front of the cylinder where the fired bullet enters the barrel) and shave off a portion of the bullet on the side striking the forcing cone. Comparing shaved spots on a bullet may be difficult in that test firing may not result in a similar shaving. Many shots may have to be fired before a similarly shaved bullet can be obtained.

In an effort to avoid detection, criminals may flatten, bend, or shorten the barrel of a firearm. Flattened barrels may be restored to round, bent barrels may be straightened, or bullets may be forced through the barrels. Marks on bullets fired through the barrel at its original length may not match bullets fired through a shortened barrel.

The conclusions that may be reached in the examination of fired bullets may be expressed in one of three ways:

1. The questioned bullet was fired from the suspect weapon.
2. The questioned bullet was not fired from the suspect weapon.
3. The results of the examinations were inconclusive.

Examination of Cartridges

In examining a fired cartridge, the examiner using a low power microscope will note:

size
shape
type (rimmed, semirimmed, rimless, belted, rimfire, centerfire)
size of firing pin impression
position of firing pin impression
location of extractor marks
location of ejector marks

The shape and location of the firing pin impression on .22 caliber, single-shot, breechloading rifles serves to identify the make and model of the rifle. The relative positions of the extractor and ejector marks on cartridges from self-loading pistols allow the same determination (Mathews, 1962).

If a suspect firearm is available and if the class characteristics of that weapon match those found on the questioned cartridge, the examiner fires test shots with the suspect weapon in order to obtain fired cartridges for comparison purposes. The cartridges are placed inside an iris diaphragm that attaches to the bullet mounting devices in the comparison microscope. Comparisons of the various marks on the fired cartridges proceeds hierarchically:

firing pin impressions

firing pin drag marks

breechblock marks

A match of these marks would show that both cartridges were fired in the same weapon. After the above observations have been completed, the examiner compares:

extractor marks

ejector marks

chambering marks

magazine (clip) marks

A match of any of these types of marks indicates that the two cartridges had been run through the action of the same weapon but does not establish that they ever passed through the barrel.

Objectives of Firearms Examination

Whenever a firearm is discharged in the commission of a crime, physical evidence is likely to be available. Such evidence in the hands of a competent firearms examiner may answer many of the following questions:

Can the crime scene bullet or cartridge casing be linked to a suspected weapon?

Is a recovered weapon capable of being fired?

Can the weapon be accidentally fired?

What is the trigger pull?

Can the serial number be restored?

Can the type of gun be determined from an examination of the class characteristics of a bullet or cartridge recovered at the crime scene?

Legal Aspects

A Virginia case decided in 1879, *Dean v. Commonwealth* (1897), is the first in which an appellate court approved of testimony regarding the similarity between fatal and test bullets (weight was the compared variable). Beginning with *Jack v. Commonwealth*, a Kentucky case decided in 1928, expert testimony concerning firearms identification began to receive objective appellate appraisal. A year later, this same court, in

Evans v. Commonwealth (1929), rendered the first exhaustive opinion treating firearms identification as a science, and sanctioning its use for the purpose of establishing the guilt of the accused.

Presently, the accuracy of firearms identification is common knowledge, and ample case law upholds the admissibility of such evidence when presented by a qualified expert. As with other expert testimony, the witness is permitted to testify that in his/her opinion a particular bullet was fired from a certain weapon. The expert's testimony is confined to the area or areas within his/her special knowledge: for example, a witness whose expertise concerns only the identification of bullets through their microscopic markings would not be permitted to testify upon the issue as to whether a certain wound was caused by a particular weapon or that the bullet travelled a particular trajectory prior to striking the victim.

In situations where bullets are mutilated beyond identification, or the suspect weapon cannot be fired, an expert may still be permitted to testify as to other relevant matters. Even though the condition of fatal bullets may preclude an identification of the evidence weapon, an identification is permissible on the basis of cartridge case breech face imprints, firing pin impressions, or ejector and extractor marks (*Williams v. State*, 1960).

Class characteristics, in the absence of a positive identification through individual markings on a bullet, may assist the jury, are relevant and therefore admissible. A firearms expert may be able to identify only the class characteristics of a badly deformed bullet. That expert may still testify to the fact that the fatal bullets fired from a gun having characteristics similar to those of a gun obtained from the accused and had physical characteristics like those of the bullets in the accused's gun (*State v. Bayless*, 1976).

Cartridge Evidence

Identification based upon a comparison of breechface imprints, firing pin impressions, and extractor and ejector marks, was recognized by the courts in *State v. Clark*. This Oregon case, decided in 1921, allowed the expert to testify that "a peculiar mark on the brass part of the primer" matched that of the suspect weapon (*State v. Clark*, 1921).

In Montana (*State v. Vuckovich*, 1921), another case was decided based upon comparative evidence. The expert in this case testified that a peculiar crimp on an empty shell found at the scene of the murder compared to a similar mark on shells fired from the defendant's pistol. Evidence was introduced to show that "their firing marks made by the lands and grooves of the barrel of the pistol were the same" on both test and fatal bullets. This decision confirmed the use of shells and bullets as comparative evidence.

Chain of Custody

As with all evidence, the chain of custody of weapons, shells, and bullets must not only be unbroken but preserved. If it is necessary for more than one examiner to handle the evidence, that should be recorded and available to the defendant upon request. Every moment of the existence of the evidence, from the time it entered into the possession of the state (through the hands of law enforcement personnel) to its introduction at the time of trial, must be accounted for and supported by the appropriate chain of custody documentation. Long periods of time may elapse between the time shots are fired and the time the bullets or shells are collected. In *State v. Boccadoro* (1929), a bullet fired into the ground a year or two prior to the commission of the murder under investigation was recovered and identified as having been fired by the murder weapon. In *State v. Lane* (1951), shells dropped into a river during target practice months before their recovery were admitted. The time spent underwater was to be considered when assigning weight to the evidence, but it was not detrimental to admissibility. Bullets that had been fired into an oak tree four months prior to the homicide were recovered and matched, in *Commonwealth v. Ellis* (1977), to the bullets found at the scene of the crime.

The destruction of ballistics evidence before the defendant has an opportunity to conduct his/her own tests may be a violation of a defendant's constitutional rights to due process and of confrontation assurances of the Sixth Amendment. Where the destruction is inadvertent, the courts have been unsympathetic to such claims. The state had made such an inadvertent destruction of the evidence in *People v. Triplett* (1976), where the alleged murder weapon and bullets were destroyed. The defendant contended that this destruction denied him his right to confront the state's firearms expert with his own expert's analysis of the physical evidence. The court rejected this assertion refusing to take an absolutist view of the confrontation clause (Moenssens, Inbau, & Starrs, 1986).

Expert Testimony

The testimony of the expert does not require a concomitant introduction of the test bullets themselves. In fact, little is to be gained by entering the bullets themselves. The expert should take photographs of the comparison microscope views and have them enlarged for courtroom use. The greater the number of striation comparisons on bullets or casing markings on shells, the easier it will be to convince the jury that the comparison was positive. Photographs of the matching bullets and shells are not required; the oral testimony of the expert is considered to be sufficient to get the matter before the jury (*Commonwealth v. Ellis,* 1977). It bolsters the expert's testimony for the jury to receive a detailed explanation of the comparisons upon which the expert has based his/her opinion. Additionally, photo enlargements go a long way in defusing the defendant's allegations that not enough points of comparisons were ascertainable to support a positive identification.

Tests performed by firearms examiners need not be conducted in the presence of the accused (*State v. Aiken,* 1967). It was held to be error in *Johnson v. State* (1971) to admit prosecution evidence in a case where the fatal bullet was not made available for an examination by the defense. But when the bullet, shell, or weapon is made available for an examination by a defense expert, it is reasonable to condition the test upon the presence of a state expert. The court, in *State v. Nutley* (1964), held that since firearms identification is a relatively exact science with a common methodology, no prejudice to the defense is incurred by prosecution representation (Moenssens, Inbau, & Starrs, 1986).

Defense Questions

In each case involving firearms identification, a litany of defense questions present themselves. Many of the questions raised by the defendant should have been raised by the examiner or the attorney expecting to call the firearms examiner as a witness. Although not exhaustive, what follows is a partial list of questions that could prove embarrassing if not addressed prior to trial:

1. Did the bullet recovery technique used in the test firing record and preserve the total capability of the firearm to produce microscopic striation marks? It is possible that the medium into which the bullet was fired could impart striations independent of those caused by the weapon

fired. It is also possible that the medium into which the bullet was fired could cleanse some of the markings that would have occurred if fired into a less resistant medium (water, ballistic gel, etc.).

2. Did two successively fired test bullets and/or casings contain the same microscopic striation marks necessary for specific identification? The more rounds that must be fired to achieve a similar result, the more suspect becomes the reliability of the comparison. The obvious question (especially in those cases involving a few points of comparison) is "how many rounds would you have fired in order to obtain a match?"

3. Did the bullet and/or casing marking details change with subsequent firings? If so, then all markings on all casings may be suspect. It is important that the examiner keep records of the order of firing of the bullets test-fired to avoid any suggestion that the weapon randomly imparts bullet striations and case markings.

4. Was the bore of the weapon changed in any way since the time of the firing of the questioned bullet? If so, the expert must be prepared to explain and demonstrate the effect if any of the changes on the riflings or markings on the bullets and cases tested.

5. Were the bullets, cases, and primers used in the laboratory tests of the same composition as those in question? Any differences in composition of the tested materials will be focused upon by the defense at the time of trial. The testifying expert must be ready to challenge any assertions that the testing materials affected the markings produced by the suspect weapon.

Expert Qualifications

Training and experience of the firearms examiner is generally gained through practical on the job training and a study of the literature. Usually a number years of work under the supervision of a competent examiner in comparing and examining weapons and ammunition is required before an examiner can properly be considered an expert. In addition to the methods employed in the examination of weapons and their components, the expert must understand and apply a standardized protocol in the examinations he/she performs. Since the majority of firearm examiners work for the state, the courts defer to the laboratory's competence and assume that if the witness is considered to be expert by the laboratory, then he should also be accepted as an expert by the court. Irrespective of the court's predisposition to accept the prosecutions' firearms expert, the defense is not likely to concur. The general acceptance of bullet and cartridge comparison in the legal community will limit the defense to a challenge of the qualifications of the proposed expert and/or to the particular testing procedures employed by the witness.

REFERENCES

Goddard, C.H. 1930. St. Valentine's Day massacre: A study in ammunition tracing. *American Journal of Police Science,* 1:60–78.

Hatcher, J.S., Jury, F.J., & Weller, J. 1977. *Firearms Investigation Identification and Evidence.* Harrisburg, PA: Stackpole.

Hall, A.L. 1931. The missile and the weapon. *American Journal of Police Science,* 2:311–21.

Hogg, I.A. 1977. *The Encyclopedia of Infantry Weapons of World War II.* New York: Thomas Y. Crowell.

Lane, A.J. 1971. *The Brownsville Affair: National Crisis and Black Reaction.* Port Washington, TX: Kennikat.

Mathews, J.H. 1962. *Firearms Identification, vol. 1.* Springfield, IL: Charles C Thomas.

Nonte, G.C. 1973. *Firearms Encyclopedia.* New York: Harper.

O'Connor, J. 1965. *Complete Book of Rifles and Shotguns.* New York: Harper.

Tarassuk, L., & Blair, C. 1979. *The Complete Encyclopedia of Arms and Weapons.* New York: Simon.

Wilbur, C.G. 1977. *Ballistic Science for the Police Officer.* Springfield, IL: Charles C Thomas.

Table of Cases

Commonwealth v. Best, 62 N.E. 748 (1902)

Commonwealth v. Ellis, 364 N.E.2d 808 (1977)

Dean v. Commonwealth, 32 Gratt (V.) 912, (1897)

Evans v. Commonwealth, 19 S.W.2d 1091 (1929)

Jack v. Commonwealth, 222 Ky. 546, 1 S.W.2d. 961 (1928)

Johnson v. State, 249 So.2d 470 (Fla.App.1971)

People v. Triplett, 243 N.W.2d 665 (1965)

State v. Aiken, 434 P.2d 10 (1967)

State v. Bayless, 357, N.E.2d 1035 (1976)

State v. Boccadoro, 144 A. 612 (1929)

State v. Clark, 196 P. 360 (1921)

State v. Lane, 223 P.2d 437 (1951)

State v. Nutley, 129 N.W.2d 155 (1964)

State v. Vuckovich, 203 P. 491 (1921)

Williams v. State, 333 S.W.2d. 846 (1960)

INDEX

Charles C Thomas
PUBLISHER • LTD.

P.O. Box 19265
Springfield, IL 62794-9265

- Brodie, Thomas G.—BOMBS AND BOMBINGS: A Handbook to Protection, Security, Detection, Disposal and Investigation for Industry, Police and Fire Departments. (3rd Ed.) '05, 320 pp. (7 x 10), 245 il.

- Molczan, George—A LEGAL AND LAW ENFORCEMENT GUIDE TO TELEPHONY: Addressing Technical, Legal, and Police Issues Relating to the Interface and Interaction with Communication Service Providers. '05, 156 pp. 93 il., 28 tables.

- Nicholson, William C.—HOMELAND SECURITY LAW AND POLICY. '05, 400 pp. (8 x 10), 9 il., 7 tables.

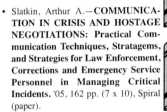

- Slatkin, Arthur A.—COMMUNICATION IN CRISIS AND HOSTAGE NEGOTIATIONS: Practical Communication Techniques, Stratagems, and Strategies for Law Enforcement, Corrections and Emergency Service Personnel in Managing Critical Incidents. '05, 162 pp. (7 x 10), Spiral (paper).

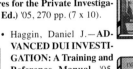

- Travers, Joseph Anthony—INTRODUCTION TO PRIVATE INVESTIGATION: Essential Knowledge and Procedures for the Private Investigator. (2nd Ed.) '05, 270 pp. (7 x 10).

- Haggin, Daniel J.—ADVANCED DUI INVESTIGATION: A Training and Reference Manual. '05, 236 pp. (8 1/2 x 11), 10 il., $34.95, (spiral) paper.

- Karagiozis, Michael & Richard Sgaglio—FORENSIC INVESTIGATION HANDBOOK: An Introduction to the Collection, Preservation, Analysis and Presentation of Evidence. '05, 380 pp. (7 1/2 x 10), 65 il.

- McDevitt, Daniel S.—MANAGING THE INVESTIGATIVE UNIT. '05, 210 pp. (7 x 10), 2 tables, $51.95, hard, $31.95, paper.

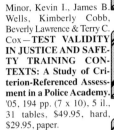

- Minor, Kevin I., James B. Wells, Kimberly Cobb, Beverly Lawrence & Terry C. Cox—TEST VALIDITY IN JUSTICE AND SAFETY TRAINING CONTEXTS: A Study of Criterion-Referenced Assessment in a Police Academy. '05, 194 pp. (7 x 10), 5 il., 31 tables, $49.95, hard, $29.95, paper.

- Moriarty, Laura J.—CRIMINAL JUSTICE TECHNOLOGY IN THE 21st CENTURY. (2nd Ed.) '05, 334 pp. (7 x 10), 5 il., 15 tables, $64.95, hard, $44.95, paper.

- Palermo, George B. & Richard N. Kocsis—OFFENDER PROFILING: An Introduction to the Sociopsychological Analysis of Violent Crime. '05, 284 pp. (7 x 10), 22 il., 2 tables, $56.95, hard, $38.95, paper.

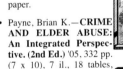

- Payne, Brian K.—CRIME AND ELDER ABUSE: An Integrated Perspective. (2nd Ed.) '05, 332 pp. (7 x 10), 7 il., 18 tables, $69.95, hard, $49.95, paper.

- Payne, Brian K. & Randy R. Gainey—DRUGS AND POLICING: A Scientific Perspective. '05, 228 pp. (7 x 10), 28 il., 4 tables, $54.95, hard, $34.95, paper.

- Bouquard, Thomas J.—ARSON INVESTIGATION: The Step-by-Step Procedure. (2nd Ed.) '04, 330 pp. (7 x 10), 1 il., $65.95, hard, $45.95, paper.

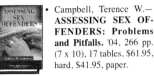

- Campbell, Terence W.—ASSESSING SEX OFFENDERS: Problems and Pitfalls. '04, 266 pp. (7 x 10), 17 tables, $61.95, hard, $41.95, paper.

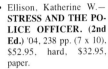

- Ellison, Katherine W.—STRESS AND THE POLICE OFFICER. (2nd Ed.) '04, 238 pp. (7 x 10), $52.95, hard, $32.95, paper.

- Schafer, John R. & Joe Navarro—ADVANCED INTERVIEWING TECHNIQUES: Proven Strategies for Law Enforcement, Military, and Security Personnel. '04, 162 pp. (7 x 10), $53.95, hard, $33.95, paper.

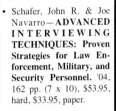

- Yeschke, Charles L.—INTERROGATION: Achieving Confessions Using Permissible Persuasion. '04, 254 pp. (7 x 10), 14 il., $54.95, hard, $35.95, paper.

- Nicholson, William C.—EMERGENCY RESPONSE AND EMERGENCY MANAGEMENT LAW: Cases and Materials. '03, 366 pp. (7 x 10), 21 il., $79.95, hard, $54.95, paper.

- Payne, Brian K.—CRIME IN THE HOME HEALTH CARE FIELD: Workplace Violence, Fraud, and Abuse. '03, 192 pp. (7 x 10), 17 il., 11 tables, $46.95, hard, $29.95, paper.

- Campbell Andrea and Ralph C. Ohm—LEGAL EASE: A Guide to Criminal Law, Evidence, and Procedure. '02, 316 pp. (7 x 10), 31 il., $68.95, hard, $47.95, paper.

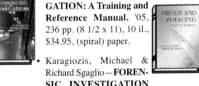

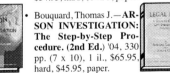

5 easy ways to order!

PHONE: 1-800-258-8980 or (217) 789-8980

FAX: (217) 789-9130

EMAIL: books@ccthomas.com
Web: www.ccthomas.com

MAIL: Charles C Thomas • Publisher, Ltd. P.O. Box 19265 Springfield, IL 62794-9265

Complete catalog available at ccthomas.com • books@ccthomas.com

Books sent on approval • Shipping charges: $6.95 min. U.S. / Outside U.S., actual shipping fees will be charged • Prices subject to change without notice